Dope

Dope

A HISTORY OF PERFORMANCE ENHANCEMENT IN SPORTS FROM THE NINETEENTH CENTURY TO TODAY

Daniel M. Rosen

 PRAEGER

Westport, Connecticut
London

Dope

A HISTORY OF PERFORMANCE ENHANCEMENT IN SPORTS FROM THE NINETEENTH CENTURY TO TODAY

Daniel M. Rosen

Westport, Connecticut
London

Library of Congress Cataloging-in-Publication Data

Rosen, Daniel M.
Dope : a history of performance enhancement in sports from the
nineteenth century to today / Daniel M. Rosen.
    p. cm.
  Includes bibliographical references and index.
  ISBN 978–0–313–34520–3 (alk. paper)
  1. Doping in sports—History. 2. Athletes—Drug use—History.
  3. Anabolic steroids—History. I. Title.
  RC1230.R65 2008
  362.2909—dc22   2008009949

British Library Cataloguing in Publication Data is available.

Library of Congress Catalog Card Number: 2008009949
ISBN: 978–0–313–34520–3

First published in 2008

Praeger Publishers, 88 Post Road West, Westport, CT 06881
An imprint of Greenwood Publishing Group, Inc.
www.praeger.com

Printed in the United States of America

The paper used in this book complies with the
Permanent Paper Standard issued by the National
Information Standards Organization (Z39.48–1984).

10 9 8 7 6 5 4 3 2 1

Contents

Preface

In the last decade, Marion Jones, Barry Bonds, Mark McGwire, Lance Armstrong, and a host of other high-profile athletes have—in one way or another—been connected to allegations of doping. With the current torrent of stories about doping in sports, one could hardly be blamed for thinking that the problem is of epidemic proportions and that the epidemic is of recent origins. Given that many of the lower-level and mid-level athletes who resort to performance-enhancing drugs rarely speak publicly about the choice they've made in order to compete, and research that yields accurate numbers is hard to come by, the exact size of the problem is difficult to determine.

The idea that doping is a relatively new phenomenon, dating back to when Ben Johnson was caught using stanozolol during the 1988 Summer Olympics in Seoul, South Korea, is fundamentally incorrect. The use of various drugs and techniques to improve athletic performance has been around much longer. Depending on how one defines what constitutes doping, some stories suggest that the practice of performance enhancement goes back to the original Olympics held in ancient Greece. At that time, athletes were said to consume certain potions or foods thought to confer some benefit on the playing field.[1] In more recent times, doping dates back to at least the mid-nineteenth century, when racehorses were doped in an effort to ensure the outcome of their races.

In modern times, the term "doping" is often bandied about to describe the use of performance-enhancing drugs, some of which may be entirely legal for one medical purpose or another, but which are outlawed in competition. Yet, some of the drugs and techniques used for performance enhancement are illegal. Among those are designer steroids developed to circumvent current drug-screening tests. There are also "nutritional supplements" that mimic certain natural hormones or are thought to enable the body to manufacture more of a given hormone in order for athletes to improve their competitive results. Regardless of a person's point of view, however, doping from today's perspective is just another form of cheating. (A century ago, however, people would have thought of such efforts as using science to push the boundaries of human performance.)

Where does the term "doping" come from? In the nineteenth century, Zulu warriors in South Africa used an alcoholic extract of grape skins that the Afrikaans settlers called "dop" to increase their strength and endurance before heading off to battle. They also used the concoction to enter into trances during religious rituals and festivals. The word entered into the Dutch language as "doop" (sauce) and "doopen" (to dip or to adulterate). By the late nineteenth or early twentieth century, the word was introduced into English as "dope" and "doping." One of the first uses of the word was to describe the act of giving racehorses illegal medications or substances, with the idea of changing (either improving or diminishing, depending on the doper's intentions) the way the horse performed. Today, there are variants of the word in other languages, such as the French "dopage" and the Spanish "dopaje."[2] And the word "dop" is still used in Afrikaans and still refers to an alcoholic drink.

The notion of what does and doesn't constitute cheating in sports affects people's thinking about doping. Today's use of the term implies that the athlete is doing something wrong, that he or she is breaking the rules. But the use of performance-enhancing drugs, at least among professional athletes, has not always been so frowned upon as it is today. Over the last fifty years, public attitude toward professional athletes' use of such drugs has changed from "whatever they need to do to do their jobs" to disdain and disapproval. Fifty years ago, the public's attitude toward doping among amateur athletes was much the same as today. Amateurs competing in the Olympics were expected to be competing purely for the love of sport, and doping was considered off-limits. As the French Olympic cycling coach Robert Oubron said in 1960, "Many pros are drugged, of course, but we don't drug amateurs."[3]

Oubron was mistaken about the amateurs competing at the time. Some were indeed doped. And some of the doping was organized by the athletes' own governments or Olympic committees. The Olympics during the Cold War era were as much about athletic performance, at least for some countries, as they were about proving which of the two competing ideologies—capitalism and communism—was superior. When the Cold War era came to an end, the truth about some of the more organized Eastern European programs finally came to light.

Some time between 1960 and the present day, attitudes toward doping in sports changed. Exactly when this happened is hard to pinpoint, but a definite turning point occurred when the Johnson scandal erupted in 1988.

By 1992, the amateurs-only philosophy of Olympic competition began a transformation. Professional athletes began competing in various sports during the Barcelona Olympics, including the first ever U.S. Olympic basketball team composed of top professional players. Other changes were afoot, as well. By the end of the 1990s, as the International Olympic Committee's drug-testing programs appeared to be failing miserably, and the IOC was also embroiled in a scandal surrounding how host cities were selected, they needed to reestablish credibility with both their sponsors and the general public.

But many had doubts about the IOC's ability to reform its antidoping enforcement. In the fallout of the 1998 Festina scandal during the Tour de France and numerous other doping scandals that occurred that year, a new independent agency (the World Anti-Doping Agency or WADA) came into existence to run the world's antidoping efforts, with the blessing of the IOC's leadership. Any sport that wished to be included in Olympic competition had to agree to abide by WADA's rules and accept their antidoping regulations. This meant that professional cyclists, as well as other professional athletes who wished to compete in the Olympics, would be subject to WADA's rules and regulations. (One of the notable exceptions was basketball, where some creative policy-making enabled the athletes to only be subject to WADA's rules during international competition.)

In contrast to an earlier era where someone might be considered innocent until proven guilty, when a modern-day news story accuses an athlete of doping, the person in question—whether a professional or amateur athlete—is instantly vilified. And the damage to his or her career and earning potential can be tremendous, all the more so for an athlete who may be innocent and falsely accused.

Not only have attitudes changed toward doping over the years, but the techniques themselves have changed. Performance enhancement techniques have become more and more sophisticated, and at the same time, increasingly more difficult to detect. What was impossible in the early 1970s—using genetically engineered artificial hormones such as erythropoietin to stimulate the production of red blood cells—is not only possible today, but (at least according to the news stories) is an oft-used method for improving an endurance athlete's results.

In the early 2000s, designer steroids manufactured specifically to avoid the current drug-testing methods made their way into sports, courtesy of Victor Conte and the Bay Area Laboratory Co-operative. Conte also found ways of using existing hormones to circumvent the antidoping tests of the times. In one case, a product he called "the cream" was a mixture of a performance-enhancing hormone (testosterone) with a benign hormone (epitestosterone) in amounts designed to beat the initial drug-screening tests.

To understand today's situation in sports, with the controversies over doping and allegations of doping, it's important to know how today's situation came about. This book presents an overview of the history of doping in sports, but it is not an encyclopedic look at each and every case where athletes have been caught using—or been alleged to have used—performance-enhancing drugs. The history of doping ranges from how and why various drugs were developed, to how various drugs and techniques (blood doping, for instance) came to be used in sports, to various notable doping cases. As new drugs and methods became available, those looking for a performance boost found ways to incorporate those drugs or methods into their training and competition practices. With each decade, new methods came into being, while older methods found new uses in other sports. While this book isn't an exhaustive recitation of the entire history of doping in sports, it should give the reader a good basic understanding of doping issues past and present.

Doping occurs in many sports, not just a few. While there are efforts to eradicate doping from competitive sports, the temptation to cheat, to take the easy way to victory, is all too human. Illegal or unethical performance enhancement techniques in sports are likely to be around for some time to come. What may change, however, are the means, methods, and techniques in which some athletes will manipulate their bodies in their never-ending quest for perfection.

Acknowledgments

Over the last year, while researching and writing *Dope*, I've had the opportunity to meet, correspond with, and receive tips and advice from a number of people. The end result is the greater for all of the input and assistance I've received. I'd like to offer my thanks to the following individuals: David Brower, Paula Kirsch, the Honorable Judge William Hue, Marc Cogan, Marco Colbert, Michael Henson, Floyd Landis, Dr. Arnie Baker, Dr. Paul Strauss, Robin Parisotto, Dr. Denise Demir, Dr. Wolfram Meier-Augenstein, Jeff Adams, Will Geoghegan, and the many people who have left comments at Rant Your Head Off (http://rant-your-head-off.com), the blog I've been publishing since August 2006. Among those whose comments have contributed to the development of this book are: Luc, Jean Culeasec, Morgan Hunter, Steve, Susie B, Cheryl, Theresa, Sara, T.G., Ludwig, William Schart, Mike Solberg, ddt240, A-Town, Steve Ballow, Whareagle, Jim Bianco, and Larry Behrendt. For those whose names or monikers don't appear here, your comments and suggestions were also greatly appreciated.

Dope would not have happened had not my editor, Debby Adams, contacted me and suggested the project in the autumn of 2006. I am very grateful for the confidence she has in me, for the comments and suggestions she made to improve each chapter, and especially for the opportunity she gave me.

In addition, I would like to acknowledge all the help and support I've received from my family—including my sister Sarah, my mom, and my dad, who I told about the project shortly before he passed away. As sick as my dad was at the time, I saw his face light up with pride that his son would someday be a published author. I only wish he could have seen the end result.

A special thanks to my sister-in-law, Ira Heimler, who went above and beyond to provide me with a large number of scientific articles on various aspects of doping, along with many textbooks and reference materials that greatly contributed to my understanding of the subject.

To my wife, Heidi, goes the greatest thanks. Over the last year, she's heard me babble on about doping in sports ad nauseam, and always listened with interest. She read all of the early drafts of the chapters in this book, offering many valuable comments and suggestions along the way. Without her love and support and insights, this book would not be nearly as good.

Daniel M. Rosen
January 14, 2008

Chapter 1

The Early History of Performance Enhancement Drugs, 1860–1959

THE FIRST CENTURY OF DOPING—A QUICK OVERVIEW

It may seem hard to believe, given the many doping scandals that have rocked the sports world over the last decade, but doping in sports was not always as frowned upon as it is today. In the nineteenth century and the early twentieth century, there was a belief that through science and medicine, the limits of human athletic achievement could be stretched. If a new drug or a potion could help an athlete run or cycle or swim faster than his opponents, many people saw no problem with the athlete using it. Science and medicine were viewed as ways to improve life, and for athletes, that meant doing better in competition.

Athletes of the era looked to medical science, in particular, to extend the boundaries of human athletic achievement. Using new drugs as a means to improve one's performance wasn't considered scandalous. On the contrary, it was considered cutting edge. And because of the different attitude toward the use of performance-enhancing drugs in this earlier time, the history of what we now call doping was not as well documented as it has become over the last fifty or sixty years.

For human athletes, doping has generally been a way to improve results, although that has not always been the case. At least a few incidents occurred during the late nineteenth and early twentieth centuries where athletes were unknowingly doped by their managers or trainers with the intention that the athlete perform worse rather than better. This happened for a number of reasons, most commonly to fix the outcome of a race, due to an arrangement with (or payoff from) another manager. Incidents like this were common among the horseracing community at the time, and had been for most of the nineteenth century. A number of athletic managers had experience in the horseracing world before working with humans. Those managers brought many of the practices of their previous community into the world of competitive sports.

In some sports, such as professional cycling, a culture of doping—or an assumed culture of doping—has existed for a long time. For sports such as running, cycling, and swimming, records of athletes competing with the assistance of various drugs goes back to the second half of the nineteenth century. The first known instance of athletes doping dates back to 1865, when Dutch canal swimmers in Amsterdam used stimulants in competition.[1] But even though some of the first instances of doping involve swimmers, it's the sport of cycling that has most often been associated with doping and other forms of performance enhancement.

By the 1870s swimmers, cyclists, distance runners, boxers, and other athletes were using stimulants in order to boost their performance. Six-day bicycle races and six-day ultramarathons (a professional sport known at the time as "pedestrianism") placed a premium on the athletes' ability to stay alert and functioning for long periods of time. The demands of such ultraendurance events made it easy for a culture of artificial performance enhancement to develop. And develop it did. Trainers for the athletes competing in these extreme events had to find ways of keeping their athletes going, by whatever means necessary.

To maintain or increase their energy and prevent fatigue, various trainers and athletes experimented with a wide variety of compounds thought to be stimulants. Some, like strychnine, had to be used very carefully, as too large a dose could prove to be poisonous, or even deadly. Caffeine, cocaine, alcohol, sugar cubes dipped in ether and nitroglycerine were often the stimulants of choice during this time period, and even into the first third of the twentieth century.

For the most part, the athletes' use of performance-enhancing drugs during this time was out in the open. But a few trainers and coaches had their own magic formulas that they guarded as carefully as any businessman would guard his trade secrets. This was to prevent other trainers from giving the same treatments to their athletes, which would then neutralize whatever advantage someone might gain by using a certain drug, potion, or formula. And doping wasn't illegal. At the time, no rules specifically prevented athletes from doping with stimulants or other performance-enhancing drugs.[2]

By the mid-1930s, testosterone had been isolated and synthesized. Over the coming decades medical researchers, as well as a number of coaches, trainers, and athletes, would experiment with testosterone as a way of increasing strength and aggressiveness, among other things. Amphetamines came into wide use, during the Second World War among the warring militaries, and later among athletes looking for a way to increase concentration, reduce fatigue, and perform better. In the 1950s, the first anabolic steroid came into use. Also during the 1950s, the first modern-style doping scandals occurred, setting the example for how many future scandals and stories would play out in the media and beyond.

Over the years, the expectations of why amateur and professional athletes engaged in sport, and how they achieved on the field of competition changed. From the beginning of the twentieth century, at least up until the 1960s, the difference between amateur and professional athletes was that amateurs were expected to compete based on their own inherent abilities merely for the love of the game. Professionals, on the other hand, who competed to earn a living and were paid to perform, were assumed to be using drugs and doping. And a number of the athletic organizations, including the International Olympic Committee, openly scoffed at professionals, as if to imply that somehow being a professional athlete was less noteworthy than being an amateur. As the modern doping era began, the expectation that professional athletes should compete without a chemical boost began to take hold.

This chapter will follow the story of drugs in sport, chronicling some of the better known incidents. Some of them happened just as the conventional wisdom leads us to believe, and some of them didn't. The story of Arthur Linton, in the following section, is a good example of an often-cited story in which the truth—the straight dope—turns out to be much different than the legend.

THE FIRST DOPING DEATH—OR NOT?

According to a number of writers, historians, and doping experts, the first person to die from doping was Arthur Linton, a British cyclist who supposedly overdosed on a drug known as "trimethyl" during or after a derny race from Bordeaux to Paris. Derny races are motorcycle-paced road races. The Bordeaux-to-Paris race covered 560 kilometers, or about 350 miles, during the years that it was run. Some versions of the Linton story claim that he died from strychnine abuse in 1886, or even as early as 1879, in the Tour de France.[3]

Who was Arthur Linton, and what really happened? Did he die after the Bordeaux-to-Paris race in 1886 or not?

To begin, Linton was one of three brothers from Aberaman (also referred to as Aberdare in a number of sources), a small mining town in South Wales. Each of the brothers—Arthur, Tom, and Samuel—was an accomplished cyclist. Arthur and another cyclist from Aberaman named Jimmy Michael became world champions during the early era of professional cycling competition.

Linton started racing around his hometown in his teens and by 1892 had built a reputation as a superb cyclist in the South Wales area. The following year, he burst onto the UK national cycling scene. Linton was soon signed to a professional contract to race for "Choppy" Warburton, a well-known trainer and manager of the era. In 1894, Arthur Linton had a very successful racing season, ultimately earning the title "Champion Cyclist of the World." When he returned home in December of that year, he received a hero's welcome.[4]

Having risen to the height of his profession in 1894, Linton suffered setbacks in 1895, including a knee injury that took a huge toll on his training and racing. After a bad 1895 racing season, Linton recovered and came back in 1896 to score his biggest victory, the Bordeaux-to-Paris derny race. His victory came with some controversy, as Linton took a wrong turn entering Paris. When Linton's wrong turn was discovered, the race victory was awarded to Gastone Rivière. After an appeal, the two men shared the title and the prize money.[5] Linton, however, contracted typhoid fever shortly after his victory. He died less than two months afterward.[6]

So where does the story connecting Linton's death with doping come from? It turns out that Warburton was a well-known advocate of performance-enhancing methods. He was known for carrying a little black bottle that contained a mysterious liquid, which would come out if one of his cyclists were suffering too greatly during a race. One publication in 1903 described Warburton's bottle this way: "If his charge showed any undue signs of distress, out came the black bottle, the contents of which seemed to act like magic on the distressed rider."[7]

The story about Linton, connecting his death to doping, seems to have gained traction in 1897 or so, when Linton's protégé, Jimmy Michael was involved in a doping controversy. Michael was banned from racing in Britain and emigrated to the United States, where he continued to flourish as a cyclist for several years.[8]

Claims that Linton was the first athlete to die from doping or doping-related causes, however, are incorrect. To begin with, Arthur Linton was just fourteen years old in 1886. He had not yet established himself on the local Aberaman cycling scene, much less the national or international stage.

Also, the Bordeaux-to-Paris race was first run in 1891, five years after Linton's supposed death. If a cyclist did die from doping at a race in 1886, it wasn't Arthur Linton and it wasn't a participant in the Bordeaux-to-Paris derny race. If the story is true, that a cyclist died as a result of doping following a race in 1886, the identity of the rider and the race he was competing in has been lost.

Having won the 1896 edition of Bordeaux to Paris, Arthur Linton did die from typhoid fever about two months later. To say that Linton died shortly after winning the Bordeaux-to-Paris race is correct. However, he died in 1896 at the age of 24, ten years later than many accounts of the time would have one believe.

JIMMY MICHAEL GOES THE WRONG WAY

Jimmy Michael was a cycling protégé of Arthur Linton, from the same area in South Wales. Due to his small size—barely 5 feet tall and 100 pounds—Michael acquired the nickname "Midget" somewhere along the way.[9]

Michael first entered the public eye in 1894 when he won the Herne Hill race. He signed on with Arthur Linton's manager, Choppy Warburton, that same year. In 1895 Jimmy Michael did very well, although it turned out to be a less than stellar year for Arthur Linton. By the end of the year, Michael had won the World Middle Distance title in Cologne.[10] Jimmy Michael became the Linton brothers' rival, to such an extent that he issued a challenge to both Thomas and Arthur Linton.

In an advertisement, Michael stated, "Seeing that Tom Linton has been boasting in the South Wales papers that he can beat me, and that he would be willing to ride me any time, and also that his brother Arthur was 'champion of the world,' I will ride either of them." Michael also said he would compete against them at any time, at either of two tracks in Paris, for a purse of £100 plus all gate receipts, maintaining that he was the true middle distance champion of the world. He even offered to give either of the Lintons two laps in every 100 kilometers, three in every 100 miles or 4 in 6 hours. No record exists of whether either brother took Michael up on his challenge.[11]

After Arthur Linton's death, Jimmy Michael and Choppy Warburton had a falling out over Michael's desire to race in America. Warburton was so angry, according to some accounts, that he doped Michael in a race against an American rider. But Warburton's doping effort was not so that Michael would go faster than the other rider, instead, Warburton wanted Jimmy Michael to go slower. This was the same type of doping technique that had been first used on racehorses in the early part of the nineteenth century.[12]

Apparently, whatever Warburton used to dope Jimmy Michael worked too well. At one point during the race, Michael fell off his bicycle. When he remounted the bike and got back on the track, Michael was so disoriented that he had no idea he was going the wrong way. The crowd went wild at the sight, yelling "Dope!"[13]

CHOPPY WARBURTON—THE FIRST MANAGER
TO DOPE HIS ATHLETES?

Choppy Warburton, the manager/trainer for both Arthur Linton and Jimmy Michael, was a colorful figure in the world of nineteenth-century bicycle racing. Part Svengali, part coach, part manager, he was known for discovering young riders with a great deal of ability who would go on to great professional accomplishments. Warburton—whose given name was actually James—came from Haslingden, a small town in Lancashire in the north of England, where he was born in 1842. He took the name "Choppy" from his father (although some stories credit his uncle), a seafaring man who was fond of describing the rough seas he sailed as "choppy water."[14] Warburton liked the daredevil image the name "Choppy" projected, so he appropriated it as his own.

Before his involvement in cycling, Warburton was an accomplished runner. He would compete in races of almost any length—2 miles or 20 miles, it didn't matter. Warburton may even have been the first ultramarathon runner, as some stories claim he once ran for 24 consecutive hours. Choppy Warburton was a dominant runner in Britain, and also in America, where he was a favorite amongst running fans. When his professional running days were through, he turned his attention to training cyclists. During his days as a runner he may have used, or learned how to use, various drugs to modify his own performance. Some have suggested that Warburton carried this knowledge of doping over to cycling, once he became a coach and manager of professional cyclists.

At least two of his young charges, Arthur Linton and Jimmy Michael, died at very young ages—24 and 29, respectively. The relatively quick rise to prominence, followed by the early deaths of his two star riders, has led a number of people to speculate that these riders succeeded with a little "boost" from some sort of doping administered by their manager.

When Warburton's riders were racing, Choppy could be found running from one side of the track to the other, offering the riders encouragement and a little more. Perhaps the reason Warburton was able to get such great performances out of his riders was because the magic potion he carried in a small black bottle contained a drug that revitalized his riders. Warburton, like many managers of his era, closely guarded his secret formula, so the actual contents of the bottle were never known. It could have been sugar water, for all we know, or it could have been laced with strychnine, trimethyl, cocaine, heroin, or a combination of any of these. Or the bottle may have contained different contents, depending on the effect Warburton wished to achieve on his athletes. Whatever the case, the one thing that is certain is that Warburton's riders would often be greatly revived by a swig of its contents.

Shortly before his death in 1897, Warburton was "warned-off" of the velodromes and tracks of Great Britain. Two incidents, one involving Arthur Linton and the other involving Jimmy Michael were said to have contributed to the ban. In Linton's case, his appearance and behavior throughout the 1896 Bordeaux-to-Paris race suggested that the rider had been significantly drugged in order to win.[15]

About halfway through the race, one witness who saw Linton said the racer seemed glassy-eyed, shaky, and speaking in a state of nervous excitement. Toward the end of the race, even Warburton described his rider as a corpse. And yet, Linton managed to finish the course in record time—although that was partly due to a wrong turn taken in the last miles. But Linton's result was also partly due to whatever care Warburton had provided the cyclist during the race.[16]

The other incident that led to Warburton's banishment involved his other star rider, Jimmy Michael. Michael had been approached by Tom Eck, the coach and manager of the American cyclists sponsored by Schwinn Bicycles, to come and race in America. He reportedly planned to accept the offer. Warburton, however, would have been cut out of the deal and was not happy about losing the income his star rider generated. John S. Johnson, a Schwinn rider, raced against Michael in England when Eck brought his riders over to Britain and Europe to compete against a number of well-known cyclists at various velodromes.[17]

During the races between Michael and Johnson, Warburton apparently doped his star rider—not to make him go faster, but to make him go slower, resulting in a poor performance by the Welsh racer. Exactly what happened is unclear. In some versions of the story, Michael was beaten badly by the American rider. In other versions he was acting strangely throughout the race. At one point he fell off the bike. Not realizing what he was doing, Michael got back on to the track and headed in the wrong direction.

The poor performances did not ultimately jeopardize Jimmy Michael's chances to race in the United States. But the combination of Michael's inexplicable performances against Johnson, and Linton's odd behavior during the 1896 Bordeaux-to-Paris race were enough for Britain's National Cyclists' Union. Warburton was warned-off of every track in Britain. In other words, he was banned.

After being banned from the tracks in Britain, Warburton went to Germany and France and for a brief period wound up coaching the young Albert Champion, a French cyclist who won some of the early cycling classics. After his cycling career was over, Champion went on to found the Champion spark plug company in the United States. Warburton died at Christmastime in 1897 at the age of 54.

AMPHETAMINES ENTER THE PICTURE

One important development of the late 1880s was the new drug, alpha-methylphenylethylamine, more commonly known as amphetamine. Amphetamine was first synthesized in 1887. Methamphetamine, a related compound, may have been discovered as early as 1893, but it was first crystallized by some Japanese researchers in 1919. Methamphetamine is a more powerful and easier-to-consume drug than its relative. It can be dissolved in liquid, smoked, injected, snorted, or manufactured in pill form.

By the 1930s, scientists had discovered that methamphetamine was good for opening blocked nasal passages and airways, and that it stimulated the central nervous system. In 1932, Smith Kline and French brought out a version known as Benzedrine, which was marketed as an inhaler to open nasal passages. By 1937, amphetamines were manufactured in pill form.

Amphetamines didn't become a highly popular drug for doping until fifty years or more after its initial discovery in 1887, in part because the properties and effects of the new drugs were not well documented or well researched until the 1920s and 1930s. In the meantime, athletes managed to find a number of ways to make their performances better, or at least to lessen their suffering during long endurance events, such as the marathon or any number of bicycle races popular at the time.

Some athletes in the 1920s and 1930s may have experimented with amphetamines, possibly including German athletes during the 1936 Olympics in Berlin. Most athletes of the time, however, stuck to the tried and true formulas of the time, which were based on the doping methods used on racehorses in the 1800s. After World War II, that would all change, with sometimes disastrous results.

THOMAS HICKS AND THE 1904 OLYMPIC MARATHON

Thomas Hicks, a British-born American runner competing in the marathon during the 1904 Olympics in St. Louis, almost became the first death in Olympic competition. St. Louis summers are well known for both heat and humidity. When Hicks and about 30 other contestants lined up at the start of the marathon at a few minutes past 3 P.M. on August 30, 1904, the temperature was hovering in the high 80s to low 90s, with the humidity to match. This was not the ideal time to start an event of the marathon's magnitude. But the organizers started the race anyway.[18]

The marathon, run mostly over dirt roads throughout St. Louis County, was treacherous—not just because of the terrain, which included seven steep hills, but because of the dust kicked up by the judges' automobiles and support vehicles pacing the race. Experience in other marathons didn't matter, as far as finishing the St. Louis race was concerned. Even veterans of the Boston marathon and other similar events fell victim to the heat, humidity, the dust, and the generally hellish conditions. And if the road conditions, themselves, weren't enough, the runners had to dodge bicycles and other obstacles, in addition to the numerous motor vehicles clogging the roads and kicking up thick clouds of dust.[19]

With about 10 miles left in the race, Hicks' energy started to flag. He asked his support crew, Charles Lucas and Hugh McGrath, to give him some water. Instead, they sponged his mouth with distilled water. At about 7 miles from the finish, his handlers gave him a concoction of brandy, raw eggs, and strychnine—a common practice at the time—to help keep him going.[20]

At about 4 miles to go, Hicks (who was now completely wiped out) begged to lie down. Lucas and McGrath wouldn't let him. They encouraged him to keep moving forward, even if he had to slow to a walk. Hicks' color turned ashen, so they gave him a second dose of the brandy/raw egg/strychnine concoction and sent him on his way. As he came over the final hill and was able to see the cheering crowds at Francis Field, where the race started, Hicks picked up the pace. After a final dose of brandy and raw eggs, Hicks managed the last mile or so to the stadium and crossed the finish line with a time of 3:28:53, the slowest winning time of any Olympic marathon. He collapsed almost immediately upon crossing the finish line. It took more than an hour to revive him enough so that he could collect his winning medal.[21]

We now know that strychnine, a powerful stimulant, mixed with alcohol, a diuretic, can have a very negative effect on an athlete's performance. Especially during hot days when the combination makes it more likely that an athlete will suffer from dehydration. Given the hot and humid conditions during the 1904 Olympic marathon, it should come as no surprise that Hicks suffered from the effects of the weather mixed with the brandy and strychnine.[22]

"I am sorry to say that the road is the hardest over which I ever ran," Hicks told the St. Louis Republic. "I have done the distance in little over two hours and a half, but today I did my best. I lost 10 pounds as it was, and you can see that I could not push myself any faster and lose more." It was the last time Thomas Hicks ran a marathon.

Later, Hicks' trainer, Charles L. J. Lucas wrote, "The Marathon race, from a medical standpoint, demonstrated that drugs are of much benefit to athletes along the road, and that warm sponging is much better than cold sponging for an athlete in action . . . Hicks was far from being the best man physically in the race, for there were three men who should have defeated him . . . but they lacked proper care on the road."[23]

THE FIRST ANTIDOPING TESTS—BUT NOT FOR HUMANS

The first tests for drugs in "athletes" were developed not for human sports, but for horse racing. Doping in horse racing became a controversial issue in the late nineteenth and early twentieth centuries. In the 1800s, doping wasn't just about making a horse go faster. Just as often as the drugs administered to the racehorses were intended to speed the horse up, the drugs administered were intended to slow the animals down, either to sabotage a particular horse's chances of winning or to otherwise fix the outcome of a race.

This manipulation of the racehorses' performance was practiced far and wide—in America, Europe, and Australia. Gambling on horse races goes back at least to the late 1700s or early 1800s. With gambling came some unscrupulous elements, intent on rigging the outcomes of races in order to maximize their profits at the expense of the ordinary gambler. At least as far back as the 1850s, professional dopers plied a secretive trade, fixing the outcomes of races by the way they doped horses. Because the stables were not very secure, dopers were even able to sneak in and administer drugs or potions to competitors' horses prior to the races in order to slow the animals down.

And it was the animals that suffered. Reports of the time mention horses pulling up in races, keeling over dead or suffering great pain after the races were run.[24] Since the gamblers who bet on the races weren't informed as to which horses were doped and which weren't, doping was considered unfair—but not to the animals or the animals' owners. The practice was considered unfair because only the people who doped the horses knew which ones to bet on in order to win.

By 1903, the English Jockey Club banned doping, and by 1910 saliva tests for cocaine and heroin, the two most common doping drugs administered to the horses, had been developed by a Russian chemist named Bukowski. The first two positive drug tests on horses occurred in Austria two years later.[25] By 1930, the International Horse Racing Organization required doping tests to be performed on all races organized under their auspices.[26]

Among the horses of that era that were widely thought to have been doped was Sir Barton, the first winner of the three races that later became known as the "Triple Crown," in 1919.[27]

THE IAAF BECOMES THE FIRST ATHLETIC FEDERATION TO BAN DOPING

By 1928, doping in track and field competitions had become a recognized problem, as far as the International Amateur Athletic Federation was concerned. In that year, they wrote the first rules banning doping in sports.

Unfortunately, however, the IAAF had to rely on the word of each athlete, as there were few tests available to detect the use of banned substances. And even though antidoping testing had begun on racehorses during the 1910s,[28] real antidoping tests would not be applied to human sporting competitions until 1968. That was the first time the International Olympic Committee implemented drug testing at both the Winter Olympics and the Summer Olympics.[29]

AMPHETAMINES COME TO THE FORE

Once Japanese scientists were able to crystallize methamphetamine in 1919, it became easier to produce and administer. Over the coming decades, amphetamines became more popular as performance-enhancing drugs. Even so, the use of the older stimulants did not completely disappear. In fact, the use of caffeine as a stimulant still occurs on a regular basis among certain types of sports, especially endurance events such as the marathon or cycling road races.

Amphetamines would be refined over the next twenty years, and by the outbreak of World War II in 1939, all of the armies in the major countries fighting the war used amphetamines or other stimulants to reduce fatigue and increase the endurance of their soldiers. Bomber pilots in the Allied air forces, as well as Japanese pilots, used amphetamines to stay alert during long missions. The Japanese air force used amphetamines to fire up Kamikaze pilots before their missions, as well. Also, watch-keepers in the various naval forces used amphetamines to stay awake on overnight watches.[30]

While amphetamines may increase concentration and endurance, they also increase an athlete's chances of suffering from heatstroke, especially during prolonged, intense efforts on hot and humid days.[31] Amphetamines would power the war effort on both sides, but the developments that had an even greater impact on the future of doping in sports were quietly being pursued in labs around the world. Testosterone and anabolic steroids would soon be entering the doping universe.

TESTOSTERONE AND THE RISE OF ANABOLIC STEROIDS

During the period between 1926 and 1946, scientific discoveries and medical breakthroughs led to the development and refinement of a new class of compound: anabolic, androgenic steroids. Anabolic, androgenic steroids, or steroids for short, are drugs that are related to testosterone. The discovery and development of testosterone in the 1930s set the stage for new doping techniques and new drugs, including the designer drugs synthesized by companies such as the Bay Area Laboratory Co-operative, also known as BALCO, in the 1990s and early 2000s. This is where one of the major chapters about the history of doping in the last fifty years begins.

The story of doping during the last half of the twentieth century actually starts in 1926, when Professor Fred Koch and Lemeul C. McGee, a young medical student at the University of Chicago, first began work that led to the discovery of the male sex hormone. After the male sex hormone was isolated, it would later be dubbed testosterone. Koch and McGee began their research by acquiring 40 pounds of bull testicles and proceeding to extract the hormone by stewing the bull testicles in alcohol, acetone, and benzene, using the era's latest organic chemistry techniques. The result of their efforts was a mere 20 milligrams of a substance they believed to be the male sex hormone. But how could they prove it?

They resorted to an old experiment performed on roosters more than a century before. Koch and McGee injected a capon (a neutered rooster) with the substance, and within two weeks the capon began to take on the appearance and behavior of a rooster. They repeated the experiment and came up with the same results.

In 1929 Koch and Dr. T. F. Gallagher refined the original technique. They were able to create a much greater quantity of the mysterious hormone by using 1,000 pounds of bull testicles, instead of the smaller amount used several years before. Having succeeded in extracting a larger amount of the hormone, the researchers set about to determine whether this was, in fact, the male sex hormone that scientists had been seeking on and off for the better part of two centuries.

One approach to determining whether they had succeeded was to try administering the hormone to men who had little or no male sex hormone, such as men who were eunuchs. The two scientists, along with Dr. A. T. Kenyon, performed experiments on a eunuch to prove that the hormone worked in humans, too. The results of this experiment left no doubt that the male sex hormone existed. Soon, the race was on to extract and synthesize the compound.

By 1935 Ernest Laqueur, a Jewish-German pharmacologist working in Amsterdam, extracted a few milligrams of pure hormone. Then he determined the hormone's molecular structure very precisely. Laqueur is the scientist credited with naming the hormone "testosterone."

During the same time period two other scientists—Ruzicka, a Yugoslav chemist, and Butendant, a German chemist—managed to synthesize the hormone from cholesterol. By the autumn of 1935, preparations of testosterone were being made available to the medical community for testing and treatment purposes. It wouldn't be long before athletes started experimenting with testosterone and other steroids (drugs derived from testosterone) in an effort to improve their performance.

The idea of performance boosters and performance enhancement was nothing new by the time researchers were isolating and testing testosterone. There were certainly as many reasons to find some magic bullet to improve an athlete's performance as there were athletes who might be willing to try new drugs or new techniques. Some of those techniques, like strength training, would be legal. Some, like the use of steroids to promote muscle growth and development, would not.

By the time German scientists had isolated and synthesized testosterone, the Nazi Party had been in power for more than two years. Among the Nazis' ideology was the idea that the German people (who the Nazis referred to as the Aryan race) were genetically superior to all other races and ethnic groups. In the athletic arena, German athletes were under tremendous pressure to win in order to help prove Hitler's notion that the Germans were the master race.

In this environment, it is possible that the Nazis experimented with testosterone to improve athletic performance at the 1936 Olympic Games held in Berlin, which they wanted to be a showcase for German superiority. Rumors have existed for some time that the Nazis treated their athletes with testosterone in the run-up to the 1936 Olympic Games, but actual documentation of the doping efforts has not yet been uncovered.

The contrast in the numbers of gold medals Germany won in 1936 versus 1932 certainly suggests the Nazis may well have been doping their athletes. In Berlin, German athletes garnered 89 gold medals, more than any other country. Four years earlier, at the Los Angeles Olympics, Germany managed only 20 gold medals, ninth in the medal count and less than a quarter of their total in 1936. Although no evidence exists that proves the Nazi government implemented a doping regime, it's hard not to wonder about the Germans' sudden change in fortunes.

By contrast, at the 1932 Los Angeles Olympics, American athletes won the most gold medals with 102, and in the 1936 games, they were second in number to the Nazis, with only 56. Perhaps some form of home field advantage accounted for the dominance of the host countries in both 1932 and 1936, instead.[32] Or, perhaps the Nazis were doping their athletes with amphetamines.

What is known is that in some women's sporting events, the "women" competitors from Germany were actually men. Clearly, the Nazis were not above using any form of subterfuge in order to win as many medals as they could, and thus demonstrate Aryan "superiority."

Whatever methods the Nazis were using, they didn't always guarantee German victories, as evidenced by the fact that Jesse Owens, an African-American athlete, won four gold medals in track and field events. Sometimes, German athletes went against the governing regime and even helped others win. In one event—the long jump—German athlete Luz Long gave Jesse Owens a bit of advice after Owens had fouled in his first two attempts: Jump from an earlier point, Long told Owens, advising him to play it safe in order to qualify for the finals.

Owens followed Long's advice and went on to win gold in the event. Afterward, Long congratulated Owens on his victory, in full view of the Nazi leader. Later, Owens would speak of the event and say, "It took a lot of courage for him to befriend me in front of Hitler. You can melt down all the medals and cups I have and they wouldn't be a plating on the 24-karat friendship I felt for Luz Long at that moment."

Despite the pressure on German athletes, and medical literature full of the information about the effects of other drugs on human performance, no mention of testosterone or its effects has been found in the German medical literature of the times. Still, the rumors persist.

John Hoberman, a professor of Germanic studies at the University of Texas in Austin, who is also a noted authority on the history and use of performance-enhancing drugs once noted, "It is likely that public anti-doping sentiment after 1933 was related to Nazi strictures against the self-serving, individualistic, record-breaking athlete and the abstract ideal of performance. It is also consistent with Nazi rhetoric about sportsmanship, e.g., the importance of the 'noble contest' and the 'chivalric' attitude of the German athlete."

Max Schmeling, on the other hand, provided Hitler with a source of pride in 1936 when he knocked out Joe Louis in the gold-medal bout in Berlin. Prior to the fight, Hitler was uncertain whether his boxer could win, but afterward he showered Schmeling with praise. Two years later, however, at a rematch in the United States, Louis knocked Schmeling out in the first round in just over 2 minutes. The German leader was subdued in the message of condolences he sent, and the German press and government propaganda machine spun the story to minimize the Nazi party's humiliation at the loss.

On the eve of World War II, in 1939, both groups of scientists who worked on the isolation and synthesis of testosterone were awarded the Nobel Prize for their efforts. Only Ruzicka accepted the award. The German scientists stayed home.

PERFORMANCE-ENHANCING DRUGS DURING
THE SECOND WORLD WAR

As World War II began, international sporting competition for the most part came to a halt, but the desire to improve performance did not. The scientists and doctors whose work led to the use of various types of drugs for performance enhancement in athletics now saw a new group interested in drugs and other methods for improving human performance: the military. The armies of both Nazi Germany and the West sought ways to keep soldiers alert and focused during long battles. They found their solutions in the form of amphetamines and other stimulants. The Nazis also wanted to develop troops with greater muscle strength and greater aggressiveness. That solution came in the form of testosterone and its derivatives.

The German Army's use of testosterone during World War II to increase troops' muscle strength and their aggressiveness is thought to have induced the first known instances of "roid rage." Testosterone was also used on inmates at such concentration camps as Auschwitz to beef up their strength so that they could work a little longer and a little harder before the wretched working conditions, environment, and treatment by their captors killed them.

On both sides, the armies used various forms of amphetamines and other stimulants in order to keep their troops going through lengthy and difficult battles. All of the experimentation on troops and others reaped a number of dividends, not the least of which was a collection of scientists knowledgeable in the ways of doping. Once the war ended, this knowledge would be transferred to other countries and other groups, and the world of sports would never be the same again.

STEROIDS AND THE COLD WAR

After World War II ended, various countries' athletics program became interested in the use of testosterone to improve strength and athletic performance. Testosterone has two types of effects: one (anabolic), increasing muscle strength; and the other (androgenic), a masculinizing effect. Eventually, the people running athletic programs in Russia and other countries sought to get the muscle-building effects of the drugs, without the excessive masculinizing effects. To do this, various researchers and drug companies developed synthetic variations of testosterone, known as anabolic steroids (steroids, for short), in hopes of reducing the masculinizing effects of the male sex hormone.[33]

Some reports suggest that the first group of athletes to experiment with testosterone were some weight lifters on America's West Coast, as early as in the late 1940s. Circumstantial evidence suggests that the Soviets were using testosterone in their training programs by the early 1950s.[34]

As the 1950s started, the Cold War between the United States and the USSR began to intensify. Both sides sought to prove the superiority of their political and economic systems. This didn't happen just in the military or political sphere, however. It also happened in sports and athletic competitions. In every facet of life where the United States and the USSR competed, each side would seek to demonstrate its supremacy.

And so, the 1950s would prove to be a seminal time in the research and development of anabolic steroids. By the mid-1950s literally hundreds of different, but related, compounds had been synthesized. Each of these compounds mimicked the strength-building effects of testosterone, with less of the masculinizing effects.

In 1954, at the world weight lifting championships in Vienna, Austria, a Soviet sports physician is said to have told Dr. John Ziegler, the U.S. weight lifting team's doctor, about the Soviets' use of testosterone. Ziegler took the Soviets' ideas back to the York Barbell Club, where he and a few other weight lifters began experimenting with testosterone, achieving some good results. In time, Dr. Ziegler became concerned about the side effects of testosterone and sought other drugs that might have the same effect.[35]

One of the first to come into use was a steroid known as Dianabol. Dianabol was developed by Ciba Pharmaceutical Company and came onto the market in 1958. Ziegler, concerned about the effects of testosterone, switched his weight lifters to the drug in order to build greater muscle mass, which in turn allowed them to lift heavier weights.[36]

Ziegler described some of the results of his experimentation in a number of journals devoted to physical training and weight lifting in that time period. Once a few of the early users started winning championships, news spread throughout the sports world about the success associated with taking the drugs. By the early 1960s, steroids were being adopted by competitors in a number of sports requiring great strength, ranging from American football to various track and field events such as shot put, javelin throw, and the discus throw.[37]

The perception that athletes who didn't use steroids were at a disadvantage surfaced as early as 1956, when Olga Fitkotova Connolly said, "There is no way in the world a woman nowadays, in the throwing events—at least the shot put and the discus—I'm not sure about the javelin—can break the record unless she is on steroids. These awful drugs have changed the complexion of track and field."[38]

THE FIRST INSTANCE OF HORMONE DOPING—1950

Many athletes, their physicians, and their trainers were experimenting with various types of performance enhancement as the 1950s began. One incident, which involved members of the Danish rowing team in 1950, is thought to be the first instance of allegations involving hormone doping in modern sports history.[39]

At a meeting of the Danish Sports Federation in 1950, Ove Bøje accused a Dr. Mathiesen of administering some "hormone pills" to Danish rowers at a competition in Milan. Although Dr. Mathiesen did admit giving the athletes the pills, he strongly objected to Bøje's statements, calling them, "a low blow." He went on to proclaim his opposition to doping, saying, "I am myself an opponent of doping, but the minor treatment I prescribed for the rowers is not doping, it does not involve an artificial stimulant, but is rather a supplement that restores natural requirements." Dr. Mathiesen was using the novel logic that doping involved stimulants to enhance performance, whereas "hormone" treatments were not so much performance enhancing as they were performance enabling.[40]

AMPHETAMINE USE IN THE 1950s

Testosterone and its derivatives weren't the only drugs being used by athletes seeking to gain a performance edge at the time. Over the next several decades, the use of steroids would become more common across a number of sports. But even as steroids would become more dominant, other doping techniques continue to this day, such as the use of stimulants to increase an athlete's speed in short-distance sprint events or to reduce fatigue in long endurance events.

And those methods were, and still are, not without their risks. Several speed skaters reportedly became ill during the 1952 Winter Olympics in Oslo, Norway, and had to seek medical attention after ingesting amphetamines. So while new techniques were coming to the fore, athletes who were bent on cheating would adapt their strategies based on the kind of performance boost they sought.

AUSTRALIAN SWIMMERS AT THE MELBOURNE GAMES

Also during the 1950s, swimmers were using amphetamines to improve their speed in the water. During the 1956 Olympic Games in Melbourne, Australia, allegations of drug use were made against the Australian swim team. Forbes Carlile, coach of the Australian swim team at the time, once described the tenor of the times this way, "This was a different, and in most parts of the world, an innocent era when anti-doping laws had not been thought of."[41] According to John Hoberman, in his book *Testosterone Dreams*, "It simply did not occur to [Carlile] that the use of performance aids might also be unethical." Whether any Australian swimmers actually used amphetamines is not clear, but swimmer Judy Joy Davies did nothing to help clear the air when she told *The New York Times* in 1957, "Some of our champion swimmers fearlessly admit they take pep pills to help them shatter records."[42] Although Davies' comments suggest a particular interpretation or understanding, exactly what type of pills the swimmers were taking isn't clear.

THE FOUR-MINUTE MILE CONTROVERSY

When Roger Bannister broke the four-minute mile on May 6, 1954, clocking a mile in 3 minutes, 59.4 seconds, he accomplished something many people of the time thought was almost impossible. The previous world record for the mile, 4:01.4, had been established by Gunder Hägg, in Malmö, Sweden, on July 17, 1945.[43] For almost nine years, no one was able to beat the record and the conventional wisdom among many was that running a sub-four-minute mile was not possible—or that it would be many decades before athletes would be able to crash through the 4-minute barrier. But Bannister did it, despite the conventional wisdom.

Three years later, in 1957, Dr. Herbert Berger became perhaps the first person to publicly question how athletes were managing to achieve what to his mind was unachievable—running the four-minute mile. In the time since Roger Bannister ran the first sub-four-minute mile, 12 runners managed to break the 4-minute barrier on 18 occasions. His contention was that the runners must have been using something, because such an accomplishment was a superhuman effort. By publicly stating his opinion, Berger set the stage for suspicions about athletic performance that still exists some fifty years later.

Dr. Berger, an expert in drug abuse and addiction who was also a consultant to the United States Public Health Service, put forth his theory while speaking at the annual meeting of the American Medical Association in New York. He postulated that the runners had used Benzedrine, a form of inhaled amphetamine, to run faster, and thus break through the long-sought-after barrier.

"When I was a college boy, the four-minute mile was as unlikely as flying to the moon," Berger said at the time. He went on to say, "The recent rash of four-minute miles is no coincidence."[44] And while Berger didn't accuse any specific athletes, he did say that he found it odd that so many runners had been able to run so many sub-four-minute miles in the three years since Bannister first broke 4 minutes. Berger felt that these runners had "turned temporarily into super-athletes by the use of drugs."[45]

As John Hoberman points out in *Amphetamine and the Four-Minute Mile*, by the late 1940s and early 1950s training techniques had advanced considerably compared to Berger's college days. During the forty years preceding Bannister's efforts, the world record for the mile dropped at a fairly steady pace. Between 1913 and 1945, when Hägg set the previous mark of 4:01.3 (officially ratified as 4:01.4 by the IAAF), the world record for the mile had dropped by more than 14 seconds. During that time, the record would stand for up to eight years before the next runner set a new record.[46]

The difference between Hägg's record time and Bannister's new record was only 1 second. And while Bannister's achievement was certainly a breakthrough, given the steady advance as the record time became shorter, it should not have been considered out of the realm of possibility. Arne Andersson, the Swede who held the record before Hägg, had managed to best his own time, 4:02.6, set on July 1, 1943 by an entire second on July 18, 1944. One year later, Hägg eclipsed his countryman's record by only two-tenths of a second (as recorded in the record books, but three-tenths according to other sources).

In what has become a pattern in the years since Berger first expressed his doubts about the athletes who broke the four-minute mile in the 1950s, a number of the athletes spoke out against his comments in the days following the initial story. Don Bowden, an American who had just broken the 4-minute mark a week before Berger's talk, called the doctor's comment, "a ridiculous and silly accusation."[47] Merv Lincoln, one of the great Australian runners, said that using drugs to run fast wouldn't be necessary.[48] The world record-holder of the time, Australian John Landy (3:58) said of Berger's assertions: "Hah, hah, hah."[49] An Irish runner, Ron Delany, echoed Bowden and Lincoln's statements, saying he hadn't used drugs, calling the idea that anyone would use drugs "absurd and crazy." He added, "Track and field is an amateur sport—a clean sport. I don't think anyone in it would want to pay such a price just to win a race or break a record."

Daniel Ferris, an official with the Amateur Athletic Union, told *The New York Times* that the AAU had no knowledge of any milers who were using drugs. He went on to tell the *Times* that the AAU, the American affiliate of the Interantional Amateur Athletic Federation, and the IAAF both had rules against the use of performance-enhancing drugs, and that anyone caught using drugs in competition could receive up to a life suspension from competition. Indeed, the IAAF had enacted the first rules against doping in 1928.

Roger Bannister stated at the time that he hadn't heard of any runners using drugs. John Hoberman, in an article published in *Sport in History*, argues that Bannister must have known something about the use of drugs, as Bannister studied exercise physiology while pursuing his medical degree at Oxford. Bannister, in his book *The First Four Minutes*, made reference to the use of oxygen as a method of performance enhancement. In the book, he stated, "[A]ll records would be beaten were we to administer oxygen to athletes in a manner similar to the one used in connection with the victorious team of Everest climbers." Bannister's point of view appears to be that it would not be ethical to do so, yet that has not stopped others from speculating about how he came by his achievement.

In *Lore of Running*, author Tim Noakes speculates, "perhaps . . . Sir Roger ran the four-minute mile because of experimental runs he performed in the research laboratory at Oxford while inhaling oxygen-enriched air."[50]

At the time, Sir Adolphe Abrahams, Honorary Medical Officer of the British Olympic team, voiced strong support for Bannister, saying that the four-minute mile "owes nothing to amphetamine (or any other drugs)."

With Berger's remarks, and the ensuing media firestorm, the pattern was set for the next fifty years. Whenever athletes would achieve what might be considered near-impossible feats, someone would question how the athlete has soared to such great, lofty heights—the assumption being, whether stated or not, that he or she had done so by doping.

Within a week of Berger's remarks to the AMA conference, a number of athletes in different sports admitted that they had, on occasion, used "pep pills." *Time* magazine, in their June 17, 1957 issue reported, "After the first angry blast at Dr. Berger's claims, a handful of sports figures—a few American pro footballers, a former Olympic swimmer from Australia, a Canadian team physician—frankly admitted that the doctor had a point."

Tom Dublinski, who played quarterback for the Detroit Lions and later switched to the Toronto Argonauts, said he once took a pep pill prior to a game when he was in college at the University of Detroit. "It hopped me up to high heaven," Dublinski told *The New York Times*. "That's no good—a quarterback has to be steady." Dublinski added that he never took pep pills during his professional career.[51]

Bruno Banducci, another football player, said that during his days on the San Francisco Forty-Niners, "Each of us usually took three [pep pills] to the game—two before kickoff and one between halves." He went on to say that this was something the players did without the management's knowledge. "I played through the games and I didn't feel tired, but I doubt that would have been the case without the 'bennies.'"[52]

Several years later, Gordon Pirie, a British runner during the 1950s, wrote that he suspected athletes from many nations were using amphetamines, although he conceded that concrete evidence was hard to come by. But there was, he felt, plenty of circumstantial evidence to support his conclusions. In his book, *Running Wild*, Pirie claimed to witness a number of runners using inhalers prior to races. At one international meet, he said, a well-known physician came into the dressing room before a race and asked the British runners if any of them wanted "any little pills" (i.e., pep pills).

Pirie felt that, "Sudden staggering performances quite out of keeping with known form can only be explained by the use of drugs."[53] Pirie may have been the first to express such sentiments, but echoes of his comments can still be heard today. Dick Pound, former head of the World Anti-Doping Agency, as well as other antidoping officials, have made similar remarks in the wake of more recent doping scandals.

While pointing the finger at others, Pirie claimed never to have used stimulants. In his book, he also wrote, "In Rome [during the 1960 Olympics] a doctor asked me what stimulants I used. When I indignantly replied that I used none, I was told, 'well, you must be one of the few mugs who don't.'"[54]

In the wake of Berger's comments and the ensuing public uproar over the use of amphetamines in sporting competition, the American College of Sports Medicine decided to look into the issue of doping. One outgrowth of their efforts was the first study to look at whether amphetamine use had any effect on athletic performance.[55] Two years later, the results of the study showed that amphetamine use could result in some small, but significant, performance improvements in several types of athletic endeavor.

THE FIRST STUDIES ON THE EFFECT OF AMPHETAMINE ON ATHLETIC PERFORMANCE

It was only in late 1950s that the true effects of amphetamines on athletic performance were first studied. Prior to this time, there was very little study or reliable data on the drugs' effects on either general athletic performance or performance in specific sports. In 1959 the American Medical Association published articles based on two studies looking into the effects of amphetamines on athletic performance. One of the papers to come out of these studies, "Amphetamine and Athletic Performance," which is considered to be a classic study of the subject, looked at what effect the drug had on highly trained runners, swimmers and shot-putters.

The study, by researchers at Harvard University, found that certain doses of amphetamines improved the performance of all three types of athletes. The maximum performance increase was for shot-putters, who were able to throw the shot between 3 and 4 percent farther, followed by runners with a performance increase of about 1.5 percent, with the performance increase for swimmers being the smallest. But even though the relative boost in performance for swimmers was the smallest (an improvement of no more than 1.16 percent), this would be enough of a boost that an Olympic-class swimmer could go from barely making it to the semifinals to winning gold in the finals.[56]

A particularly important aspect to the study is this: All three types of events that the researchers focused upon require a large effort from the athlete for a short period of time. Other studies have shown that the use of amphetamines delays the onset of fatigue, which may also help endurance athletes, such as marathon runners or cyclists racing in long one-day or multiday events.

Chapter 2

The Beginnings of Modern Doping, 1960–1969

KNUD ENEMARK JENSEN—FIRST DOCUMENTED DOPING DEATH?

As the 1960s dawned, doping in sports was coming into the public consciousness more and more. Testosterone and steroid use were spreading out from sports like weight lifting to various disciplines in track and field. They would ultimately find their way into American professional sports, including football and baseball.

But the first incident of the 1960s connected to doping involved the tragic death of a young Danish cyclist at the Rome Olympics in 1960.

Knud Enemark Jensen rode into sports history during the 100-kilometer team time trial event at the Rome Olympics. He is, unfortunately, the first person whose death during competition was linked to doping, and only the second athlete to die during competition at the Olympics. Since his tragic death, no other athletes have died while participating in Olympic events.

The heat in Rome during the 1960 Olympics was oppressive, according to a *Time* magazine article.[1] On August 25, during Jensen's race, the temperature reached the 100-degree mark in Rome. Jensen and his teammates Jørgen B. Jørgensen, Vagn Bangsborg and Niels Baunsøe started off amidst high expectations for the Danish team. In the early portions of the race, the team was on pace to win a bronze medal. But at about 33 kilometers into the event, Jørgensen was no longer able to continue and dropped out of the race. Jensen and his two remaining teammates carried on. At about 80 kilometers, Jensen started feeling ill and began weaving from one side of the road to the other. Bangsborg and Baunsøe started pushing Enemark, trying to help him continue.

Without Jensen, the team's chances for a medal were doomed. Even with him, given that Bangsborg and Baunsøe had to expend a lot of energy to push their teammate, the chances of finishing toward the top of the heap were steadily declining. At about 10 kilometers from the finish (about 6.2 miles), the two riders could no longer help their ailing compatriot.[2] Moments later, Jensen suddenly tumbled from his bike in a crash that took down his two teammates as well. Jensen was seriously injured, suffering a fractured skull, and was first taken to the local emergency room, where he lay unconscious and with a high fever. He was then transferred to a larger facility, Oespedale S. Eugenio. Jensen remained unconscious and within a couple of hours he passed away. Knud Enemark Jensen was only twenty-three years old.

The cause of death was officially listed as sunstroke, but rumors of doping quickly spread. The surviving Danish cyclists denied any doping. Some reports claim that during the autopsy, traces of methamphetamine and nicotynal alcohol[3] (a drug also known as Ronicol or roniacol and which is another stimulant) were found.[4]

Oluf Jorgensen, one of the Danish cycling team's trainers, later admitted to giving the four cyclists roniacol, traces of which were found in Jensen's system. Roniacol was often prescribed during that era to help improve blood circulation in elderly patients. In Denmark, at the time, the drug was available only by prescription. Jorgensen said that the purpose of giving the medication to the cyclists was to improve their blood flow, and he went on to claim the drug had been legally obtained. *Aktuelt*, a Danish government publication, commented, "As Roniacol is given only to elderly people with blood circulation difficulties, it must be considered highly irresponsible that the trainer ordered this remedy under the given circumstances."[5]

In 1960, the use of stimulants was not prohibited during Olympic competition. Before the decade was out, however, the International Olympic Committee would implement their first rules against doping, and the first athlete to test positive for a banned substance would have to give up his medal.

It turns out that the previous year Jensen was involved in another doping incident. At the 1959 World Championships in Holland, Jensen rode an impressive race and wound up finishing tenth. Ole Krøyer, another Danish cyclist, also competed at the 1959 World Championships, but he became ill just after finishing the race. Krøyer fainted just after he crossed the finish line. Later, he admitted that both he and Jensen had taken stimulants before and during the race. Krøyer claimed that he had gotten the drugs from Danish professional cyclist Bent Ole Retvig.

Several days after Jensen's death, Robert Oubron, the coach of the French Olympic cycling team, was quoted in *The New York Times* as saying, "I'm not surprised to hear Jensen had been drugged. A healthy young athlete does not die from sunstroke. Many pros are drugged, of course, but we don't drug amateurs."[6] In the same article, a Swiss amateur cyclist named

Bieler is mentioned as having died from drug use at the 1959 Swiss National Championships the previous summer. So was Knud Enemark Jensen's death the first documented death of an athlete as a direct result of doping?

Perhaps not. At least one author, Verner Møller, disagrees with labeling Jensen's death as doping related.[7] On March 25, 1961 the official results of the autopsy performed on Knud Enemark Jensen were announced in Rome. As reported in *The New York Times*, the three physicians involved in the autopsy stated that Jensen's death was due to heatstroke. Although some reports suggested that traces of methamphetamine and nicotynal alcohol were found during autopsy, the official report noted that no traces of drugs were found in Jensen's system.[8]

In the immediate aftermath of Jensen's death, Olympic officials took measures to minimize the effects of the heat on the athletes, adjusting the start times of various events to avoid the worst heat of the day. During the first few days of the 1960 Olympic Games, several athletes were hospitalized for heat-related problems, including Jensen's teammate Jorgensen, Raya Mohamed (who coached Pakistan's field hockey team), and Bulgarian cyclist O. Toschev.[9]

Others had trained for the hot, humid weather. The British track and field team trained in anticipation of the Roman summer conditions. "We've had our boys train in heat chambers on treadmills just to get ready," British track and field chief Geoffrey Dyson said at the time.[10]

While Jensen's death put a bright spotlight on the issue of doping in cycling, he was not the first cyclist to use stimulants. Through the 1950s a number of professional cyclists used stimulants, including such greats as Fausto Coppi. Coppi was once asked if he had ever used amphetamines while racing, to which he replied, "Only when strictly necessary." And how often might that be? "Most of the time," Coppi replied. Amphetamines would play a role in another cycling death later in the decade. And there would be no doubt about whether or not drugs were involved in that case.[11]

Knud Enemark Jensen was not the first death at the Olympic competition. Jensen was, however, the first death that had any connection to doping. Forty-eight years before, in the 1912 Olympics held in Stockholm, Sweden, the marathon proved to be fatal for a young Portuguese runner named Francisco Lazaro. Lazaro had won his country's national championship three times, and like all competitors of the time, held a doctor's certificate stating he was fit to run the event. Just like in 1960 team time trial in which Jensen participated, and in 1904, when Thomas Hicks won the marathon in St. Louis (with a boost from strychnine, brandy and raw eggs), the weather during the 1912 marathon was hot and sweltering.

Lazaro managed to run 30 kilometers (slightly more than 19 miles) before heat exhaustion got the better of him. He collapsed and was rushed to a nearby hospital, where he died the next day of complications due to heat exhaustion. Francisco Lazaro was only twenty years old when he passed away. His death, while not doping related, was the first death of an athlete at the Olympics during competition. Jensen's death in Rome is, so far, the only other time an athlete has died in Olympic competition. Several other athletes have died in training incidents, as well as terrorist incidents, over the years.[12]

THE YORK BARBELL CLUB AND THE SPREAD OF STEROIDS

If one place in the United States could be described as the epicenter of steroid use in modern athletics, that place would be the York Barbell Club in York, Pennsylvania. York Barbell in the late 1950s and early 1960s was the home of many of the United States' most prominent weight lifters. As mentioned in the previous chapter, Dr. John Ziegler worked with a number of athletes who came through the facility. Ziegler also worked with Ciba Pharmaceutical in the late 1950s on the development of one of the first artificial anabolic steroids—dianabol. And it was Ziegler who introduced dianabol and other steroids to promising athletes at the York Barbell Club.

Among those athletes who trained at the club were: Bill March, who once held the world record in the standing press; Gary Cleveland, who twice won the U.S. senior national championships; Tony Garcy, and Norbert Schemansky, who won four Olympic medals.

In developing dianabol (methandrostenolone), Ziegler was looking to lessen the androgenic effects of testosterone, while maintaining its muscle-building properties. After the drug was developed, he initially experimented on himself to see how well the drug worked. In 1960, Ziegler started giving dianabol to March and Jake Hitchens.

Ziegler had March take 10 milligrams of dianabol a day, and had March train on a power rack in his office. Within a short period of time, March noticed an increase in his strength. It wasn't long before Tom Garcy added dianabol to his training regimen. And the results were quick. Within two months, March increased his strength so much that he was able to increase the weight he lifted in competition by 100 pounds and sometimes more.

Ziegler was a strong advocate of the use of dianabol and amphetamines combined with exercise using a power rack of his own design. March, following Ziegler's training and medical advice, won the U.S. Senior Nationals from 1961 to 1965. In addition, he took home a gold medal at the 1963 Pan American games. During the Pan Am games, he set a new world record in his event.

Ziegler looked on weight lifting as one Cold War battle that the United States could win, provided the right athletes were given the right medications to help improve their strength and performance. Ever the scientist, he expected the athletes using steroids he prescribed to keep detailed training diaries recording their progress. In December 2006, Dick Smith described Ziegler's approach to a reporter for the *York Daily Record*.

Ziegler's approach, according to Smith, was, "These anabolic steroids are good for people with health problems? Why wouldn't they be good for healthy people, make them stronger?" Smith also told the newspaper that the doctor "would prescribe five milligrams to the lighter men, 10 milligrams to the middleweights and, (to) the heavier guys, 15 milligrams a day." Ziegler's program was a forerunner of today's techniques: Six weeks taking the drugs followed by five weeks off.

Louis Riecke met Ziegler shortly before competing in the 1960 Olympics in Rome. Riecke competed as a weight lifter in the 1950s, with some limited success. In 1960 he was thirty-five, an age where most lifters of the time were already past their prime. Ziegler convinced Riecke to incorporate two new items into his training regimen: isometric exercises, and dianabol. It wasn't long before Riecke noticed an increase in his strength. Soon, he was lifting much greater weights than he had before.

"[Dr. Ziegler] gave me some pills, and I really didn't know what they were," Riecke told the *York Daily Record* in December 2006. "I took them. I know they made me stronger."

The following year, at the 1961 nationals, Riecke increased the weight he lifted by 100 pounds. Riecke's performance improved so much that he placed second behind Tommy Kono—often regarded as one of the greatest, if not the greatest, American weight lifter of all time. Kono claims that he never used steroids during his weight lifting career.

Toward the end of his life, Ziegler had a different perspective on steroids. "I honestly believe that if I'd told people back then that rat manure would make them strong, they'd have eaten rat manure," Ziegler said. When he first started promoting the use of steroids, he didn't comprehend what kinds of people he would be dealing with in the sport. "What I failed to realize until it was too late was that most of the lifters had such obsessive personalities."[13]

As more and more athletes started using steroids without medical supervision, in ever-larger doses, Ziegler became concerned about the side effects and the harm they could cause to a person's health. By 1967, Ziegler had become convinced that steroids were not something athletes should use to gain an edge over their competitors. In an issue of *Strength & Health* magazine from that time, he let it be known, "Androgenic anabolic steroids... are categorically condemned for the athlete." But by then, it was too late. The genie has long since slipped out of the bottle.

TESTOSTERONE BREAKS OUT OF THE WEIGHT LIFTING WORLD

As the 1960s began, testosterone and other anabolic steroids were being used among weight lifters on both the United States and Soviet teams, and possibly other teams as well. As athletes in other sports started adding weight work to their training regimens, the use of testosterone and its related compounds spread. One of the first sports to take up the use of steroids was

American professional football. In 1963, Sid Gillman, the coach of the San Diego Chargers, hired Alvin Roy as the first strength training coach for a professional football team. Roy, who had been affiliated with the United States weight lifting team, knew a thing or two about the use of dianabol.

And like the trainers for cyclists and runners in the nineteenth century who had worked in horseracing beforehand, Roy took his knowledge of doping and applied it and adapted it for professional football players. Over the years, Roy would work not only with the Chargers, but also the Kansas City Chiefs, the Oakland Raiders, and the Dallas Cowboys. Later, Roy was elected to the USA Strength and Conditioning Coaches Association Hall of Fame. Somewhat ironically, the organization condemns the use of steroids in sports.[14]

It didn't take long before steroids found their way into baseball and other sports. "It grew from a few people and spread into other sports," March said.[15]

Eventually, though, some athletes stopped following Dr. Ziegler's instructions and started taking larger and larger doses of dianabol. According to March, "One thing led to another. Some people figured if one pill helped, what would five do for you? They wanted faster results. Then they started selling it on the side. I'm not going to name names, but I knew what was going on. Guys got caught with their hand in the cookie jar."

Dick Smith, who was March's personal trainer during the 1960s, added, "For some guys, it's never enough. If a little is good, a whole lot must be better. It started getting out of hand."

By the end of the 1960s, athletes in an ever-increasing number of sports were using steroids. And in some countries, coaches and government officials pushed the indiscriminate use of steroids in order to achieve athletic superiority and score propaganda points. The 1960s and 1970s were a turning point in the world of doping. The preferred drugs changed from amphetamines and other stimulants to steroids. Both continued to be used, but more and more athletes jumped onto the steroid bus.

THE SAN DIEGO CHARGERS CHARGE UP ON STEROIDS

In the past twenty or thirty years, steroids and football have gone hand in hand. It wasn't always that way. From the 1950s through the early 1970s the more dominant drugs in football were amphetamines. But in 1963, steroids entered the sport on the training tables of the San Diego Chargers football team.

According to football historian Jerry Magee, dinners for the San Diego Chargers included some pink pills that Alvin Roy, their strength coach, assured players would make them stronger. Sid Gillman, the team's head coach at the time, would make an announcement at the beginning of the meal, reminding the players to take their pink pills.

Roy had been affiliated with the U.S. weight lifting team when steroids first surfaced. He was also a student of Russian weight and strength training methods.[16] That being the case, it's quite likely he knew about the Russians' use of steroids, and how they used the drugs. And he was a disciple of Dr. John Ziegler when it came to using dianabol. So, when Roy was hired to be the Chargers' strength coach (he was the first strength coach in the professional football leagues), he introduced dianabol into the team's training regiment in order to get the Chargers' players "pumped up."

Ron Mix, the team captain of the 1963 Chargers (who has since been inducted into the Professional Football Hall of Fame), told the *Pittsburgh Post-Gazette* that Roy once spoke to the team about how important it was to take in more protein in order to get the full benefit of pumping iron. But Roy also told them a story about how the Russian weight lifters were able to do so well in competition.

"I learned a little secret from those Russkies," Mix recalls Roy telling the players. He then pulled out a bottle of dianabol pills from his pocket. Mix told the players it was a supplement and instructed them to take one pill with each meal. After that, a cereal bowl filled with pink pills would be on the Chargers' training tables for each meal. Sid Gillman, the head coach of the team, would stand up and announce at each meal, "Don't forget to take your pills."

The benefits of steroids were quickly realized; but the dangers of using the drugs slowly filtered out as well. After some time, player Dave Kocourek became concerned about the drug and sought advice from a physician who wasn't one of the team's doctors. What the physician told him was frightening. After six weeks of use, the drug could cause heart and liver damage, as well as shrunken testicles. Kocourek went to Mix with his concerns.

"I was as shocked as the doctor and my teammates," Mix said. "Testicle shrinkage! Our team was three weeks away from having the finest professional football men's choir in America."

Mix spoke to Gillman, and although Gillman told his captain that he had been assured that the drugs posed no risk, Mix insisted on calling a team meeting to discuss the matter with the players.

At the meeting, Mix told the players that they had been taking a dangerous drug. His teammates were shocked by the revelation, and according to Mix, from that day forward the players stopped taking the pills. "[We] may have had the unhappy distinction of introducing steroids to professional football," Mix told the *Pittsburgh Post-Gazette*, "but I am relieved to say that it was a mere early flirtation and in no way diminishes the accomplishments of that great team."

Steroids, however, didn't disappear from the Chargers after that meeting. In 1970, a former player sued the team for $1.25 million over the use of the drug, claiming that his career had been cut short as a result of the drug's side effects. In the end, he received just under $300,000 as a settlement. The steroid genie had been let out of the bottle, and there was no turning back.

Other teams would take up steroids in time, with some of those teams going on to dominate their eras.

The Chargers went on to win the American Football League championship game that year by a score of 51–10, a complete rout of the opposing team. It would be several decades before the San Diego Chargers would win another championship game.

STEROIDS AT THE TOKYO OLYMPICS, 1964

In 1964, March and Riecke earned spots on the U.S. Olympic team. Only March was able to compete at the games, however, as Riecke was suffering from injuries that prevented him from being able to perform in top condition. March came close to winning a bronze medal. He matched the lifts of Polish competitor Irenuez Palinsky, but because he outweighed his Eastern-European competitor, the medal was awarded to Palinsky.

"We knew the Russians were on something. All the communist bloc countries were doing it," March told the *Pittsburgh Post-Gazette* in October 2005. "We didn't know what caused them to gain so much weight and be so far ahead. We heard that they were taking shots of adrenaline backstage, too."[17]

In the 1960s, March didn't think of taking steroids as anything wrong. And at the time, using steroids in competition had not been banned. That would happen a number of years later, because it would take until the mid-1970s before tests would be developed that could detect steroids in an athlete's system.

"We didn't think it was any woo-hoo-hoo," Doug Stalker told the *York Daily Record* in 2005. Stalker became a protégé of March in the 1960s, while still in his teens. "You're in sports, you use substances of one kind or another. There was none of this Puritanism, bad-bad, shushing going on.

"This was another thing you used, like a lifting belt."

The same was true for March. "I never gave it any thought," he said in December 2006. "I knew I was getting bigger and stronger. It was just another supplement."[18]

Steroids would continue to be a factor in Olympic weight lifting (and increasingly, for other sports, too) for some time to come, despite being officially banned by the International Olympic Committee and the governing bodies of various sports in the latter part of the 1960s.

UCI AND FIFA BAN DRUGS

In 1966 both the International Cycling Union (known by its French-language acronym UCI) and the International Football (Soccer) Federation (known by its French-language acronym FIFA) banned the use of drugs during their championship events. But this was not the first time either federation had taken action against doping in their respective sports.

In 1955, the UCI banned a trainer after learning that he had supplied his team with performance-enhancing drugs. Then, in 1960, the organization added the following to the articles of their Sports Code:

"In view of the serious danger which the use of narcotics or drugs, which are considered as harmful by the medical profession, poses to the health of riders, any rider who is found to be under the influence of the above-mentioned substances [. . .] will mercilessly and definitively have his licence [sic] withdrawn."[19]

Not a lot of enforcement would happen over the next few years. In the meantime, doping allegations were also making news in the world of soccer.

In 1962, charges that members of the Italian team were doping rocked soccer's World Cup tournament, being played that year in Chile. The uproar became so great that the International Federation of Football (FIFA) called upon its member associations to do everything possible to eradicate doping.

Luis Murguel, a Brazilian member of FIFA's organizing committee at the time, told the Associated Press, "FIFA has asked all member associations to take drastic measures so that the doping of players is eliminated."

The scandal started when articles published in the Chilean newspaper *Clarin* charged that Italian players competing in the World Cup championships had taken pep pills prior to their match against the Chilean team. Italian officials denied that any doping had taken place.

Murguel said at the time, "These charges against the Italian team have not been investigated separately by FIFA. However, if any specific evidence comes up that any team has used dope before championship matches then we will have to take appropriate action."

FIFA had already stepped up their efforts to root out doping in soccer after an International Congress of Sports Medicine meeting in Chile that year passed a resolution urging all countries to continue their fight against doping. Although Italian officials denied that any World Cup players had doped, six Italian major league players were accused of doping earlier in the 1962 season.

The situation in Chile in the wake of the doping allegations became so polarized that at least one newspaper account of the times reported an anti-Italian feeling spreading throughout the country. Some restaurants, bars, and shops went so far as to display "No Italians Admitted" signs.[20]

Two years later, in 1964, the Italian Soccer Federation's antidoping campaign was conducting random spot checks of players from each team in the league. These spot checks were an outgrowth of the 1962 scandal.[21] When tests on some of the Bologna players, taken at a match between Bologna and Torino, revealed traces of stimulants, a new doping scandal broke out. In March 1966, however, the scandal came to an end when an Italian magistrate acquitted all of the players from the Bologna Soccer Club.[22]

Also in 1964, the UCI established their own Medical Commission, one of the first of its kind in sports. The idea was that the commission would be comprised of experts who would work to educate the athletes and to ensure the athletes' health. Two years later, the International Olympic Committee would establish their own medical commission, shortly before they would ban doping in Olympic sports.

In 1965, the Council of Europe held the first International Conference on Doping in Strasbourg. Afterwards, the UCI decided to implement the conference's conclusions into their medical commission's work. So in 1966, they added new rules aimed at combating doping among professional cyclists. These new rules stated that any athlete caught in the act of using banned substances would be fined, and that UCI officials had the right to analyze riders "refreshments" and their "bodily fluids." They also spelled out the fines for those found guilty of committing doping infractions. The punishment for a first offence was 1,500 francs, for the second offence 4,500 francs, and on the third offence the rider's license would be revoked.

With the pressure from the previous doping scandals at the 1962 World Cup in Chile, combined with the Italian doping scandal a couple of years later, FIFA, in 1966, also banned the use of drugs during World Cup championship play. By 1970, the sports federation had introduced a doping control system to test athletes for prohibited drugs.

In 1967, the first full racing calendar after the new UCI rules had been adopted, 14 amateur and professional riders were caught doping. By September of that year, the UCI's medical commission published its first list of banned substances, drawn up by a group of doctors and pharmacologists. The UCI's new rules were prescient. Doping in cycling was very much in the public's eye in July 1967, when an English cyclist died as a result of amphetamine use during the Tour de France.

TOM SIMPSON DIES ON THE SLOPES OF MONT VENTOUX

Tom Simpson was probably Britain's greatest professional cyclist. As a young amateur, Simpson won a bronze medal at the 1956 Olympics in Sydney, Australia. Two years later, he won a silver medal in the Commonwealth Games. The following year, 1959, Simpson turned professional. Within a few years, he had established himself as one of the great riders in the pro peloton. In 1962, he became the first British cyclist to wear the Maillot Jaune (the yellow jersey), which symbolizes the race leader in the Tour de France. Simpson only wore the yellow jersey for a single day, but even so, it was a remarkable moment in Tour history. At the time relatively few English or English-speaking riders raced the Tour. Three years later, Simpson won the world championship road race. But what many know Simpson for is not how great a cyclist he was, but for the way he perished in the 1967 Tour de France, while riding up Mont Ventoux in southern France on a blisteringly hot day.

Mont Ventoux is the largest mountain in Provence, the only mountain of its size for miles around. Although Mont Ventoux is geographically part of the Alps, many consider it to be separate from them, due to the lack of any similarly sized peaks nearby. Trees once covered the mountain almost completely, but from the twelfth century onward, the demand for wood by the shipbuilding industry in Toulon led to the mountain's deforestation.

Since the 1860s parts of the mountain have been reforested, but not the peak, which is covered in limestone and has the appearance of being snow-covered all year round. The rocky landscape on top of Mont Ventoux gives the mountaintop an almost moonlike appearance. Due to the exposed rocky surface, on sunny summer days the heat reflects from the rocks and the tarmac to make riding up and over the mountain a truly brutal experience. Almost like a trip through Hell. One other thing the mountain is known for: wind. The summit of Mont Ventoux also happens to be the place where some of the highest wind speeds have ever been recorded—320 kilometers per hour, or approximately 200 miles per hour.[23]

Simpson once said that his lucky number was 13. His daughter and his wife were both born on the 13th day of their respective birth months. So Thursday, July 13, 1967 should have been a lucky day for him. It was the 13th stage of that year's Tour de France, being held on the 13th of the month. The route: Marseille to Carpentras. On the way: Mont Ventoux, a brutal climb any time of year, but especially so in the heat of summer. And the day was nothing if not hot. Accounts vary as to just how hot, with the cooler versions claiming it was 40C (104F). Other reports suggest that at points along the road to the top the temperature was perhaps as hot as 45C (113F) or even 55C (131F) as Simpson climbed the 1,910-meter (6,200-foot) bald-topped mountain.[24]

When the day's racing began, Simpson was in seventh place overall, and gunning for a spot on the podium once the Tour ended in Paris on the Champs-Elysées. Although Simpson's team was not noted for its strength, the riders were loyal and worked well together. Overall, the team's race strategy was working pretty well. But race rules and the extreme heat would take a heavy toll by day's end. Among the Tour's rules at the time was a restriction on how much a rider could drink. Even in the extreme heat, riders were limited to 4 bidons—or about 2 liters—of water for the entire stage. No water bottle hand-ups were allowed from team cars.

The riders, however, had figured a way around the rules. They would stop and raid cafes, restaurants, and bars en route in order to refill their water bottles. At his final stop, near the base of Mont Ventoux, Simpson didn't fill with water. Instead, he took at least a few sips from a communal bottle of cognac being passed around. Today, we know that consuming alcohol on a hot day will cause dehydration. In the 1960s, exercise science was not so precise.

Add wicked temperatures, a determined cyclist going all out, and a little bit of amphetamines and alcohol in the system can be a potentially fatal combination.

Simpson attacked early on the climb up Mont Ventoux, gaining a bit of time on Julio Jiminez, the eventual stage winner, and a number of other riders. But he was not able to sustain his pace, and soon Jiminez, Ray Poulidor, and a couple of other riders passed him. Simpson fell in with one of the chase groups. For a large part of the climb, Tom Simpson could see the leading riders. He kept trying to bridge the gap between the groups so that he could get into the winning breakaway. As Simpson tired, fans would run beside him and give him a push.

As the temperature rose, the heat took its toll on Simpson. Less than 2 miles from the summit, he started to weave erratically from one side of the road to the other. A bit more than a mile from the summit, Simpson fell off his bike. According to popular legends of the time, Simpson asked the people around him to, "Put me back on my bloody bike." The reality, said Harry Hall (the mechanic for Simpson's team that year), is that Simpson just managed to get out the words, "On! On! On!"[25] Several fans helped Simpson back onto his bike, but it was all for nought. Simpson wobbled along the road for no more than another half kilometer or so and collapsed again.

Dr. Pierre Dumas, the Tour's doctor, and others tried administering CPR, which seemed to help, as far as Hall, Simpson's mechanic, could see. During mouth-to-mouth resuscitation, Simpson's chest would rise and fall, as if he were breathing. The stricken cyclist was airlifted to a nearby hospital. Despite the first aid and the hospital's efforts, Simpson never regained consciousness. He was pronounced dead about half an hour after he arrived at the hospital.

In the aftermath of Simpson's death an inquiry was launched. An autopsy found traces of amphetamine and methamphetamine in his system. This was not a huge surprise, as amphetamines were found in Simpson's cycling jersey that day. And while amphetamine was not listed as the cause of death, the official report left no doubt that Simpson's use of amphetamines that day enabled him to push his body beyond its normal limits, which resulted in the officially listed cause of death—dehydration, oxygen deprivation, and overwork.[26] Given that the temperature on Mont Ventoux was more severe than during the 1960 Olympic team time trial, perhaps the most surprising aspect of the day's race is that more riders didn't succumb to the heat.

The news of Simpson's death sent shockwaves through his team and through the entire peloton. That night, the remaining members of Simpson's team voted on whether to continue with the race or to withdraw. They decided to continue, but left open the option of changing their minds the following morning before the next stage began. They didn't change their minds. Instead, they carried on, wearing black tape armbands around their left arms as a symbol of mourning for their fallen comrade. The other riders had mixed feelings about whether the stage should go on. Eventually, they agreed to continue, but only if a British rider would be allowed to win the stage, as a tribute to the fallen star. As riders lined up for the start of the day's race to Sete, some wept. French rider Jean Stablinski made his way over to Simpson's teammate, Vin Denson.

"You were Tom's closest friend," Stablinski said to Denson. "He has gone and now you are pere de famille. You must win today for Tom. Just go to the front and take a lead of a couple of minutes and do not race too hard. Nobody wants to race hard today."

The day's racing began, and Simpson's teammates rode at the front of the peloton. Denson, at times, could not help weeping. Denson said, "I was riding along in a complete trance and every now and again I would just break down in tears. When I saw another English rider, I kept looking and thinking it was Tom again. I kept listening to Tom—I could hear his voice all the while."

It wasn't Denson who took the stage victory; it was another British rider—Barry Hoban. Hoban afterward said of that day's events, "We were all riding at the front and the next thing, I looked round and there was no one there.

"To this day, I do not know how far I rode on my own. I could give you every inch of Ghent-Wevelgem which I won, but I cannot tell you much about that."

Simpson was known for his sense of humor. Once, in speaking about using stimulants while racing, he quipped, "if it takes ten to kill you, I'll take nine and win." After Simpson's death his joke about drug use would resonate much differently.

A year after Simpson's death, a monument honoring the great British cyclist was placed near the site where he collapsed by the roadside on the ascent of Mont Ventoux. Simpson's widow, Helen, unveiled the monument, paid for by a number of British cyclists. On it are inscribed the words, "Put me back on my bloody bike," that are now believed to have been crafted by Sid Saltmarsh, who was a writer for *Cycling* and *The Sun* at the time of Simpson's death. While Simpson did not speak the words, they sum up his determination to carry on, even when his body could no longer oblige. Each year, thousands of tourists and cycling fans stop at the memorial and place flowers, bicycle parts, and other items to honor the British cycling hero.[27]

In 1968, another cyclist, a French rider named Yves Mottin, would die during a race after using amphetamines. Despite the tragic death of Tom Simpson, some riders did not heed the lessons of Simpson's tragic death and continued to use pep pills. And at least one more paid with his life.

THE IOC BANS PERFORMANCE-ENHANCING DRUGS

Following the death of Knud Enemark Jensen at the 1960 Olympic Games, the International Olympic Committee began discussions on banning the use of performance-enhancing drugs in competition. During the 1962 annual meeting of the committee, the organization responded to concerns over the growing emphasis on winning medals at any cost, including by doping. One outgrowth of the meeting was the formation of a Medical Commission to look into the use of performance-enhancing drugs in Olympic competition.

The commission's charter was to investigate drug use in competition and to make recommendations on what should be done to ensure the integrity of the Olympics.

Two years later, at the IOC meeting held in Tokyo, the commission had an answer. Ban drug use, begin testing for drugs, and make every athlete sign a statement that he or she was competing drug-free. In addition, the commission recommended penalizing national sports organizations implicated in drug cases.

But it wasn't until May 1967, only a couple of months before the death of Tom Simpson, that the International Olympic Committee outlawed the use of performance-enhancing drugs. The new rule banned "the use of substances or techniques in any form [. . .] with the exclusive aim of obtaining an artificial or unfair increase of performance in competition." In 1967 The IOC had two main goals in mind in banning doping. First, they were concerned about the health effects that the use or abuse of drugs would have on the athletes. Second, and just as important as the athletes' health, was to ensure fair competition and remove any disadvantages nonusers would experience when competing against athletes who were doping. Even though professional cyclists were not allowed to compete in the Olympics at that time, the uproar over Simpson's death and other doping scandals inside and outside the Olympic movement ensured that doping in sports could no longer be ignored.

Over the coming months, the IOC's Medical Commission drew up a list of prohibited drugs, substances and methods that would be outlawed starting with the 1968 games. The list was short, comprising 20 stimulants and narcotics felt to be dangerous to athletes' health.[28] Today, the list of banned drugs is much, much larger. And up to 90 percent—or more—of the current list of banned drugs are legal medicines in many countries.

Banned Substances at the 1968 Winter and Summer Olympics

Prior to 1968, the International Olympic Committee did not test for the presence of banned substances during Olympic competition. Starting with the Grenoble Olympics in the winter of 1968 that changed. The IOC embarked on their effort to ensure clean competition. For the 1968 Winter Olympics, the following substances were banned:

1. Sympaticomimetic amines (e.g., amphetamine), ephedrine, and similar substances.
2. Central nervous system stimulants (strychnine) and analeptics
3. Narcotics and analgesics (e.g., morphine) and similar substances
4. Antidepressives (e.g., MAO inhibitors) imipramine and similar substances
5. Major [i.e., powerful] tranquilizers (e.g., phenothasine)

The list shown above was not meant to be an exhaustive list. According to the minutes of the IOC's Medical Commission meeting on December 20, 1967 (where the list was drawn up), the IOC's Medical Commission decided to concentrate on products that could be abused by healthy athletes during competition, even though the medications could be used for legitimate medical purposes under different circumstances.[29]

During the Summer Olympics held that year in Mexico City, the following substances were banned:

1. Sympathicomimetic amines (ex. amphetamine) ephedrine and similar drugs
2. Stimulants for the central nervous system (strychnine) and analeptic and similar drugs
3. Analgesic narcotics (ex. morphine), methadone, and other similar drugs

In addition, the IOC Medical Commission's meeting minutes from July 13 and 14, 1968 also note that for any nonalimentary drugs that excite a normal effort either by their composition or by their dosages if used, even therapeutically, they will be considered as doping products. As with the December 1967 meeting that drew up the list for the Grenoble Winter Olympics, the July 1968 meeting's minutes also went on to say that the list was not meant to be restrictive, and that it was well known that the drugs banned could and often were employed for therapeutic uses outside of sport.

Strangely, the list for the Mexico City Olympics doesn't specifically name ethyl alcohol as a banned substance, and yet, the only positive test result that came from either the Summer or Winter Olympics in 1968 was for a Swedish athlete competing in the modern pentathlon, who tested positive for alcohol.

Among the drugs left off the original list were steroids, due to two reasons. First, no reliable tests existed yet for the detection of artificial steroids in an athlete's body. And second, the exact amounts and ratios of naturally occurring steroids were not completely known. Within ten years, however, the first tests for the presence of testosterone and other steroids would come into existence.

Were steroids being used by athletes at the 1968 Olympics? In 1973, Harold Connolly told a U.S. Senate Committee looking into drug use by athletes, "I know any number of athletes in the 1968 Olympic team who had so much scar tissue and so many puncture holes on their backsides that it was difficult to find a fresh spot to give them a new shot."[30] Connolly, who won a gold medal at the 1956 Melbourne Olympics in the hammer throw, admitted to the committee that by 1964 he was "hooked" on steroids.[31]

Dr. Tom Waddell, another athlete who competed in the 1968 Olympic Games, told *The New York Times* that about one-third of the U.S. Track and Field team had used steroids at a training camp held in Lake Tahoe before the 1968 games.[32]

THE FIRST OLYMPIC ATHLETE WHO TESTED POSITIVE FOR A BANNED SUBSTANCE

Although some athletic organizations had banned doping before the International Olympic Committee took action, drug testing on athletes was still in its infancy when the IOC implemented antidoping measures in 1968. For some tests, research still needed to be done, and the 1968 Games would provide a perfect opportunity. So it might not be a surprise to learn that much of the antidoping testing done at the Mexico City Olympics in 1968 was for research purposes.

The tests that were performed and did matter were tests for the so-called hard drugs, like amphetamines, heroin, cocaine, and the like. But the first Olympic athlete to test positive for a banned substance in Olympic competition didn't come up positive for any of the drugs listed above. Instead, it was something simpler. Alcohol.

Hans-Gunnar Liljenwall, a Swedish athlete who competed in the modern pentathlon, was the unlucky person to test positive. Although testing began at the 1968 Winter Olympics, it wasn't until the summer games that an athlete tested positive. Liljenwall was the first and only Olympic athlete to test positive that year.

Liljenwall claimed that he only had two beers prior to his event, the pistol shooting competition, to relax and calm himself down. By the time the dust settled on the scandal, Liljenwall and the rest of the Swedish modern pentathlon team had to return their bronze medals.

STEROIDS CROSS OVER TO BASEBALL

By the mid- to late-1960s, testosterone and other steroids found their way into the training regimens of a number of baseball players. Former major-league pitcher Tom House, who played for the Atlanta Braves, Boston Red Sox, and the Seattle Mariners during twelve seasons as a pro starting in 1968, admitted to using steroids during his professional days. House told a reporter for the *San Francisco Chronicle* that the use of performance-enhancing drugs was common during the late 1960s and early 1970s.

House claimed that he and several of his Braves teammates used amphetamines, human growth hormone, and "whatever steroid" they could get in order to keep up with all the other players who were using the drugs.

"We were doing steroids they wouldn't give to horses. That was the '60s, when nobody knew. The good thing is, we know now. There's a lot more research and understanding."

House once estimated that six or seven players on each team were experimenting with some form of steroid or human growth hormone during his days as a major-league player. Also, players often talked about their concerns they would be beaten by others who were using better, more effective drugs.

"We didn't get beat, we got out-milligrammed," he told the *San Francisco Chronicle* in 2005. "And when you found out what they were taking, you started taking them."

For House, using steroids began during the 1969 off-season, when he was still playing on the Triple-A farm team of the Atlanta Braves. At the time, House lived in Santa Monica, California, and was secretly working out at a gym—against his manager's orders. He asked some of the weight lifters training there what they used to get so big. They told him they used dianabol.

Steroids were easy to get and relatively inexpensive in California, where House lived during the off-season, so he decided to try them. He wrote in *ESPN The Magazine*, that he did steroids during two off-seasons, but that he would have done the drugs during the regular season, if he could have. But he was playing in Richmond, Virginia, where getting steroids was not as easy as in California.

House felt the effects of steroids almost immediately. He gained size; going from 185 pounds up to 225 pounds in the two years that he used the drugs. And even though he was gaining the benefits, he felt the side effects, too.

According to House, "I was more aggressive about everything. I was on the freeway fighting with people. My wife would say, 'Hi, how are you doing?' and I would scream at her for asking how I was doing."[33]

House told the *San Francisco Chronicle* that the drugs improved recovery time and helped him train harder. But he also gained an extra 30 pounds while taking performance-enhancing drugs, and he blames the extra weight, in part, for knee problems during his professional career.

Despite the benefits of taking steroids, House said that they had no effect on his fastball. "I tried everything known to man to improve my fastball," he once said, "and it still didn't go faster than 82 miles per hour. I was a failed experiment."

"I'd like to say we were smart, but we didn't know what was going on," he said. "We were at the tail end of a generation that wasn't afraid to ingest anything. As research showed up, guys stopped." House said he stopped taking the drugs as soon as he learned about their side effects.

Today, Tom House is a well-known and respected pitching coach. Over the years, his attitude toward steroids has changed.

"As an instructor, I'm about as anti-steroid as you can be, not through research but through first-hand knowledge. I try to aim people toward research and make it clear it's an unacceptable choice. It's OK to ask questions, but it's not OK to experiment.

"The risk-reward isn't worth it. You may get lucky in the short term, but the medium- and long-term effects are if not life threatening, then close to life threatening."[34]

Soon enough, however, baseball players would again be taking steroids and other performance-enhancing drugs as they chased old records and set new ones. Thirty years after House stopped playing professional ball, scandals involving steroid use in baseball would heat up into what became known as the BALCO scandal.

Doping in baseball, however, didn't begin with the use of steroids. Ten years before Tom House started using steroids, another big league player wrote about his experience as a major-league ballplayer. In the book *The Long Season*, Jim Brosnan detailed his life as a major-league pitcher in 1959. In the book, Brosnan wrote about how major-league players used amphetamines to survive the sport's lengthy schedule. Two other authors, Jim Bouton and Leonard Schechter, also wrote about amphetamine use in their best-selling book, *Ball Four*.[35] Steroid use by baseball players would continue up until the present day. Eventually, some of baseball's most hallowed and revered records would be broken by athletes rumored to be using the performance-enhancing drugs.

Chapter 3

The Rise of East German Athletics and Other Tales of Doping, 1970–1979

AGE OF AQUARIUS OR AGE OF STEROIDS? THE DAWN OF THE 1970s

By the beginning of the 1970s, steroids had made inroads into both professional football and professional baseball. Athletes in an ever-expanding circle of sports were using the drugs to excel. Steroids and other drugs found their way into swimming pools, the Tour de France and by the end of the decade even the sideshow of professional sports—wrestling. Most of all, the drugs had their greatest impact during the 1970s on East German athletics. At the beginning of the decade, East Germany was not considered an athletic powerhouse. By the end of the 1970s, the East Germans would have an edge on Olympic competition vastly out of proportion to the country's size.

Antidoping tests improved and new tests developed. By the end of the decade, tests for steroids arrived on the scene and the drugs were banned in Olympic competition. As the steroid tests continued to improve, those athletes who used the drugs had to become more creative in order to avoid getting caught. And while steroids are a major part of the history of doping during the 1970s, another technique gained in popularity during that time, as well. Blood doping.

WE'LL SEE WHOSE ARE BETTER

Steroids and weight lifting have gone hand in hand since the 1950s, when the Russians started giving testosterone to their athletes in order to make them stronger and perform better than their competitors. Perhaps one of the best examples of the Russians' supremacy in weight lifting was Vasily

Alexeyev, who dominated competitions in the early 1970s. Alexeyev was rumored to be using steroids, and his development—both in size and strength—strongly suggested a link. Alexeyev, over a period of years, went from about 220 pounds to 340 pounds, gaining mostly—if not all—muscle. During this time, he became the weight lifter to beat in competition. Few could actually do so.

Alexeyev managed to evade doping controls by knowing the effects of steroids, when to use them and when to taper off prior to competition. He would scale back his use of steroids so that by the time competitions came—and he would have to be tested—his samples would come out clean. Even with the new testing protocols introduced at the 1976 Olympics, Alexeyev was able to evade detection.[1]

Suspicions over Alexeyev's use of steroids date back to at least 1971. In a *New York Times* article, Ken Patera, an American weight lifter, spoke openly about his use of steroids to prepare for the 1972 Olympics. Patera was looking forward to the matchup.

"Last year the only difference between me and him was that I couldn't afford his drug bill," Patera was quoted as saying. "Now I can. When I hit Munich next year, I'll weigh in at about 340, maybe 350. Then we'll see whose are better—his steroids or mine."[2]

Apparently, Alexeyev's were better. He won the gold medal in the super heavyweight classification. Patera didn't win a medal during the 1972 games.[3]

ARNOLD, THE AUSTRIAN OAK

Arnold Schwarzenegger, before he was a movie star or politician, was one of the most award-winning bodybuilders of the 1970s. From 1970 through 1975, Schwarzenegger, nicknamed "The Austrian Oak," won the Mr. Olympia contest six consecutive times. How did he do it? In part, with a little boost from steroids. Schwarzenegger, unlike many other athletes, does not shy away from the topic of steroids. In fact, he's been open about using the drugs since he wrote and published the booklet *Arnold: Developing a Mr. Universe Physique* in 1977. Schwarzenegger marketed the booklet through *Muscle & Fitness* magazine for a number of years.

"I will not speak for my colleagues, but I will write of my experience with tissue-building drugs. Yes, I have used them, but no, they didn't make me what I am. Anabolic steroids were helpful to me in maintaining muscle size while on a strict diet in preparation for a contest. I did not use them for muscle growth, but rather for muscle maintenance when cutting up."[4]

Schwarzenegger has always maintained that he only used steroids while they were legal. "In those days you didn't have to deal with the black market," Schwarzenegger said in a 1992 interview with *U.S. News and World Report*, "You could go to your physician and just say, 'Listen, I want to gain some weight, and I want to take something.' Then the physician would say, 'Do it six weeks before the competition, then it will be safe.' And that's what you would do. The dosage that was taken then vs. what is taken now is not even 10 percent. It's probably 5 percent."[5]

While most articles and stories about Arnold Schwarzenegger state that he started using steroids in the 1970s, at least one individual claims Arnold began using the drugs much earlier. In 1961, Kurt Marnul, a former Mr. Austria, became Arnold's weight-training mentor. In an unauthorized biography of Schwarzenegger written by Nigel Andrews, the author writes, "Marnul introduced Arnold to steroids, which were then legal. In the early 1960s, the trainer claims, 'There was no weightlifter in the world who did not take them. You could get prescriptions for them from the doctor. Arnold never took them, though, without my supervision.'"[6]

Although he retired from competition for good after winning a seventh Mr. Olympia title in 1980 (Arnold originally retired from competition after winning his sixth Mr. Olympia title in 1975, but came out of retirement in 1980 to compete one final time), Schwarzenegger still cuts an imposing figure in the world of bodybuilding. The annual Arnold Classic bodybuilding competition honors his legacy. Also, Schwarzenegger holds the largely honorary position of executive editor for both *Muscle & Fitness* and *Flex* magazines.[7]

STEROIDS AND PROFESSIONAL WRESTLING

In 1976, Terry Bollea, a young professional wrestler whose stage name was and still is Hulk Hogan, did what a number of others in his sport were doing at the time—bulk up by using anabolic steroids, seeking to get an edge on his fellow wrestlers. The use of steroids by wrestlers would continue for years before a true scandal erupted in 1994, when Vince McMahon was put on trial for distributing steroids to various professional wrestlers. Hogan would be one of the athletes who testified against his former boss.[8]

THE SWIMMING SCANDAL THAT SHOULDN'T HAVE BEEN

When people talk about swimming and the 1972 Olympics in Munich, perhaps the most well-known story of that time is Mark Spitz winning seven gold medals. But another swimmer hit the headlines in 1972, and in his case, he was forced to give up his medal because of bureaucratic bungling.

The athlete was sixteen-year-old Rick DeMont, an American swimmer and teammate of Spitz', who won gold in the 400 meter freestyle. The night before he competed in the 400-meter freestyle finals, DeMont was wheezing from an asthma attack. He took an antiasthma drug called Marax, which had been prescribed by his doctor, to ease his breathing. The following morning, when he woke up, he was still having difficulty breathing, so he took another Marax and didn't think anything was wrong.

Before he went to the Olympics, DeMont filled out the standard medical questionnaire, listing the medications he was taking at the time. He assumed that this meant the proper authorities had been notified about his asthma and the medications he was taking because of the condition. Since he was actually at the Olympics, competing, he figured that everything was OK.

DeMont won the 400-meter freestyle by an extraordinarily close margin, beating Australia's Brad Cooper by just one one-hundredth of a second. It was an exciting race. DeMont was behind until the final length of the 50-meter pool. On the last turn, he came up even with Cooper, who had been leading the race to that point.

"At the 350, we flipped even and I thought I can get this guy on the last lap," DeMont later recalled. "He was a lot stronger than I thought he would be. We were toe to toe the whole length."[9] The two swimmers battled side by side to the end, with DeMont touching the wall just before Cooper.

How did DeMont pull out the win? "I skipped one breath in there and I think that gave it to me."

Two days later, after qualifying for the 1,500-meter freestyle finals—an event he held the world record in—DeMont was prevented from competing. The reason? After the 400-meter freestyle, like all medalists, DeMont had to submit a urine sample to be tested for banned substances.

Unfortunately, DeMont tested positive for a banned substance—ephedrine, which is a component of the drug Marax that had been prescribed for his asthma. According to the IOC Medical Commission's statement at the time, DeMont was disqualified and banned from the games "because of the use of forbidden preparations." Ephedrine has been on the IOC's list of prohibited substances since 1968.[10]

DeMont had suffered from asthma for years, and had competed prior to the Olympics without any problems regarding his prescription medication. U.S. officials protested that the IOC had been informed of DeMont's condition and the medication he used.

Prince Alexandre de Merode, a member of the IOC's Medical Commission, told the Reuters wire service that the IOC had not been informed, and suggested that some official on the U.S. team should be disciplined as a result of the scandal. De Merode went on to tell Reuters that all teams had been informed that the drug was unacceptable, and that the U.S. team failed to heed the warning.

What happened in the DeMont case was simple: U.S. team physicians didn't look over his medical forms prior to the 1972 Olympics and failed to pass his information on to the IOC Medical Commission. During a congressional investigation in 1975, Douglas Roby, then a member of the IOC, testified that had the team physicians passed DeMont's information to the appropriate authorities, DeMont would have been able to keep his gold medal.[11]

In the aftermath of DeMont's positive result, the IOC Medical Commission declared, when it upheld DeMont's disqualification, that there would be no gold medal awarded in the 400-meter freestyle. Originally, the IOC decided that Brad Cooper, the Australian swimmer who finished second to DeMont, would remain the silver medalist and that the official list of results would show no gold medal winner. After a protest by Australian officials, IOC officials reconsidered and awarded the gold medal to Cooper.

Cooper's time in the event, 4:00.27 became the official Olympic record rather than DeMont's 4:00.26. DeMont left the Olympics with his gold medal, but was required to return the medal to the IOC in order to maintain eligibility for other international competitions.

After news that DeMont had been stripped of his Olympic victory, the media was all over the story. "I got more attention than I think anybody can ever handle," DeMont recalled years later. "People were sympathetic, that was nice, but it was still in my mind a terribly negative thing."

DeMont became the first Olympian in sixty years to be told to relinquish his gold medal. The last time a gold medalist was required to return his medals was in 1912, when the International Olympic Committee disqualified Jim Thorpe, an American track star of the early twentieth century, and voided his results because he had played minor-league baseball and was considered to be a pro.

After the 1972 Olympics, DeMont continued to compete as a swimmer. "Prior to the Olympics, I was powered by optimism, dreams, and desire. After that, I was pretty much just powered by anger."

In 1973, about a year after DeMont's Olympics fiasco, he channeled that anger into a new world record in the 400-meter freestyle. And in the process, he beat Brad Cooper of Australia a second time. This time, however, he wasn't disqualified and DeMont became the first swimmer to break the 4-minute barrier in the 400, clocking in at 3:58.18. After his victory, DeMont won the World Swimmer of the Year award.[12]

The DeMont story doesn't end in 1972, however, but in 2001, almost twenty-nine years after his fateful race in Munich. After years of trying to get the US Olympic Committee to take responsibility for what happened in Munich, DeMont finally got a measure of satisfaction. The USOC acknowledged their mistakes and took DeMont back into their good graces, by admitting that DeMont did not dope during the 1972 Olympics. Rather, bureaucratic bungling was at the heart of DeMont's positive test.

"It was nice to be acknowledged [by the USOC], to be recognized, and for the truth to come out," DeMont said after the announcement that he'd been cleared. "It wasn't just me. It was my coach. It was my family. Everyone had to live with this stigma."[13]

The International Olympic Committee, however, at a meeting in Dakar, Senegal, in February 2001, decided not to give DeMont his gold medal back. Instead, they chose to let the decision from the Munich Olympics stand, leaving Brad Cooper as the gold medalist. In addition, the IOC chose not to give DeMont any special recognition after all the years that had passed.[14]

Years later, DeMont became an accomplished painter, as well as a highly regarded swimming coach at the University of Arizona. In 2004, he helped coach the South African swimming team at the Olympic Games in Athens.

As Dan Patrick wrote on *ESPN.com* in 2001, "[I]n 1972, Rick DeMont won a gold medal and then had it wrongfully taken away. No honor, no parade in his hometown. No sweet memories of being the best in the world. Just snickers and raised eyebrows when he tried to defend himself.

"Still, justice is sweet. Even if it takes 29 years to arrive."

SOMEONE SLIPPED TORINO A MICKEY

About one month after the DeMont scandal hit the Olympics, allegations of doping of a different kind struck the world of soccer. After a devastating loss to Las Palmas during a Union of European Football Associations (UEFA) Cup match, the president of the Torino soccer club charged that someone had slipped reflex-slowing drugs to several of his players.

Club president Orfeo Pianelli told a news conference that traces of the drugs were found in doping tests performed about 60 hours after the match's conclusion. After the club lost 4–0 to Las Palmas, Pianelli decided to have the doping tests performed to determine what had happened. Even though the deadline for making a challenge to the game's results had already past when the test results came back, Pianelli decided to forward the information to UEFA, in order to avoid criticism of his players' poor performance during the match.[15]

Three years later, in Greece, a similar incident occurred. In April 1975, the president of the Olympos soccer club in Larissa, Greece, filed suit against one of his own players for doping other members of the team. According to a story run on the United Press International wire service, Nikos Constantinidis claimed that forward George Skedros gave his teammates some pills to help them in a match against their local rival Anthoupolis. The match was for the Greek Third Division soccer championship that year.

It turned out, however, that the pills supplied by Skedros to the other players were actually tranquilizers, resulting in the players becoming drowsy during the game and losing the match instead of winning.[16]

A CANADIAN RUNNER BANNED

Thirteen years before Ben Johnson became one of the most well-known athletes caught in a doping scandal, another Canadian runner faced sanctions due to a positive doping test. This earlier runner was Joan Wenzel, a sprinter who ran the 400-meter and 800-meter distances. The International Amateur Athletic Federation initially gave Wenzel a lifetime ban in November 1975, after she tested positive for a banned substance at the Pan American Games held in Mexico City one month earlier.

According to an article in *The New York Times*, Wenzel tested positive for a banned substance after having taken a cold-cure preparation.[17]

John Holt, the executive director of the IAAF, was quoted by the newspaper as saying, "A doping offense means an automatic ban. But the rules allow for reinstatement through an appeal by an athlete's national association. The IAAF, of course, would consider any appeal made by the Canadians on Mrs. Wenzel's behalf."

Few records exist to document whether such an appeal was made on Wenzel's behalf. Canadian records, however, show her participating in a meet in Sudbury, Ontario, in September 1977. Wenzel placed second in the 800-meter race, clocking the distance in 2:08.6.[18] This suggests that at some point, the lifetime ban preventing Wenzel from competing had been reduced. Or perhaps the original punishment was not as severe as news reports of the time suggested.

STEROIDS BANNED IN OLYMPIC COMPETITION

In the mid-1970s tests to detect the presence of anabolic steroids became available for use. The International Olympic Committee announced new testing protocols in 1974 that could determine testosterone levels and whether other hormones or steroids were present, and in what concentration. The IOC decided that testing for testosterone and other steroids would begin at the Montreal Olympics in 1976. The initial tests were much simpler and less accurate in their detection capabilities, and would be refined over the next few years. So while cheaters were able to get around the original tests at the Montreal Olympics, as the East Germans managed to do, newer and more sophisticated testing techniques came into use by 1978. With some further refinements, those tests are still being used in Olympic and WADA-affiliated testing programs today.[19]

THE SUPER STEELERS—SUPERPOWERED OR STEROID-POWERED?

In the history of American football, one team had a run of success during the 1970s like few others. Between 1975 and 1980, the Pittsburgh Steelers (nicknamed the Super Steelers) won the Super Bowl four times. Did they win their championships the old-fashioned way, based on hard work and a strong desire to be the best? Or did they win with the aid of modern medicine, by using anabolic steroids?

Rumors and suspicions about steroid use by the Steelers teams of that era have been around for years. In his 1990 book, *God's Coach*, Skip Bayless tells the story of Randy White, a Dallas Cowboys player who used steroids during the 1970s. White, a defensive lineman who's in the Professional Football Hall of Fame, says he started using the drugs after feeling intimidated by the Steelers' linemen.

"Man," White told Bayless, "I'd look across the line at those Steelers with their sleeves rolled up on those huge arms, and well, I had to do something. I figured they were using steroids too."[20] And at a certain point, White would have been correct. Steve Courson, who played on the Steelers during the late 1970s and early 1980s, would eventually admit to using steroids when he played on the Pittsburgh football team.

And Jim Haslett, another former NFL player who was head coach of the New Orleans Saints in 2005, once claimed that the Super Steelers of the 1970s were influential in making steroids popular among NFL players. Haslett (who currently serves as the defensive coordinator of the St. Louis Rams) began his football career when he was drafted by the Buffalo Bills in 1979. In March 2005, he was quoted in the *Pittsburgh Post-Gazette* as saying he felt the need to use steroids during his early days as a professional football player. Haslett spoke about his steroid use at a meeting of the National Football League held in Maui, Hawaii. At the time he was playing, Haslett told the NFL meeting, he estimated that about half of the league's players were taking performance-enhancing drugs. He described the strength of the NFL linemen of his era this way: "They tossed you around, they were strong. So everybody wanted an advantage, so you tried it; I tried it. I mean I tried it, everybody tried it."

The only way to stay competitive, Haslett felt, was to take steroids. At the time, the league had not banned use of steroids, so any player using the drugs was not breaking any established rules.

"If you didn't [take steroids], you weren't as strong as everybody else, you weren't as fast as everybody else," Haslett said at the time. "That's the only reason to do it. Everybody's looking for a competitive edge."[21]

Reaction to Haslett's accusations from the Steelers organization was swift.

"This is totally, totally false when he says it started with the Steelers in the '70s," Dan Rooney, the Steelers' owner, told the *Pittsburgh Post-Gazette*'s Ed Bouchette. "Chuck Noll was totally against it. He looked into it, examined it, talked to people. Haslett, maybe it affected his mind."

Rooney also pointed out that the Steelers offensive lines of that era were noted for their speed, among other things, and not for being large players. In fact, Steelers linemen were among the smallest linemen playing in the league during the 1970s.[22]

The uproar in the sports world caused by Haslett's claims was swift. The next day, Haslett retracted his allegations, saying, "I have a lot of respect for that team, that organization and Mr. (Dan) Rooney. That's just what we believed when I played. And, later, one of their players admitted using steroids. But I didn't mean to cause them any harm."

Haslett went on to say that he didn't like the side effects of the drugs and eventually stopped using them. He also said that anyone who takes the drugs still has to work hard, "[I]f you take [steroids] you still have to eat right and you have to work your ass off. If you take them and you don't do anything, that doesn't do anything for you."[23]

In 1991, Steve Courson published a book called *False Glory*, which was an exposé of steroid use in the NFL. But as exposés go, it wasn't much. Courson claimed a large percentage of NFL players used steroids in the late 1970s and early 1980s, but he didn't name names. Courson did, however, say that Jack Ham and Jack Lambert, two of his Steelers teammates, adamantly refused to touch steroids.[24]

In his book, Courson admitted to using steroids while playing on the Pittsburgh Steelers in 1979. His admission may have been the catalyst that led Haslett to believe a number of players on the team had been using steroids during the Super Steelers era.[25]

Courson later suffered heart problems that may have been an indirect result of his steroid use. After he retired from football in 1986, Courson's physical condition hung in the balance. In 1988, he was diagnosed with cardiomyopathy, a weakening and enlarging of the heart muscle that can be fatal. Courson's condition at the time was so serious that he was put on the list for a heart transplant. At a Pittsburgh Steelers reunion in 1994, other players wondered if he would survive much longer.

"I know they all wondered it, and with good reason," Courson told the *Pittsburgh Post-Gazette*'s Chuck Finder in November 2004. "When I was sitting there at 330 pounds with a beeper for the heart-transplant list, I definitely understood. I was a sick puppy. I didn't look good. I didn't feel good. It was hard getting out of bed every day. It was a very humbling experience."[26]

For Steve Courson, the increased body mass that came from using steroids may have contributed to his later obesity, which would take its toll on his heart. Amazingly, Courson managed to pull his life together, lose weight, and restore his heart function back to normal.[27]

Roger Staubach, quarterback of the Dallas Cowboys during their heyday in the late 1970s and early 1980s, once said, "I'm sure that the '70s had its steroid issues. I wasn't aware of steroids back then. The Olympics recognized it years ago. The rest of sports did not. It haunts us now. We lost two tough games to the Steelers. (Lynn) Swann, (Terry) Bradshaw, (John) Stallworth—I don't think they were on steroids. Jack Lambert was phenomenal and he weighed 220 pounds. He sure didn't look like he was on steroids. Neither did Jack Ham nor Andy Russell."[28]

THE TOUR DE TESTOSTERONE

In 1975 and 1977, Bernard Thevenet won the Tour de France with a little boost. He used testosterone and other steroids during his training and racing. At the time, professional cyclists and their trainers considered steroids to be like vitamins or other health supplements, and the Union Cycliste International (UCI) had no rules that banned their use.

"It was thought that just like riders take vitamins, for example, they should take cortisone and anabolic steroids," Thevenet, now a Tour de

France official, told the Associated Press. "It wasn't to get a boost, but . . . to recuperate."[29]

Thevenet tested positive for doping during the 1977 Paris-Nice race, and was hospitalized later in the year for a liver ailment that he claimed was due to long-term use of steroids. The 1977 Tour was his second, and last, victory in France's most storied bicycle race.

After Thevenet retired from professional cycling, a number of newspapers reported that he had used various doping products during his career. "I think everybody did because in that era it wasn't just not forbidden, it was recommended," Thevenet said.[30]

After his retirement, Thevenet admitted his use of steroids and called for a ban on the use of performance-enhancing drugs by professional cyclists.

LE TOUR DE BEAKER: THE YELLOW JERSEY CAUGHT—AND EXPELLED

Before 1978, no rider leading the Tour de France had ever been ejected from the race because of a failed doping test or because he'd tried to beat the doping tests. In fact, no yellow jersey holder had ever been expelled from the race for any reasons before 1978. But after the 13th stage of that year's race, Michel Pollentier of Belgium became the first rider to achieve that dubious honor. At the start of the stage, Pollentier was wearing the polka-dot jersey signifying the cyclist who had won the most points in the mountain-climbing competition within the race.

While many nonfans might recognize the yellow jersey signifying the overall leader, there are three other individual competitions within the tour. The white jersey signifies the best rider under the age of 25, the green jersey signifies the best sprinter, and the polka-dot jersey signifies the rider who is the best climber. As the race progresses and cyclists gain points in any of these competitions, these jerseys can change hands just like the yellow jersey.

So Pollentier was holding the polka-dot jersey on heading into the 13th stage of the 1978 Tour. The stage was long—240 kilometers (approximately 150 miles) from St. Étienne to l'Alpe d'Huez—and grueling. The race finished with an epic battle up the 21 switchbacks and hairpin turns that l'Alpe d'Huez is known for.

Bernard Hinault, who would go on to win the race, was more worried about his rival, Joop Zoeltemelk, and Zoeltemelk was so concerned about Hinault that neither rider responded when Pollentier broke away on the climb to Chamrousse. Each wanted the other rider to do the work, and neither rider did. Pollentier, at one point, had a three-minute advantage over the other two, putting himself in the position of perhaps being able to take the yellow jersey and the overall lead—if he could hold onto his lead. By the time he reached the bottom of l'Alpe d'Huez, Pollentier was still ahead of his rivals, but he progressively lost time to them over the course of the mountain's many twists and turns. Still, by the time he reached the summit, he had maintained enough of a time gap on both Hinault and Zoeltemelk that he would claim the leader's yellow jersey.

And then came the doping test. Pollentier, who had taken amphetamines to help him during the race, had a device to beat the system—or so he thought. It was a contraption that used a rubber ball hidden in one of his armpits, some tubing and pipes, and a bottle containing clean urine. One of the officials at the doping control area became suspicious of another rider, and then he became suspicious of Pollentier. The official raised Pollentier's jersey and exposed the contraption.

Pollentier was fined 5,000 Swiss francs, ejected from the Tour and suspended from competition for two months. Although he came back to cycling after his suspension ended, Pollentier suffered from depression over the years. He won the Tour of Flanders in 1980 and continued on without any major results until retiring from the sport in October 1984.[31]

THE EAST GERMAN DOPING MACHINE MAKES WAVES IN MONTREAL

When an athlete, team, or an entire country's sports establishment decides to undertake an illicit doping program, they are not likely to publicly announce that such a decision has been taken. In 1970, Dr. Manfred Höppner, the director of sports medicine for the East German athletic establishment, made a momentous decision. He authorized the use of performance-enhancing drugs, including steroids, as part of the training regimen for all athletes in their sports development programs. This decision was taken in preparation for the 1972 Olympics to be held in Munich, in what was then known as the Federal Republic of Germany, or more commonly, West Germany.[32]

At the time Höppner made his fateful decision, steroids had not yet been outlawed in Olympic competition. In fact, that would not happen until the middle of the decade, when a reliable test to determine the presence of steroids would become available. But secrecy was paramount. East Germany's program was just a microcosm of the athletic programs—both formal and informal—in both the Soviet Union and the United States.

East Germany's focus, like many of the countries on either side of the Cold War, was to prove its superiority, and by extension, the superiority of the East German economic and political system. So the focus was not just on developing athletes who could perform well in international competition, but athletes who would be able to beat the West Germans, and who would dominate various sports in the process. Nowhere was this more evident, perhaps, than the East German women's swim team.

From that moment forward, the East German athletic establishment, with the backing of their government, began a relentless drive to dominate the Olympic games. The full extent of how willing East German officials were to win at all costs, despite any dangers to their athletes, would not be known until 1998.

Sports in East Germany (also known as the German Democratic Republic, or GDR) were organized in such a way as to encourage a more scientific approach to the selection of potential star athletes for further coaching and development. Some of that development included the use of steroids, unbeknownst to the athletes who were the guinea pigs for these experiments. The physicians, coaches, trainers, and others involved in the program would often refer to the little blue pills and pink pills as "vitamin supplements." Since the 1950s, the East German program had been giving athletes in various disciplines supplements in order to improve the country's results.

In fact, the East Germans started experimenting with the use of steroids back in the 1950s. The athletes who received the drugs were then put through grueling workouts. Over time, the leaders of the programs—and those who participated in them—discovered the many side effects and problems from the early forms of steroids, especially when given in excessive doses. Eventually, they would find that a system of three- to four-week cycles on and off the drugs produced optimum results. But it would only be after 1970 when the program would be put to broader use. In those early days, most of the athletes who were doped came from a discipline involving strength, such as weight lifting, discus throwing, and so forth.[33]

In the 1970s, what was already an efficient system for finding and nurturing gifted athletes would turn into an efficient system for doping athletes and avoiding detection—for the most part.

During this period, East Germany morphed from a small country with the occasional Olympic medal into a full-fledged powerhouse, in some cases totally dominating entire sports for an extended period of time. Even though the GDR were quick to find new methods to beat drug testing in foreign competition, they were also quick to find ways of masking the use of steroids by East German athletes. Creativity in scheduling the doping was the key to East Germany's success.

Although Dr. Höppner had formally approved the use of drugs to improve athletic performances in 1970, there's evidence that the use of steroid might have been happening in East Germany well before that time. In 1968, Brigitte Berendonk, a West German Olympian, noticed competitors from the East who bore the hallmarks of steroid use, including a more masculine appearance, aggression, and unusual body hair.[34]

After being badly beaten by athletes she felt showed obvious signs of doping at the 1972 Olympics in Munich, Berendonk spoke out publicly and demanded that something be done. The German press ridiculed her at the time, but she continued to speak out.[35]

Speaking about her Olympic experiences, Berendonk told Steven Ungerleider (author of *Faust's Gold*, a well-documented chronicle of the East

German doping machine), "[W]hen I think about my years as an Olympian, both in my competition in 1968 in Mexico City and then in the Munich Olympics [when she took eleventh place], it seemed natural at that time that we all looked like well-trained athletes, conditioned athletes. But I knew deep in my soul that doping was wrong. The GDR, the system I escaped from, had created monsters. These were not real people, just engineered experiments."

Berendonk was intimately acquainted with the East German athletic machine. She had seen the program up close and from the inside. In the 1950s she had been an athlete in the East German development program, until her parents decided to defect to the West. Once in West Germany, Berendonk embarked on an athletic career that would take her all the way to the Olympics, not once, but several times.[36]

Athletes and officials from the GDR didn't need to worry about getting caught using steroid before the mid-1970s. No reliable testing technique existed for steroid use until 1975. These testing techniques were still fairly crude by today's standards, but they were enough to start catching the most obvious of drug cheats. Although many suspected that the GDR was dope-fueled, it wasn't until 1977 that an East German swimmer—Ilona Slupianek—tested positive in and was disqualified from a competition.[37] For the most part, the East German program was able to avoid such embarrassments. After 1977, they would need to work a little harder to do so.

Not only were testing methods not as advanced as today, but East German sports officials had a devastatingly simple plan to avoid getting caught. First, as antidoping labs were being established and certified by the IOC, they set up their own lab in Kreischa in 1977. By doing so, they gained access to the IOC's testing protocols and procedures. This gave the doping program a crucial advantage. The institution could not only test for whether an athlete had taken banned substances, they could also use data gathered from their own experiments, and from antidoping research they were privy to, in order to further their national Olympic ambitions.

The plan to avoid detection worked like this: Athletes scheduled to compete outside East Germany would be required to give urine samples before leaving the country. Only those who could test clean would be allowed to compete. If an athlete's urine didn't come up clean, the athlete would continue to be tested until it did—and only when it came up clean could he or she attend the games. If the athlete couldn't pass the tests, he or she would not be allowed to attend international competitions. The athlete would be "ill" and unable to attend.

How did East Germans manage to beat the system? Part of their success in Olympic competition came from having the resources and equipment to be on the forefront of doping research. For example, when the initial testing methods were developed to monitor the use of testosterone, through the use of the testosterone to epitestosterone (T/E) ratio, the GDR's antidoping lab learned how to conduct such tests. By carefully monitoring an athlete's

T/E level and ensuring that all athletes leaving the country would pass the screening tests, they were able to avoid detection.

This worked well for the 1976 Olympics, where the women's swim team, especially, dominated their sport. Of 13 gold medals in women's swimming that year, the East German team won 11. The GDR were well on their way to becoming an athletic powerhouse.

And then, in 1978, they hit a snag. Newer testing protocols to detect the use of testosterone and other steroids were coming into use. And while the East German program had managed to avoid detection in 1976 by taking their athletes off steroids shortly before competition, these new techniques were more sophisticated and able to measure the presence of banned substances in much smaller concentrations.

Up to that time, coaches tried to keep their athletes on the doping program until the last possible minute. So when preparing for the 1978 World Swimming Championships in West Berlin that year, the coaches prepared their athletes in their usual manner. And, as was typical at the time, the East German sports authorities did their prescreening tests as close to competition as possible. With the newer techniques being implemented, suddenly it turned out that a number of East Germany's women's swimming stars would very likely test positive if they went to the World Championships in West Berlin.

The East Germans learned of the problem with their doping program ahead of time because their antidoping lab at Kreischa was among the first to purchase the Hewlett-Packard gas chromatography/mass spectrometry testing instruments that were then being used to determine the presence of steroids and a number of other banned substances. The Kreischa lab purchased their new HP testing equipment in the spring of 1978 for approximately $187,000.

Using their newly acquired equipment, the East German authorities tested 13 swimmers during a routine testing period in the lead-up to the 1978 World Swimming Championships in West Berlin. Of the 13 swimmers, 10 came up positive for banned drugs. Then, they were retested. This time, only two swimmers came up positive for Nandralone: Petra Thümer and Christiane Sommer. The two women were sent to the lab in Kreischa, where further testing was carried out. But even with testing every several hours, Thümer's and Sommer's samples kept coming up positive. Concerned that their athletes would test positive at the swimming competition in West Berlin, a directive was issued that all doping treatments should cease.

The East German team fared poorly and suffered a humiliating defeat. However, the long-term impact of this experience was that the East German program learned how to better avoid detection. And they developed a new way to circumvent the testing procedures—using testosterone esters, which were undetectable by the testing methods of the times. By doing so, they ensured that their athletes maintained the performance advantages gained by the use of anabolic steroids as part of their training regime.

But the GDR didn't settle for just one way to beat the system. In addition to monitoring athlete's levels of steroids prior to competition, athletes were also given epitestosterone, in order to balance out his or her T/E ratio. Epitestosterone, a naturally occurring hormone, has no known function in humans. In the late 1970s, an East German pharmaceutical company managed to isolate the hormone and make an easily administered form.

With careful manipulation of an athlete's T/E ratio by giving epitestosterone (the E in T/E) the GDR program was able to ensure that their athletes would pass through the initial screenings undetected. The more sophisticated techniques, called Isotope Ratio Mass Spectrometry (or IRMS, for short), are only used when an athlete's T/E ratio exceeds a certain amount.

At the time, the ratio was fixed at 6:1. As long as an individual's T/E value was less than that, the antidoping labs would not perform the more sophisticated (and expensive) test. While the current threshold value is lower (currently set at 4:1), modern antidoping labs testing for the presence of testosterone follow the same general process: Use the T/E ratio to screen for suspicious values and then subject the suspect samples to the more rigorous testing.[38]

When necessary, the East Germans, would also resort to another painful, but almost foolproof method: Switching urine. By switching an athlete's contaminated urine with "clean" urine, athletes could continue to dope and still manage to evade detection. Sometimes this meant using a fake bladder or other apparatus to store the clean urine. In other cases, it meant actually filling the athlete's bladder with the clean urine—a very uncomfortable procedure.[39]

Even if East German athletes avoided testing positive for banned substances, other athletes competing against them noted changes in the appearance and mannerisms of some of East Germany's elite sportsmen and sportswomen. Brigitte Berendonk, who would play a major role in Germany's doping trials more than twenty years after the Montreal Games, as well as a number of others, recalled that the appearance of East Germany's female athletes was intimidating, to say the least.

Physical appearances may have intimidated competitors from other nations, but what was even more intimidating was their total dominance in a few select sports, like swimming. For a long time, East Germany was able to take advantage of their ability to circumvent the IOC's antidoping rules. Rarely, if ever, did an East German athlete test positive for any banned substance.

BLOOD DOPING: THE LASSE VIREN CONTROVERSY

Just as Rick DeMont has been associated with doping at the Olympics, so has Finnish runner Lasse Viren been subjected to suspicions of doping in his run (literally) into the Olympic record books by scoring what sports commentators have called a "double-double." Viren, a Finnish middle-distance runner known as "The Flying Finn," managed to win gold medals in both the 5,000- and 10,000-meter races in both 1972 Summer Olympics held in Munich and the 1976 Summer Olympics held in Montreal. While DeMont's name has been associated with the use of ephedrine, a stimulant, Viren's name has long been associated with a new and different form of doping that may have first come into use in the 1970s—blood doping.

If the technique that became known as blood doping actually was used before 1972, no clear records exist. In 1972, a Swedish researcher looking for a way to improve an athlete's performance without subjecting the athlete to potential harm developed a technique he referred to as "blood packing" or "blood boosting." Later, someone coined the term "blood doping."

So what is blood doping and how does it work? The idea behind blood doping is simple, if an athlete has more red blood cells to carry oxygen to his or her muscles, the athlete will be able to perform for a longer period of time. So someone who intends to blood dope stores a quantity of blood sometime before an important event. Shortly before the race, that blood is then reinjected back into the athlete. Does it work? For endurance athletes, yes, it works very well. For sprinters or athletes whose sports require sudden, short bursts of strength, blood doping offers very little, if any, advantage.

Dr. Bjorn Ekblöm pioneered research into blood doping in 1972 when he tested the basic idea on four athletes in Sweden. He removed a quart of blood from each athlete, separated out the red blood cells and then about a month later reinjected the red blood cells back into the athletes. Before he removed their blood, he tested them on treadmills, noting the level of exertion each athlete attained and how long the athlete was able to continue exercise. After adding the extra red blood cells, he again tested the athletes. What he found was that they could work at the same level of exertion for about 25 percent longer once the extra red blood cells were added to their systems.[40]

At the time, blood doping was not illegal in Olympic competition. In fact, blood doping wouldn't be outlawed until some fourteen years later, in 1986. In the interim, blood doping was a technique used by a number of athletes from different countries. Many coaches and athletes, even though the practice was not banned, considered it to be unethical and contrary to the true nature of sport.

But was Lasse Viren the first athlete to use the technique to win a major event? Those who are skeptical of Viren's accomplishments point out that in competitions outside of the Olympics, he didn't fare nearly so well. Added to that, the skeptics point out, Viren didn't really race much in between 1972 and 1976. They argue that in order to compete at a high level, one must continually compete at that level. Put another way, the idea is that the only way one can be in race condition is to race.

Viren didn't do that. He and his coach maintained a training schedule that included a lot of base-level training and a gradual buildup to peak fitness for a specific event. In his case, the event he was training for in 1972 was the 5,000-meter run. The 10,000-meter run came about as a bit of fluke. Viren did so well in the 5,000 that his coach encouraged him to attempt the 10,000 as well. When he did so, he won a second gold medal. Four years later, Viren would do it all over again.

Given the seemingly few and admittedly poor results in between the Olympics, some have argued that there must have been a secret source from which Viren obtained his speed. Viren, on the other hand, insists that he has never blood doped and never needed to. By focusing on the Olympics, to the exclusion of other events, he built up his fitness specifically for those few events every four years.

The truth is a bit more complicated. First, there are two types of blood doping. One, called homologous blood doping, involves injecting someone else's blood into an individual's system. Since 2004, a test has existed to detect the presence of blood cells from another person. If the science of the test is correct, then athletes who use homologous blood doping are more and more likely to get caught.

The other type of blood doping is what Dr. Ekblöm was researching in 1972. This form of blood doping, known as autologous blood doping, involves reinjecting an athlete's own red blood cells back into his/her system. So far, no test has been developed that can reliably detect, by direct observation, whether an athlete has used his own blood, stored for a number of months.

By measuring an athlete's hematocrit, or the percentage of red blood cells in a person's blood, it is possible to determine whether an athlete has an unusual amount of red blood cells in his or her system. But because hematocrit values can vary from one individual to the next, it's not a surefire indicator that anything is amiss. In fact, the only way to tell for certain is to conduct a number of tests over an extended period of time to determine what is normal for a given athlete. But the hematocrit level is just an indicator that something might be wrong. It's not proof positive that an athlete has been engaged in doping, unless a series of tests show that the level is not normal for the individual, or other tests show that the athlete in question has someone else's blood cells.

So whether or not Viren blood doped in the 1970s, even if a blood sample from the era had been stored over the years, it would be impossible to prove that he had engaged in such practices—unless he was using someone else's blood.

For many years, Viren has had to deal with questions about blood doping from fans, from journalists, and from others. Viren knows what happened, and willingly offers to tell his side of the story. In a 2004 interview with James Raia, Viren said, "I know what happened and what I did or didn't take. They (the media) always want to know about the big games and why, why, why (he won). I have no problems answering the question. I trained many times at high altitude. High altitude training started at that time. People did not [know] what was happening or who was coming up, but it's not a problem for me when people ask."[41]

Chapter 4

Blood Doping, EPO, and Human Growth Hormone, 1980–1989

USHERING IN THE 1980s

By the beginning of the 1980s, doping was becoming more and more commonplace across a wide range of sports. At the same time, the IOC and various national Olympic committees were building momentum in their fight against doping. For the twelve years after the first antidoping tests in the 1968 Winter and Summer Olympics, more and more cheaters were caught in each successive Olympic games.

And then a strange thing happened. In both the 1980 Winter Olympics in Lake Placid, New York, and the Summer Olympics in Moscow, no one tested positive. This was the one and only time since the start of drug testing that not a single person was found to be using performance-enhancing drugs in both the Summer and Winter games when both were held during the same year. (Currently, the Summer and Winter games alternate every other year.) There have been a number of instances since 1980—especially during the Winter Olympics—where no athletes were found to be doping. Was it a sudden attack of conscience that prevented the competitors from doping? Or were the athletes and those who helped them dope smarter than the people trying to catch them?

If the East German experience of the 1970s is any guide, then more likely it was the latter. But a number of other things happened that year that affected competition at the Olympic Games. The most prominent event to affect the Olympics was the Soviet invasion of Afghanistan on Christmas Day, 1979. In the aftermath of the invasion and continued occupation of the country, U.S. President Jimmy Carter asked the International Olympic Committee to move the Summer Olympics to another location. When the

IOC refused, Carter called for a boycott of the Olympics. The U.S. Olympic Committee decided to boycott, as did the Olympic committees of a number of American allies.

With American athletes not attending the 1980 Moscow Olympics, along with athletes from other countries, it's possible that some athletes who might otherwise have been caught doping were not caught simply by virtue of their absence. On the other hand, the East German sports program, and no doubt the sports programs of a number of other countries, had learned techniques for getting around the drug tests.

In 1984, a number of countries, led by the Soviet Union, stayed away from the Summer Olympics in Los Angeles, citing fears for their athletes' safety. Whether it was really the safety issue, or whether it was merely retaliation for the boycott of 1980 can be argued either way. Again, however, athletes who might have been doping were not caught for the simple reason that they weren't competing. But the 1984 Winter and Summer Olympics were not free of doping scandals.

Blood doping allegations swirled around a number of athletes, including members of the U.S. cycling team and a Finnish runner. But at the time of the 1984 Summer Olympics, blood doping was not a specifically banned technique.

During the 1980s, two of the bigger stories in the world of doping were the use of blood doping, and, at the close of the decade, the development of synthetic hormones that could be used for a different kind of blood doping. In the latter case, one of the biggest dangers was the possibility of death—a high price to pay for a brief moment of athletic glory. The new hormone was called recombinant erythropoietin (EPO). EPO was developed by a biotechnology company in Massachusetts that eventually became known as Amgen, and it was originally intended to help patients who suffered from anemia. Soon enough, someone figured out a different use for the drug—synthetic blood doping.

By the mid-1980s, the International Olympic Committee would ban blood doping. But not much later, EPO would come on the scene, eliminating the need for storing and reinfusing blood cells prior to competition. Reliable tests to determine whether an athlete had used EPO or had received transfusions of another person's blood would not be developed until the early 2000s. So while the use of blood doping was banned in the 1980s, the drug-testing programs could not prove that a person had blood doped until twenty years later. And even now, no direct test exists that can determine whether an athlete doped with his or her own blood.

THE BAY AREA LABORATORY CO-OPERATIVE FORMS

In 1984, Victor Conte, a former bassist for the San Francisco funk-rock group Tower of Power, founded the Bay Area Laboratory Co-operative

(BALCO). BALCO started out as a company that did medical testing and provided nutritional supplements to athletes. Within a few years, Conte had made a reputation among elite American athletes for being able to determine, through blood and urine tests, the overall state of an athlete's fitness. On the basis of those test results, Conte would recommend various vitamins and nutritional supplements to help athletes perform better.

By 1988, he managed to convince coaches of various Olympic sports to try his methods. One of those coaches, Wes Cahill, took the entire U.S. Olympic Judo team to visit Conte's offices in Burlingame, California, to have blood work done and their fitness levels assessed. To Cahill's amazement, based on the test results, Conte correctly predicted which member of the judo team would go on to win a medal in Seoul, South Korea.

"[Conte] made predictions about each member of the team, based on what he saw in the test results," Cahill told *The New York Times* in 2003. "There was one guy, Kevin Asano, and Victor said he was in the best shape to win an Olympic medal. We were shocked. Kevin was a good athlete, but he wasn't considered a medal favorite. But Victor was right. Kevin fought for the gold medal. He ended up winning the silver medal."

Conte found his way into the nutritional supplements business through his wife, Audrey Stein. She had a holistic health shop in the Bay Area. In the late 1970s and early 1980s, at a time when his music career was flagging, Conte became interested in his wife's business. Conte was also no stranger to the sports world, having competed as a triple-jumper in both high school and college.

He started visiting the library at Stanford University to read and learn everything he could about the manner in which the human body's metabolism functions. Eventually, he felt confident enough to open his new business, the Bay Area Laboratory Co-operative, in a small trailer.

Articles in the local papers started describing the work that BALCO provided, and over time the company's clientele grew. It wouldn't be until the 1990s when BALCO would move into new lines of business that would eventually make the company's name synonymous with steroids and doping.[1]

MARTTI VAINIO, ONE OF THE FLYING FINNS, BUSTED IN LOS ANGELES

If drug testing in 1984 were like antidoping testing twenty years later, perhaps Martti Vainio would never have participated in the Los Angeles Olympics. Earlier in 1984, Vainio competed at the Rotterdam Marathon in Holland. At the time, Vainio was so pumped up on steroids and other supplements that he easily cruised to a third-place. He was 33 at the time, an age when most distance runners are beginning their long, gradual decline in performance.

Vainio should have been easily caught. The latest techniques in drug detection, even at that time, were capable of detecting tiny amounts of steroids or their remnants. But at the time, the home country of each athlete handled drug testing and its results. So, although the tests found traces of steroids in Vainio's system, the Finnish sports establishment covered it up. Antti Lanamaki, the Finnish Athletic Association's chief coach, destroyed the records, rather than forwarding them to the International Olympic Committee.

The cover-up would not last too long, however. At the Summer Olympics in Los Angeles later that year, Vainio won the silver medal in the 10,000-meter run. Routine drug testing after the race detected miniscule amounts of a steroid called primobolan. According to some reports, the small traces of primobolan may have come from blood stored prior to the Los Angeles games and reinjected into Vainio shortly before the 10,000-meter race. Vainio, or whoever reinjected him with the old blood, may not have realized that the stored blood had been taken at a time when the anabolic steroid had not completely cleared from his system.[2] It's also possible that he'd either taken the drug on his own, or had been given the drug without his knowledge.

Six weeks after Vainio was stripped of his Olympic medal, he went on Finnish television and apologized for the positive drug test. Vainio said, "My own tests were positive a long time after the Games. That indicated an injection, and I have gotten a confession from people whom I have trusted. They thought I should be helped against being overtrained, and they gave me testosterone and anabolic steroids without me knowing it."[3]

When the cover-up became public, Antti Lanamaki was forced to resign as the chief coach of the Finnish Athletic Association.[4]

ALEXI GREWAL ALMOST MISSES THE 1984 OLYMPICS

At the 1984 Los Angeles Olympics, the U.S. Cycling Team turned in a very successful performance. Under the guidance of famed Eastern European coach Eddie Borysewicz, the United States won nine medals, four of them gold, including a gold medal in an epic duel between American cyclist Alexi Grewal and Canadian cyclist Steve Bauer during the men's road race. It was the first time since 1912 that Americans won any Olympic medals in the sport.[5]

Grewal almost didn't make it to the Olympics, however. After he won a stage in the Coors Classic in 1984, he went to doping control and provided a urine sample. Grewal was stunned to find out that he tested positive for the banned substance phenylethylamine. He was given a thirty-day suspension with the right to appeal.

At first, Grewal thought that the positive test happened because of an herbal supplement an assistant gave him moments prior to the race. Later on, it turned out that the asthma medication Grewal was using (with permission

from the United States Cycling Federation, now known as USA Cycling),
albuterol, sometimes shows up as phenylethylamine in testing, depending
on exactly which test is run. Due to some confusion regarding the testing
methods used, Grewal was reinstated four days after he had been suspended.
Had he not been reinstated, Grewal would have been ineligible to participate
in cycling events at the Los Angeles games, nine days later.[6]

BLOOD DOPING IN LA

Bigger than Grewal's near miss, however, were rumors of blood doping on
the U.S. cycling team during the 1984 summer games. At the time, a number
of sports federations and governing bodies frowned upon the practice, but
no rules specifically prevented athletes from using the technique. Partly due
to the blood doping scandal surrounding the U.S. cycling team, the U.S.
Olympic Committee (USOC) outlawed the practice the following year. In
1986, the IOC banned blood doping, too.

In November 1984, Dr. Thomas B. Dickson, an orthopedic surgeon from
Pennsylvania, blew the whistle on blood doping that he witnessed several days before the start of the Los Angeles Olympics. According to Dr.
Dickson's account, eight members of the U.S. cycling team received blood
transfusions. Five of those who received the extra blood went on to win
medals—Brett Emery, Steve Hegg, Pat McDonough, Leonard Nitz, and
Rebecca Twigg. Three other cyclists, according to Dr. Dickson, received
transfusions but then went on to perform below their abilities, ostensibly
due to illness. They were John Beckman, Danny Van Haute, and Mark
Whitehead. Dr. Dickson identified the physician who performed the transfusions as Dr. Herman Falsetti, a prominent cardiologist from Iowa who
had not previously been involved with the cycling team. "[The transfusions]
were certainly unethical, whether they were illegal is something I still don't
know," he told *The New York Times*, going on to say the International
Olympic Committee's rules at the time were ambiguous.

One of Dr. Dickson's concerns over the episode was the source of the
blood used for the transfusions. What he observed was athletes being given
whole blood from their relatives. This type of transfusion would not contain
enough red blood cells to offer any real benefit. At the same time, the
transfusions exposed the athletes to a number of potential health problems.

"There is no reason to think that whole blood transfusions would have
any benefit for an athlete and plenty of reason to think they might cause
harm," Dr. Dickson told the *Times* in January 1985. He also told the paper
that he regretted not saying something at the time the incident occurred,
rather than waiting a few months to report what he'd seen.[7]

The whole plan to try blood doping at the 1984 Los Angeles Olympics was
hatched, apparently, by Ed Burke, who had a Ph.D. in physiology and was
both a member of the USCF Board of Directors and a member of the USCF

staff. In 1983 he approached the USCF staff with his idea. They expressed some interest, provided that he got approval from senior USCF officials.

Dave Prouty, the executive director of the USCF, informed Burke on October 1, 1983 that in order to proceed with his project, he would need the approval of the USCF's Board of Directors. Burke never submitted his proposal.[8]

Interest in the procedure didn't completely vanish, however. One rider, Danny Van Haute, whose father happened to be a medical doctor, decided to try blood doping on his own. Van Haute performed exceptionally well at the selection races for the 1984 Olympics, and ascribed his success to blood doping. The USCF national staff, as well as certain other riders, took notice and quietly decided to find a way to use the technique for Olympic competition.

There was just one problem. Most blood doping is done by removing an athlete's blood, processing and storing the blood, and then reinfusing it at a later date. To do this requires enough time for the athlete's body to replenish its own blood supply. In 1984, by the time the coaching staff and athletes started considering the technique, there was not enough time to do so.

And that was when the idea to transfuse the athletes with blood from their relatives came into play. The decision to try transfusions stepped into quicksand—both from the standpoint of medical ethics and also the standpoint of medical safety. When one person receives blood from another, the two people need to have matching blood types in order for the procedure to be safe. This may not have been the case for all of the donors and recipients. And even if the blood types did match, there was still the possibility of the donor transmitting a disease like hepatitis or AIDS to the recipient if the blood wasn't properly screened before transfusion. Complicating matters was the fact that there was no reliable blood test for AIDS at the time.

In deciding to use this form of blood doping, the athletes were put in a position of great risk. And as mentioned earlier, several of the athletes who received transfusions became ill or performed worse after receiving the extra blood, perhaps due to a mismatch between the donors' blood types and those of the recipients. Dr. Falsetti, the man who actually performed the transfusions in a Ramada Inn, did manage to at least have the athletes' and donors' blood types determined by a local hospital. The doctor's cover story was that the athletes' blood needed to be typed in case of a terrorist attack, playing on the memories of Munich in 1972.[9]

A former USCF official leaked documents relating to the USCF's internal investigation to a reporter for *Rolling Stone* magazine in late 1984 or early 1985. On January 4, 1985, Les Earnest received a call from *Rolling Stone*'s reporter who asked him questions relating to the matters discussed within the leaked documents. Within several days, he received calls from a number of reporters, for both print and broadcast media. From that point onward, virtually every major news organization in the United States picked up the story. Earnest confirmed the contents of the leaked documents to reporters, but would not comment on information not contained within the leaked material.

At the time, some cyclists were not only experimenting with blood doping, but also with the use of caffeine. Dr. Irving Dardik, a top medical official with the USOC during the mid-1980s, told *The New York Times* in early 1985 that several cyclists, their coaches, and their doctors had experimented with caffeine to see how much could be used without getting caught or suffering any ill effects. When Dr. Dardik spoke to the *Times*, he was heading an investigation into the use of blood doping by American cyclists competing in the Los Angeles Olympics.

Dr. Dardik also noted that the athletes involved were not using caffeine in amounts greater than what was allowed under the IOC's rules. But, he said, "Some of the same individuals [being investigated for blood-doping] stated that they felt this was an appropriate approach to see if they could improve performance, but not illegally.

"But this, in the view of the Olympic committee, is to come as close to cheating as you can and not get caught." In order to account for consumption of coffee, tea, soda, or other products containing caffeine, the IOC had set a maximum allowable level of caffeine in an athlete's system during competition.[10]

One final note: Of the more than 2,200 American athletes tested prior to the Winter and Summer Olympics in 1984, only 86 failed drug screening tests, according to a statement by the USOC the following year. And all of the athletes who failed the screening tests did so during Olympic trials.

Only two athletes testing positive had qualified to compete in the Olympics, but both of those athletes were barred from competing. Other athletes took their places on the U.S. Olympic Team.[11]

BLOOD DOPING OUTLAWED

The drive to ban blood doping in sporting competition began in earnest when the United States Cycling Federation (now known as USA Cycling) voted to ban the practice at a meeting on January 19, 1985. At the same time, the USCF sanctioned the three officials implicated in the blood doping scandal that came out of the 1984 Los Angeles Olympics. They also issued apologies to the American public, to the other cyclists who competed at the 1984 Summer Olympics, and to the USOC for the behavior of the coaches and trainers involved. None of the athletes involved in the scandal lost any of the medals they won in competition.

"No athletes will be held or considered responsible for the incident. Those athletes underwent incredible physical, emotional, and intellectual preparation in preparing for and participating in the ultimate athletic event in the world," David Prouty, executive director of the USCF told the Associated Press at the time of the announcement.

The officials held responsible for the scandal were Eddy Borysewicz, the national and Olympic cycling coach; Ed Burke, the USCF's Elite Athlete Program director at the time; and Mike Fraysse, a former president of the federation who was then serving as first vice president. Borysewicz and Burke were suspended without pay for thirty days, and each was given a letter of reprimand. Fraysse was demoted from first vice president to third vice president.

Although no specific rules of the USOC prohibited blood doping in 1984, Dr. Irving Dardik described the practice as an "unethical procedure" that had been banned, in effect, by various USOC directives and instructions. Dr. Dardik also said that those responsible should be held to account, and that the matter was "under the review of the Bureau of Quality Medical Assurance of the state medical licensing board of California."[12]

In June 1985, the USOC followed suit by banning blood doping. By 1986, the International Olympic Committee formally banned blood doping, too.

BASEBALL'S FIRST DRUG TESTS—EXCEPT FOR MAJOR LEAGUE PLAYERS

In the spring of 1985, following years of allegations of doping in baseball, the sport's commissioner, Peter Ueberroth, decided to implement a drug-testing program for professional baseball. Ueberroth, in announcing the testing program, said that he wanted baseball to be at the forefront of the efforts to eliminate drug use in society. The program, as Ueberroth conceived it, was established to test every athlete in the minor leagues, team employees, and even employees of the commissioner's office. Ueberroth said he would also submit to the tests. In all, about 4,000 individuals would be subjected to the commissioner's drug-testing program.

One group was not a part of Ueberroth's original plan, even though he said at the time he hoped they would voluntarily participate. That group included the biggest stars of baseball—the major league players. The major league players are all members of the Major League Baseball Players Association, the union that negotiates a collective bargaining agreement with the major league owners. The agreement between the players and the owners sets forth a number of terms and conditions that apply equally to both sides.

Donald Fehr, executive director of the players' union, called Ueberroth's efforts "grandstanding."

"What he's doing is engaging in a public relations effort to co-opt the collective bargaining process to get the players to go along with his unilateral decision. It won't work," Fehr told *The New York Times* in May 1985.

In the 1980s, drug testing could be carried out on major league players in only under very well-defined circumstances, which were limited by the collective bargaining agreement made the previous summer. Major league players, in 1985, could only be tested for drug use after a medical panel determined the need for such testing. Ueberroth wanted the players to voluntarily join his plan, which would have a much wider scope, at a time when the players and owners were negotiating a new basic contract. The players didn't go along.

When the commissioner made his initial announcement on the NBC television network, it came as a complete surprise to the major league's team owners. While Ueberroth was publicly backed by a number of major league owners, executives, and managers, at least one baseball executive had some misgivings.

"I think Ueberroth is trying to force the players to submit to the testing," an anonymous executive for a National League baseball team told *The New York Times*.

"When individual liberties and presumptions of guilt and innocence are violated it doesn't make us happy even if players are not involved," Fehr said. He went on to say, "Powerful people tend to issue edicts."

About six weeks following Ueberroth's initial announcement that such a program would be implemented, he released details of what the testing regime would entail. Ueberroth described his new program as a deterrent, designed to help athletes or staff who were currently using drugs quit, and to prevent future athletes from falling into the trap of drug abuse. One thing missing, however, was a penalty for anyone caught by the program.[13]

Ueberroth said, "If somebody is addicted and won't accept help, we may have to contemplate some negative actions. But I don't expect that to happen." Athletes who underwent treatment would still receive their salary, but would not be able to return to the game until they proved themselves to be drug-free over a period of time. Ueberroth's plan had some basis in existing drug-testing programs, as well as some unique features.

Like the Olympic drug-testing programs of the time, each athlete's sample would be split into two. An "A" sample for testing, and a "B" sample for any confirmation tests that might be necessary, should the initial results show signs of any banned substances. Unlike other drug-testing programs then or now, if an athlete tested positive, he would be contacted by a doctor to arrange for a thorough examination and any necessary medical treatment. This policy would continue on well into the future.

Like antidoping testing in other sports, the commissioner's program would code the samples to protect the athlete's privacy. Unlike other antidoping programs, if a player tested positive, that result would not become part of his employment record, and the player would not be disciplined or suffer any penalties.[14]

In September 1985, Ueberroth tried to go around the player's union by appealing directly to the major league players to submit to his drug-testing program. While some expressed general support with the commissioner's plan and goals, the players refused to go along without the involvement of the union. Over the course of the next year, Ueberroth tried to bring the player's association on board. It never happened.

In fact, it would be many years before the major league players would accept any sort of drug-testing program that dealt with anything other than the so-called recreational drugs, even one that—compared to other programs of the day, or even modern programs— would be fairly easy on the athletes.

SWISS TRACK STAR EMBROILED IN CONTROVERSIAL DOPING RESULTS

Long before the high-profile and highly contentious doping cases in track and field in the early to mid-2000s, Swiss track star Sandra Gasser became embroiled in a controversial one. Gasser, who won a bronze medal in the 1,500-meter race at the world track and field championships in September 1987, allegedly tested positive for methyltestosterone,[15] an anabolic steroid. The International Amateur Athletic Federation (IAAF) almost immediately banned her from competition, and stripped her of the bronze medal she won at the world championships, as well as of her victory at the Mobil Grand Prix Final held in Brussels, Belgium, six days later. The IAAF also made her forfeit approximately $10,000 that she won for finishing first in the Mobil Grand Prix season standings.[16]

In October 1987, Gasser's attorneys filed a lawsuit seeking her immediate reinstatement. They claimed that the IAAF's testing procedures did not meet minimum legal standards.[17] This was the beginning of a long, drawn-out, and expensive battle by the Swiss athlete to clear her name. In fact, Gasser would become one of the first athletes to aggressively defend herself against the doping charges.[18]

The following month, she filed an appeal with the IAAF seeking to over-turn her ban, claiming that there were discrepancies in the results of the two tests performed on her urine sample from the world championships. Joining her in the appeal was the Swiss Athletic Federation.[19]

Gasser's samples had been tested at an IAAF-sanctioned antidoping lab-oratory in Rome, following the World Championships in early September. Her A sample came back with results showing traces of methyltestosterone. About two and a half weeks later, Gasser's B sample was tested in the same lab. According to an account of the testing in John Hoberman's book, *Mortal Engines*, the chemical profiles of the two samples were very different. The B sample actually showed much greater amounts of methyltestosterone than the A sample did, a rather unusual turn of events. Despite the anomalies in the test results, the lab reported their findings to the IAAF and Gasser was handed a two-year ban from competition, which was to end on September 5, 1989.[20]

Gasser's response to the allegations was strong. "Honestly, I took nothing that is prohibited; I never doped," she said at the time. "I was always against that and I have said so publicly many times." Gasser tried distancing herself from the people she referred to as "real dopers."

"Whenever I see Martti Vainio, a real doper, I think, what does he think he's doing among us. He doesn't belong here anymore," Gasser said. But it wouldn't be too long before she, herself, fell from grace in the eyes of other Swiss athletes. In part, this was due to suggestions made by her lawyers that perhaps someone had sabotaged Gasser by slipping the drug into a drink. Among those with whom she fell out with was Cornelia Bürki. Bürki, a former roommate who had initially supported Gasser, was angered by comments and suggestions by Gasser that she might have spiked a drink with the steroid.[21]

In defending herself against the doping allegations, a number of procedural errors that occurred during Gasser's test came to light, beginning almost at the moment of collection. It turns out that the official who was in charge of splitting Gasser's urine into an A and B sample spilled some of the sample on his hands. The upshot of this clumsiness was that the sample sent to the antidoping lab in Rome was less than half the minimum volume the rules of the time demanded.

But the staff member receiving the sample in Rome paid no attention, accepted the sample and began the testing process. The A and B sample tests, which produced radically different results for the amount of methyltestosterone present, were performed differently.[22] Dr. Manfred Donike, a famous expert at the German College of Sports Medicine in Cologne, suggested that due to the great differences in the results of the two samples, they may have actually come from different people. And two Swiss scientists offered the opinion that the B sample could be just about anything, including dog urine.

Donike, a member of the IAAF panel adjudicating Gasser's case, cast the sole vote against finding her guilty of doping. In an interesting bit of irony, the Rome lab that performed Gasser's test lost its accreditation a short time after her case ended.[23]

KERRY LYNCH ADMITS BLOOD DOPING IN 1987

In January 1988, a month before the 1988 Winter Olympics, U.S. Nordic Combined skier Kerry Lynch admitted that he had blood doped at the 1987 world championships held in Oberstdorf, Germany. In doing so, he became the first athlete to be sanctioned for blood doping. The International Ski Federation banned Lynch from competition through the end of 1988. They also stripped him of the silver medal he won at Oberstdorf in the men's Nordic Combined competition.[*]

Doug Peterson, head coach of the U.S. Nordic Combined team, and Jim Page, the chief U.S. Nordic ski coach received lifetime bans by the FIS for involvement in covering up Lynch's blood doping. Page's lifetime ban was eventually rescinded in 1990, and he now serves as the executive director of sport at the USOC.[24]

---

[*]Nordic Combined is a mixture of cross-country skiing and ski jumping.

BEN JOHNSON: GREATER SPEED THROUGH CHEMISTRY?

At the 1988 Olympics in Seoul, South Korea, Canadian sprinter Ben Johnson put in an incredible effort during the 100-meter finals, beating the world record he established at the 1987 world championships in Rome the previous year. Going into the finals, Johnson's world record stood at 9.83 seconds for the 100-meter dash. In a fast and exciting race, Johnson beat his nemesis, Carl Lewis, and set a new world record—9.79 seconds. The only person who had ever run a faster time in competition was Carl Lewis. Lewis clocked the 100 meters in 9.78 seconds with the help of a tailwind during the U.S. Olympic trials.

Ben Johnson beat Lewis in the one place where he most wanted to beat him—in the finals of the 1988 Olympics, after having suffered a bitter loss to Lewis in the 1984 Olympics. Johnson's new record would not last long, and though he won a gold medal, it would soon be taken away.

In September 1988, Ben Johnson was a bona fide track hero. And it was a feat all the more impressive because of the season he'd been having. Johnson's year, up to the Olympics, was marked by injuries and subpar results. During a meet in February, he suffered a serious hamstring injury, and he reinjured the muscle the following May. This turn of events was certainly frustrating for the Canadian.

"Ben was pretty depressed about it," Johnson's coach Charlie Francis told *The New York Times*. "They found a tear low in his hamstring, an injury that takes a long time to heal. He was off completely for two weeks before he could work on other parts of his body, and it must have been five weeks before he got back on the track."[25]

Johnson spent the entire summer recovering and training in an attempt to regain form prior to the Summer Olympics. His results during competition at the end of the summer paled by comparison to his record-setting time at the 1987 World's in Rome. By the time the Olympics rolled around, a number of people were wondering about Johnson's condition. But after Johnson's medal-winning final, one reporter suggested that perhaps it had all been an effort to psych out the competition.

While Johnson predicted he would win, to many the words rang hollow in light of his results over the summer. Carl Lewis, on the other hand, spoke confidently about being in good form, but never predicted he would win. Lewis, in contrast to Johnson, was having one of his best seasons on the track. For those inclined to gamble on sports, betting on Carl Lewis to win the 100-meter dash in Seoul would have seemed like the logical choice.

Before the finals, the two athletes' results would bear out such a guess. During the preliminary heats, Lewis was winning his events with times faster than Johnson's, but slower than the times either athlete would run in the finals. When the showdown between the American and Canadian sprinters finally happened, Johnson got a slight jump on Lewis right out of the starting blocks, accelerated to top speed quicker and held on longer for the win. In all of 9.79 seconds, Ben Johnson had achieved what he'd dreamed of: beating Carl Lewis at the Olympics. And he won a gold medal for the effort.

The glory of Johnson's sprint into history didn't last long. Two days later came word that he failed a drug test for stanozolol. The day after that he returned to Toronto, stripped of his gold medal by the International Olympic Committee. Johnson's positive test marked a turning point in the war on doping, but it would take more than ten years before some of the changes brought about by his scandal would fully play themselves out.

Dick Pound, one of the Canadian officials at the Seoul Olympics was a 40-something tax attorney and former Olympic swimmer who was also a rising star at the International Olympic Committee. While Pound would eventually become both loved and reviled by sports fans around the world, when the Ben Johnson affair happened, he was relatively unknown outside the Olympic movement.

In the early 1980s, Pound shrewdly negotiated the first television broadcast rights contract to pay the IOC a large sum of money—$309 million for the U.S. broadcast rights to the 1988 Winter Olympics in Calgary, Alberta, Canada.[26] Pound continued as the IOC's broadcast rights negotiator for a number of years, but he had his eye on a bigger prize. He wanted to become head of the International Olympic Committee when the current head, Juan Antonio Samaranch, would step down. And he was steadily positioning himself for the job, eventually becoming Samaranch's right-hand man.

Even though his specialty is tax law, Canadian Olympic officials turned to Pound to represent Johnson before the IOC as they deliberated over what to do about Johnson's positive test. Before agreeing to represent Johnson, Pound asked him if he was guilty of the charges. Johnson assured Pound that he was innocent. Pound agreed to represent Johnson on the basis of Johnson's reassurances. As Michael Sokolove described in *The New York Times Magazine*:

"After Johnson assured Pound he was clean, Pound asked him, Could someone have spiked his post-race beer? No, he got his own beer. Anything unusual in the collection of his urine sample? No, nothing. 'Give me some bullets,' Pound remembers thinking. 'I've got nothing to say.' But there wasn't much of a defense to offer. Johnson was stripped of his medal, and it was awarded to the second-place finisher, the American Carl Lewis."[27]

In the first few days surrounding Ben Johnson's positive test, Dick Pound protested the Canadian athlete's innocence.

"This is a disaster for Ben, a disaster for the Games, and a disaster for track and field. But let's turn this around to make the slate clean and show the world that we do mean business. We are prepared to act, not just to pick out a low-profile athlete in a low-profile sport. If it happens to the best, the same thing will happen," Pound told *The New York Times* in late September 1988.

Pound went on to say, "He sat there looking like a trapped animal. He had no idea what was going on all around him. He said he didn't do anything wrong and he hadn't taken anything. Sitting there, he was nervous and he could hardly speak."

James Worrall, who was also an IOC member from Canada, told *The New York Times* "If this results in telling every young aspiring athlete, no matter what the sport, that drug-taking just doesn't pay, then perhaps we have achieved something."[28]

But it wasn't long before Johnson owned up to having doped at the 1988 Olympics. And during the course of a Canadian government inquiry into the matter, Johnson would eventually admit that he had been taking steroids throughout most of the 1980s.

Only a couple of weeks after his positive test for steroids at the Olympics, Ben Johnson found himself in a different kind of trouble—this time with the law. A motorist reported to Toronto police that a man driving a Porsche on Highway 401 during the evening rush hour waved a gun at him. When the police traced the license plate number given to them by the motorist, they discovered that the car belonged to none other than Ben Johnson. When they searched the car, they discovered a starter's pistol, a kind of gun that fires blanks.

Johnson admitted to police that he had been driving on the 401 at the time the driver claims, but initially claimed he had not waved the gun at the motorist.[29] Five days after the incident took place, however, Canadian prosecutors charged Johnson with assault and dangerous use of a weapon.[30]

Pound would write about the Johnson scandal in his book *Inside Dope*, saying that Johnson's coach felt that Canadian athletes and others had to dope, because everyone else was. One question echoed in the aftermath of Johnson's positive test: Given how sophisticated drug testing had become by 1988, how was it that Johnson had not tested positive before the Olympics? Over the seventeen months prior to the Olympics, Johnson was tested eight times. He had competed in at least two meets in August 1988, one being the Canadian Olympic trials, as well as several international meets in Europe that ended about two weeks prior to the start of the Seoul games.

It turns out that Johnson wasn't tested during the Canadian Olympic trials. How could that be? Drug testing is expensive, so Canadian officials only tested two of the three top finishers in an event, along with one other athlete chosen at random. "He had a 33-percent chance he wouldn't get picked, and by the luck of the draw he wasn't," Abby Hoffman, Sport Canada's director general at the time, told *The New York Times*. Johnson was lucky not to have been tested at the 1988 Canadian Olympic trials.

Johnson wasn't tested after the European meets, either. How was it that Canadian officials didn't test Johnson in between the European meets and the Seoul games? Hoffman told *The New York Times* several days after Johnson's scandal broke, "If someone is competing in major international meets in Europe in August, just 14 or 15 days before Seoul, and it's likely that he'll be tested at those meets, it could be regarded almost as harassment to make him be tested again here."

Of course, another possibility exists on how he evaded detection: masking. The East German athletic machine had figured out how to beat steroid screenings by using other drugs to mask the presence of banned substances. Perhaps Johnson, or someone close to him, had figured out how to mask the presence of stanozolol successfully prior to the 1988 Summer Olympics.

And it was also possible that Johnson had stopped taking steroids far enough in advance of competition that the drugs would not show up in the drug screenings.[31]

In the aftermath of Johnson's positive test, the Canadian government launched an inquiry into his case, and into doping in general. According to news reports, 39 witnesses testified before the panel prior to Johnson's own testimony. Two of those who testified were Charlie Francis, Johnson's coach, and Dr. George (Jamie) Astaphan, Johnson's physician for the five years leading up to the Seoul Olympics. Both told the panel that Johnson had used steroids and other performance-enhancing drugs.

When the scandal first broke, Johnson denied having used stanozolol or any other drugs. Several weeks later, he appeared to moderate his story by saying that he had never knowingly used steroids. And then came his testimony before the commission. Johnson's story changed for the inquiry. On June 13, 1989, Ben Johnson admitted that he had used various banned drugs beginning in 1981.[32]

In contrast to Francis' and Astaphan's previous testimony that they told Johnson about the risks of using performance-enhancing drugs, Johnson recalled events differently. "Nobody took the time to tell me what the side effects were," Johnson said. "They were all happy making their money, and stuff like that. So, no."[33]

Johnson told the inquiry that his drug program started in 1981, on the advice of his coach, Charlie Francis. He went on to say that Francis broached the topic after a training session, telling him that he had the potential to be a world-class sprinter. But to be a world-class sprinter would require the use of various drugs, because "the only way to win is to use drugs" and everyone else was already using them.

Johnson, in his testimony, said that he relied on the advice of both Francis and Astaphan. He said that he trusted the advice of his coach completely. "If Charlie comes to me and tells me to take [drugs], yes, I take them."

According to Johnson's account of his drug use, it was not until a couple of years after he started taking whatever Francis was giving him that he realized the drugs were anabolic steroids. By that point, Johnson was completely immersed in Francis' doping program and he was well aware of the risks of getting caught.[34]

The Canadian government's inquiry into doping went on for the better part of 1989. In September of that year, Dick Pound, who was then an IOC vice president, testified before the panel. In Pound's testimony, he criticized a new rule enacted by the IAAF that would require any records held by athletes who doped to be nullified if those records were set in the six years preceding the athlete's confession.

The rule, which was slated to go into effect on January 1, 1990, would have affected only two athletes, both Canadian. Ben Johnson, and Angella Issajenko. Johnson held the records in the 60-meter and 100-meter dashes, and Issajenko held the record in the 50-meter dash. During the Canadian government's inquiry into doping among Canadian athletes, Issajenko testified that she had injected Johnson and another athlete with a mixture of human growth hormone and a steroid during a training camp on the island of Guadalupe in 1984.

"I would not have given him drugs without him knowing," Issajenko responded to questioning by Robert Armstrong, the inquiry's chief counsel, as to whether Johnson knew he was being injected with steroids.[35]

Pound, while praising the IAAF's efforts, also said that the sports world needed a coordinated, uniform set of antidoping strategies to fight the use of performance-enhancing drugs. He suggested that it would take between five and ten years' time to clean up the drug problem in sports—but only if the IOC and the various international federations developed a single approach to fighting the problem.[36]

In the middle of June 1989, Johnson finally came clean. In emotional testimony, Johnson told the inquiry, "I lied. I was ashamed for my family and friends and kids who looked up to me as a Canadian athlete and wanted to be in my position. I was just in a mess." Johnson told the inquiry that he was sorry for what he had done, and would like to become a leader in the fight against doping in sports. He said his message for young people would be, "Don't take drugs. It happened to me; I was there. I know what it's like to cheat. I've got four nephews who might be in track. I would warn them not to take drugs. If anybody wants to give them drugs, they should tell their parents and family."

Johnson told reporters as he left the hearings that he was happy to have finally told the truth, and he expressed hope that he might be able to represent Canada again in competition. "I like to run for this country," he said. "If it happens, that's the way it's supposed to be."[37]

In the end, Johnson's suspension was not reduced. He served the full two years and then mounted a comeback in the early 1990s. As an athlete, Johnson would never rise to the same heights he achieved in 1987 and 1988.

MORE POSITIVE DOPING TESTS IN SEOUL

Ben Johnson wasn't the only athlete at the Seoul Olympics to test positive for banned substances. Weight lifters from both Hungary and Bulgaria failed drug screenings during the 1988 Summer Olympics, too. Kalman Csengari, a Hungarian weight lifter who competed in the 165-pound category, tested positive for testosterone. And Andor Szanyi tested positive for the same drug Johnson was using—stanozolol. The twenty-four-year-old Szanyi, who was the world champion in his weight class during 1985, had won the silver medal in the 220-pound category by lifting a total of 896 ½ pounds.

In the aftermath of Szanyi and Csengari testing positive for banned substances, the Hungarian weight lifting team returned home. While some say they left to avoid further positive tests, the Hungarians' story at the time was that they left on schedule. They claimed to not have an athlete entered in the final category of competition.

The Hungarians weren't the only Eastern bloc athletes to be caught using banned drugs. During the Olympic, two Bulgarian lifters were caught using diuretics, and the entire team withdrew from further competition.[38]

Linford Christie, the British track star, tested positive for drug use after finishing in fourth place during the finals of the 200-meter run. If he were found guilty, Christie could have been thrown out of the games and stripped of his silver medal from the 100-meter run. However, upon investigation by the IOC, the positive test was linked to an herbal medicine that he had taken. The IOC dropped the charges against Christie, and he was allowed to keep his silver medal.[39]

In the aftermath of the Ben Johnson scandal, sports officials and sports ministers from around the world met at a conference sponsored by UNESCO. At the conference, they considered a new weapon in the struggle to eliminate doping from sports: year-round testing of athletes, in addition to testing during competition. In-competition steroid tests had proven, up to that point, not to be enough of a deterrent for those who would use drugs to better their performance. By performing unannounced tests during training, the participants hoped, steroid use among athletes would be eradicated.[40] Over the next twenty years, those who wished to dope found new ways to beat the system.

EPO EMERGES

At the beginning of the 1980s, blood doping was already a practice gaining momentum among endurance athletes. By 1986, however, it was banned from competition. Even though there were no reliable tests yet that could prove an athlete had blood doped, those who would cheat were on the lookout for new techniques.

With scientific advances, recombinant DNA techniques were coming into use. These techniques enabled scientists (and pharmaceutical companies) to create artificial versions of natural hormones. One hormone of interest at the time was erythropoietin, or EPO. EPO is produced by the kidneys, and enables the body to produce red blood cells. People who are anemic, for example, might be treated with EPO to raise the amount of red blood cells in their bodies.

With the new recombinant DNA techniques that made the production of EPO in mass quantities possible, and with the approval by the FDA for the first EPO-related drugs in 1989, a new weapon entered the medical arsenal. One that could serve as a real medical treatment, but also could serve as a way to dope. Even though it might sound simple enough, blood doping is a complicated procedure. To do so safely requires that an athlete withdraw a certain amount of blood (usually a pint) and store it six weeks or so before competition. If the athlete sets aside the blood too close to competition, the body can't compensate for the reduced blood volume by making more. And if that were the case, then the athlete wouldn't really get much benefit from doping him/herself back up to a normal level.

The idea is to have more blood than normal so that the blood can help carry more oxygen to hardworking muscles. So timing, as the old saying goes, is everything. With the advent of EPO, however, the need for drawing blood from the athlete, and reinjecting it later, vanished. EPO allows the body to create those additional red blood cells without having to donate blood: Blood doping in a syringe instead of intravenously.

Clinical trials of EPO started in Europe in 1986. Large quantities of the drug were available, and according to some sources, within a short period of time, professional athletes such as cyclists, marathon runners and cross-country skiers found ways of acquiring and using the drug. From 1987 through 1989, approximately 15 professional cyclists died under mysterious circumstances. Five Dutch racers died suddenly in 1987, followed by a Belgian and two Dutch riders in 1988, and five more Dutch cyclists in 1989. A number of those deaths may have been due to the use of EPO, but evidence was hard to come by.

"There is no absolute proof, but there's so much smoke that most of us are convinced. You just don't get 18 deaths in four years, mysteriously, with 10 of them attributed to cardiac problems," Dr. Randy Eichner, chief of hematology at the University of Oklahoma, told *The New York Times* in 1991.

As indicated earlier, EPO causes the body to create more red blood cells. The more EPO is used, the greater the percentage of red blood cells in a person's blood. But by increasing the number of these cells, the blood thickens. And when the blood becomes too thick, the heart can no longer beat, causing a heart attack. Other risks associated with EPO abuse include blood clotting and strokes. Or as Dr. Eichner told *The New York Times*, "Pretty soon you have mud instead of blood; then you have trouble."[41]

This thickening of the blood is especially worrisome for professional cyclists and other endurance athletes who compete in the heat for long periods of time. As a person becomes dehydrated, the blood gets thicker still. So even if an athlete's blood was not so thick that his or her heart could pump it at rest, it could become too thick to pump during strenuous exercise, which could lead to tragic consequences.

Because EPO is a naturally occurring hormone, the genetically engineered version is almost identical to the version produced by the human body. In the late 1980s and early 1990s, no test existed that could distinguish one from the other. The only method that could suggest a link would be determining the percentage of red blood cells (known as the hematocrit) in a person's blood sample. If a person's hematocrit exceeds a certain cutoff above which few, if any, documented cases of natural occurrences happen, one could presume that the person was doping with either blood or EPO. But this method is fraught with problems, as each individual can have a different "normal" hematocrit value, and humans are, almost by definition, quite variable.

It wouldn't be until the turn of the century that a test that could detect the use of genetically engineered EPO would come into use. During the intervening years, a number of athletes—both amateur and professional—may well have been using the drug and managed to avoid detection. Exactly how many is something that may never be known.

HUMAN GROWTH HORMONE: FROM CADAVERS TO GENETIC ENGINEERING

EPO was not the first genetically engineered drug to find its way into the locker room. Before EPO came a genetically engineered form of human growth hormone (HGH), a drug originally developed by Genentech Inc. to treat the problem of dwarfism in children. But even before Genentech's development of an artificial version of growth hormone, a limited supply of natural HGH was available. This natural version was extracted from the pituitary glands of cadavers.

Due to the source of the natural hormone, it was possible for patients using the drug to become infected with various diseases. One such malady is Creutzfeldt-Jakob disease, which is the human equivalent of mad cow disease. When four boys who were treated with naturally derived growth hormone developed Creutzfeldt-Jakob disease, the use of all pituitary-derived hormones and drugs was discontinued. Fortunately, synthetic growth hormone came along at about the same time, enabling continued treatment for those whose bodies didn't produce enough HGH on their own.

While the amount of HGH available was still limited even after the synthetic form came into use, athletes began trying to acquire the drug and use it for their own benefit. Through the end of the 1980s, Genentech kept a tight lid on the drug. But other varieties also existed, including natural variants from monkeys, cows, and other animals. Some of what was sold as growth hormone in the mid- to late-1980s was not growth hormone at all. Rather, it was simply colored water. And while growth hormone from cows won't work for humans—the hormone has to come from the same species to be of any benefit—the health effects of those alternative forms of growth hormones were less innocuous.

"Taking growth hormone when it's not medically necessary is serious business, because you're fiddling with a very delicate chemical feedback mechanism, which may have very serious side effects," Dr. Joseph Fetto, an assistant professor of sports medicine at New York University, told *The New York Times* in 1984.

There were, however, doctors who prescribed the drug for various types of athletes. Although the use of HGH was a relatively new phenomenon in 1984, word-of-mouth stories among bodybuilders and other athletes made the drug popular, very quickly. Soon, black market trafficking in the drug emerged. Athletes in some countries, like Sweden and Italy, were rumored to be spending as much as $500 a week for their supply of the hormone.

Dr. Terry Todd, a professor of physical education at the University of Texas said, "Growth hormone has become the new 'in' drug among athletes seeking to put on muscle mass." The fact that growth hormone helped athletes gain weight and muscle mass was well established by then. Whether it was safe to use was still being debated.

Another physician, Dr. Alan Rogol said, "The use of growth hormone came into sports very suddenly, so fast that word of its potential dangers has yet to catch up with the glowing reports of its value to athletes. I do everything I can to discourage the use of growth hormone, yet it is apparent that athletes are not listening and that there is an underground source of supply."

The high price of the drug at the time may have prevented a number of athletes from obtaining HGH. But a real concern was what would happen when the cost of the drug dropped. Some doctors worried that once the HGH became more affordable, more athletes would try it. Others worried more about the quality of the drugs being sold.

Another concern was the potential side effects of HGH. Those athletes who took excessive quantities of growth hormone developed a condition called acromegalia, or gigantism. As Dr. Fetto told *The New York Times*, "It's known in medicine that a small number of individuals secrete too much growth hormone, which in adulthood can lead to bizarre growth of the jaw, feet and bones, as well as diabetes and severe problems with the endocrine glands. There are no beneficial effects from its use with athletes except for putting on weight."[42]

Because drug testing could pick up the presence of anabolic steroids, but could not yet detect the presence of human growth hormone, a number of

U.S. Olympic athletes using steroids may have used HGH as a means of avoiding detection. They would taper off of the steroids and replace those drugs with human growth hormone in the run-up to an event.

At the American College of Sports Medicine annual meeting in San Diego in May 1984, reports surfaced that a number of athletes on the U.S. Olympic track and field team were using both anabolic steroids and human growth hormone. The physicians who discussed the situation expressed concern that the athletes might harm themselves through such hormonal manipulations.[43]

By the end of the 1980s, efforts were being made to regulate both the use of anabolic steroids and human growth hormone. These efforts included legislation that would criminalize the distribution of these drugs for non-medical purposes.[44] In contrast, by 1989 some scientific studies were beginning to show potential antiaging benefits to the use of human growth hormone, prompting even more interest in the drug.[45]

Chapter 5

An Explosion of Doping Cases and the Rise of Custom-Tailored Drugs, 1990–1999

THE DAWN OF THE 1990s

As the 1980s came to a close and the 1990s began, the new drug of choice—at least in endurance sports—was synthetic erythropoietin (EPO). The drug had come into use in the late 1980s, and by 1990 was already making its presence known—in a bad way. In the last years of the preceding decade, a number of cyclists died under mysterious circumstances. Over the course of the 1990s, new drugs, undetectable by the current testing techniques, would come into the picture. And at least a few athletic records would be broken with the use, or alleged use, of performance-enhancing drugs.

With the Ben Johnson scandal at the 1988 Summer Olympics in Seoul, South Korea, the news media began to notice a large doping problem and they started covering doping more conscientiously. As the 1990s wore on, more and more doping scandals would hit the pages of every major media outlet. In *The New York Times*, for example, a recent search of the paper's Web site for stories mentioning the term "doping" turned up approximately 160 articles published during the period from 1981 through 1989. For the period from 1990 through 1999, the newspaper published in excess of 400 stories, more than doubling the number of the previous decade.[1]

Also during the 1990s, political upheaval in Europe would find its way into the world of sports. In 1990, what seemed unthinkable a few years before became reality: The two Germanys reunited as one country. Later in the decade, a number of the East German apparatchiks who ran that country's sports doping program would be put on trial and held to account. As the 1990s dawned, the wild ride that is the world of doping scandals was really beginning to take off.

MORE MYSTERIOUS DEATHS OF CYCLISTS

In 1990, five more cyclists died under mysterious circumstances, possibly connected to the use of EPO. One of the cyclists, twenty-seven-year-old Johannes Draaijer, died of a heart attack in his sleep. Draaijer, a strong cyclist who finished 20th in the 1989 Tour de France, had completed a race in Italy only days before. His widow, speaking on television a short time later, said she hoped her husband's death would serve as a warning to other athletes using EPO. Interestingly, the report of the autopsy performed on Draaijer did not include a cause of death.

Several companies were seeking approval to sell EPO in Europe in 1990, which also meant that significant quantities of the drug were available for clinical trials. Some doses of EPO, however, may have been diverted to other uses. By the spring of 1991, articles about the great benefits of the drug for patients with anemia began appearing in such medical journals as the *New England Journal of Medicine*. These same articles also noted that EPO abuse, coupled with dehydration, could lead to heart attacks in athletes.

Word of the drug's ability to improve an athlete's performance had already spread among runners and cyclists. "I began hearing about EPO two to three years ago through the grapevine in running circles. The story was there was this new drug that would take over from blood doping, and that it was much better," John Treacy, who won the silver medal in the marathon at the 1984 Los Angeles Olympics, told *The New York Times* in 1991.

Len Pettyjohn, coach of the Coors Light professional cycling team, agreed. "We've all heard about EPO. I could only speculate on its use now, but it wouldn't surprise me. I don't think any Americans are using it, but anybody doing something like that is certainly not going to talk about it."

Both Amgen, the manufacturer and distributor of EPO for patients with kidney failure, and Ortho, who was licensed to sell the drug for other uses, responded to the threat of EPO abuse by developing and implementing programs geared toward educating athletes the dangers of EPO abuse. Jan Gibers, the directeur sportif of the Dutch cycling team PDM, told *The New York Times* that any cyclist on his team using drugs without approval of the PDM team doctors would be thrown off the team.

Edmund Burke, who was involved in the U.S. cycling team's blood doping scandal at the 1984 Olympics, said of EPO, "You have to tell them [the athletes], EPO can do wonders for your aerobic capacity. The problem is, it can also kill you."[2] Even one publication generally favorable to the use of steroids and other performance-enhancing drugs concluded that "EPO's risks outweigh the benefits."

In 1990, the IOC banned the use of EPO, following the first scandal over the deaths of a dozen or more young, promising professional cyclists. It would take another decade before a test would be developed to detect the use of EPO. Despite the deaths and warnings about the dangers of EPO abuse, athletes have continued using the drug.

STEROIDS IN THE WORLD WRESTING FEDERATION

The use of steroids by professional wrestlers came out into the open as a result of two trials in the early 1990s. In November 1991, Federal prosecutors put Dr. George T. Zaharian III, of Harrisburg, Pennsylvania, on trial for distributing steroids to professional wrestlers. During Dr. Zaharian's trial, four professional wrestlers testified that he had provided them with steroids—Rowdy Roddy Piper, Rick Martel, Dan Spivey, and Brian Blair. Each wrestler testified that he had received steroids from Dr. Zaharian in the late 1980s, after it had become illegal to sell the drugs without a proper prescription.

At his trial, Dr. Zaharian testified that he was unaware of the change in laws making the distribution of steroids or providing the drugs for nonmedical uses illegal as of November 1988. Dr. Zaharian also testified that as a ringside physician, he maintained a watchful eye on the wrestlers.

Hulk Hogan, one of professional wrestling's biggest stars, had also been called to testify against Dr. Zaharian. Hogan was excused from testifying after his attorney argued that requiring Hogan to testify would be an invasion of his privacy. Hogan, however, eventually admitted that he used the drugs from 1976 until 1989.

Dr. Zaharian was convicted in late 1991. But the story doesn't end with his conviction. A new case involving the use of steroids in professional wrestling went to trial in 1994, partly as a result of Dr. Zaharian's cooperation with Federal prosecutors. This time, the case involved Vincent McMahon, the wrestling promoter who operated both Titan Sports—an agency that promoted wrestling in various venues—and the World Wrestling Federation (WWF), which is now known as World Wrestling Entertainment (WWE).[3]

During McMahon's 1994 trial, Hulk Hogan testified under a grant of immunity from prosecution for anything he might disclose in court. On the witness stand, Hogan (whose real name is Terry Gene Bollea) said that the use of steroids in the WWF was fairly common during the 1980s, when he worked for the organization. Hogan also spoke of sharing steroids with McMahon during the filming of No Holds Barred in 1989. He told the court how he got the drugs, saying that while working and touring as part of the WWF, he would call McMahon's executive secretary and ask her to place an order (for steroids) with Dr. Zaharian.

Hogan would then pick up the drugs from Titan Sports headquarters at the same time he picked up his paycheck or fan mail. Hogan told the court that he took steroids "to heal injuries, to keep on going," adding that he was no longer using the drugs. While on the witness stand, Hogan estimated that 80 percent of all WWF professional wrestlers were using the drugs during the 1980s.[4] During cross-examination, McMahon's laywer, Laura A. Brevetti, tried to demonstrate that the drugs had not been distributed illegally.

"I believed it was legal because I had a prescription for it," Hogan told the court. He added that McMahon never instructed him to take steroids and never purchased the drugs for him.[5]

Ultimately, Vince McMahon was found not guilty. But the seamy underbelly of professional wrestling came into clear view as a result of his trial and the trial of Dr. Zaharian.

BEN JOHNSON RETURNS, BUT NOT FOR LONG

After testing positive for nandrolone at the 1988 Seoul Olympics, Ben Johnson served a two-year suspension from competition. Shortly before his suspension ended, no less a figure than the head of the IAAF spoke positively about Johnson's return to racing. At the Goodwill Games in July 1990, about two months before Johnson's suspension would come to an end, Primo Nebiolo told *The New York Times* that Johnson could be a "great champion" if he steered clear of performance-enhancing drugs. One of the conditions of Johnson's return was that he had to submit to regular drug testing. Three of the four tests he passed were on 48 hours notice, and the fourth was a surprise test with no notice. Nebiolo also noted that over the previous year, each drug test that Johnson submitted to came up negative.

"In life, one must have the opportunity to come back. He has paid. Logically, he must be careful. He knows the rules. If he makes another mistake, he will pay again. But I wish him the best," Nebiolo told the *Times*.[6]

Johnson's comeback, however, would be short-lived. When he returned to competition in 1991, Johnson's results were lackluster. During 1992 and into the beginning of 1993, his form improved, and his results got better, too. But in January 1993, Johnson again found himself confronting charges of doping—this time with testosterone.

A urine test at a meet in Montreal on January 17, 1993 returned a testosterone to epitestosterone (T/E) ratio of 10.3:1. At the time, the highest allowable T/E ratio was 6:1. Two other tests administered around the same time—one two days before and the other two days after—came back negative. However, the five-person panel reviewing Johnson's case, after what was called "an extensive and thorough investigation," reached a unanimous decision: They found the Canadian athlete guilty of doping. In the end, Ben Johnson was banned from competition for life.[7]

DID LYLE ALZADO DIE BECAUSE OF STEROID ABUSE?

In 1992, former professional football player Lyle Alzado passed away at the age of 43. Alzado, who had been a much-feared All-Pro defensive end during his NFL career, was an admitted user of steroids. As he fought a rare form of brain cancer, Alzado spoke of how his disease was caused by his steroid abuse as a player.

During his days as an NFL player, Alzado claimed that he took steroids for most of his time as a pro. "Big massive guy that I was, I don't like to admit this but it was all phoney," Alzado told one journalist. "It got me where I wanted, but it also got me very sick."[8]

Off the field, Alzado was said to be a very mild-mannered individual. On the field, he was an entirely different person.

"The guy had a split personality. On the field, he had this tough image that he projected. Off the field he was the gentle giant. So caring, so warm, so giving," Los Angeles Raiders defensive end Greg Townsend once told *ESPN*.[9] If "'roid rage" exists, then one moment out of Lyle Alzado's career would be an almost perfect illustration of the phenomenon.

During a playoff game between the Los Angeles Raiders and the New York Jets, Alzado ripped the helmet off Jets' lineman Chris Ward and flung it at Ward. Alzado had become enraged because he felt that Ward had been holding him during a play. During the off-season, the NFL enacted a new rule, dubbed "The Alzado Rule," barring such action. The penalty for such behavior? Ejection from the game, as well as a possible fine.[10]

In 1990, when Alzado was trying to launch a comeback, he told television personality Maria Shriver during an interview, "I'm clean. I've always been clean." A year later, he would admit to Shriver that he had been using steroids his whole career. "In my comeback attempt," Alzado told Shriver, "I used a certain steroid that caused me to lower my immune system." It was that suppression of his immune system due to his long-time abuse of steroids, Alzado believed, that led to the brain cancer that ultimately claimed his life.

During his second interview with Shriver, Alzado didn't identify which drugs he took or provide any medical records to back up his claims. Whether Alzado's death was a result of steroid abuse or not has been widely debated over the years. When Alzado spoke out about his steroid abuse, he linked that abuse to his affliction with brain cancer.

In July 1991, Dr. Forest Tennant, a former drug adviser to the NFL, told The Associated Press, "Anabolic steroids depress the immune system and lymphocytes. He has lymphoma. You don't have to be a rocket scientist to figure out the connection."[11]

However, Dr. Gary Wadler, a well-known expert on the abuse of drugs in sports who is now a member of the World Anti-Doping Agency, told *The New York Times* in 1991, "There is zero correlation between brain tumors and steroids."

"I've talked to everyone and his brother in the field, scientists, endocrinologists," Dr. Wadler added, "and no one sees any evidence of relationship between his story and his cancer, other than the very real concern we all have about AIDS-related lymphomas, particularly when needles may have been shared, or bottles containing chemicals may have been shared."

Dr. Wadler also critiqued the media's handling of Alzado's announcement of his cancer through a *Sports Illustrated* story, and a follow-up interview with Maria Shriver, by noting that "the result was a media feeding frenzy and it wasn't responsible."[12]

What was the ultimate cause of Lyle Alzado's death at the age of 43? It depends who you talk to. Even today, a search on Google, Yahoo, or other Web search engine will turn up Web sites that back Alzado's contention, as well as Web sites that back the contention of experts like Dr. Wadler.

One thing is clear: Steroids played a major part in Lyle Alzado's career. As former NFL defensive back Keith Lee told *The New York Times* in 1991, "We all knew Lyle was a 'roid monster, but those were the days of what I came to think of as the Fridge Syndrome. The league was in love with size-plus-speed, and there was a lot of pressure on linemen. Like a lot of smaller guys who weren't using, I thought, 'O.K., it helps the team.' I thought of steroids as vitamins for big guys."

Lee, who played with the Buffalo Bills, New England Patriots, and the Indianapolis Colts during his NFL days, went on to say, "Lyle wasn't naturally that fast or big or skilled. Who knows if he would have had that career without drugs? Steroids helped his body perform what was in his heart."[13]

CLENBUTEROL TAKES A TOLL AT THE 1992 OLYMPICS

Clenbuterol, an asthma medication with similar muscle-building effects as anabolic steroids, caused a number of athletes at the 1992 Summer Olympics in Barcelona to be disqualified from competition, lose their medals, and be sent home. Among those disqualified and sent home was Jud Logan, a thirty-three-year-old U.S. track and field athlete who competed in the hammer throw. Logan, a five-time national champion, finished fourth in the hammer throw in Barcelona prior to testing positive for the drug and being disqualified from competition.

Logan denied ever having used steroids, but in a handwritten note he left before leaving Barcelona, he admitted that he had used Clenbuterol from October 1991 until February 1992, when he learned that the drug was being added to the IOC's list of banned substances. "Upon hearing Clenbuterol was to be put on the banned list," Logan said in his note, "I immediately stopped its use." Logan also said that he used the drug, "as a safe alternative to steroids" and that "all high level athletes look for safe, legal vitamins and minerals to enhance performance."

In his statement, he also noted that, "six months later it is possible to test positive for asthma medication." Logan took full responsibility for his actions, and felt sad that his career would be marred by the test results. "The thing that is most devastating to me," he said in his note, "is after three Olympics and 15 years of drug-free training that my accomplishments will somehow be tainted."[14]

Logan, however, wasn't the only athlete to test positive for Clenbuterol in Barcelona. German athletes Katrina Krabbe and Grite Breur also were found to be using the drug. In addition, within days after Logan tested positive for Clenbuterol, another American athlete would be caught. This time it was Bonnie Dasse, a thirty-three-year-old shot-putter who tested positive for the banned substance. She became the fourth athlete to test positive for the asthma medication during the Barcelona games. Dasse was a two-time Olympian who had ranked among the top 10 American female shot-putters for the previous nine years.

In appearing before the IOC's doping commission, Dasse admitted that she had taken the drug several days before she gave the sample that, upon analysis, showed the presence of Clenbuterol in her system. According to the IOC's antidoping commission, Dasse had appeared before the commission, answered all their questions straightforwardly and admitted to receiving the drug from a friend.

"She recognized having taken the product. She didn't try to lie and to give false explanations," commission chairman Prince Alexandre de Merode told the Associated Press.

Dasse, Logan, Krabbe, and Breur became some of the first individuals to be punished not for testing positive for a specifically banned drug, but because of a clause in the IAAF's rules that banned the use of substances "related" to those on their prohibited list.[15]

CHINESE SWIMMERS' SUDDEN SUCCESS

In the late 1980s, China's swimming program began to show signs that they would emerge as a major player in competition over the coming years, after never being a factor in competition before that time. In 1988, China's women's swim team won four silver medals at the Seoul Olympics. At the 1992 Olympics in Barcelona, Spain, China started to dominate the sport, much like the East Germans had done in the late 1970s and 1980s.

A number of competitors started raising questions about the Chinese team. How had they managed to get so good, so quickly? Was it by using steroids or other performance-enhancing drugs? Members of the U.S. women's swim team were especially frustrated by their losses to the Chinese. Rumors and speculation about whether the Chinese women were fueled by performance-enhancing substances ran rife.

When swimmer Lin Li came under fire after she barely outtouched Summer Sanders in the 200-meter individual medley finals, her coach Zhang Xiong responded defensively, saying, "An East German coach came to China in 1986. But I have been with Lin for 11 years, since she was a child taking her first steps. She has never trained with East German coaches. To go into such matters is meaningless."

Lin set a new world record—2 minutes, 11.65 seconds—beating the previous world record (2:11.73) set by Ute Geweniger of East Germany in 1981. In doing so, Lin managed to beat her previous best time by four seconds, an astonishing improvement. Lin hit the wall 0.26 seconds ahead of Sanders, who took the silver medal.

The same day that Lin outtouched Sanders for gold, FINA (the governing body for swimming competition) changed their antidoping testing policy. Previously, they tested two of the top four finishers from each race, chosen at random. Under FINA's new system, all of the medal winners from each event would be subjected to drug testing.

The Chinese team again surprised their competitors with their performance in the 400 medley event at the Olympics. When the finals for the 400 medley relay took place, China's top swimmer Zhuang Yong, who normally would have swum the last leg of the event (the anchor leg), did not compete. Zhuang, according to the Chinese team's story, was "too exhausted" to compete. The rumor mill had a different story—that the stricter testing program was to blame. Zhuang had won the 100-meter freestyle event several days earlier, but as luck would have it he hadn't been tested.

In fact, no Chinese swimmers tested positive for banned substances in Barcelona. Over the coming years, however, Chinese swimmers would find themselves at the center of a number of doping scandals.[16]

During the 1994 world swimming championships, the Chinese women's swim team would again come under scrutiny. Prior to the competition in Rome, two Chinese swimmers tested positive for elevated testosterone to epitestosterone ratios. Zhong Weiyue returned an elevated T/E ratio during competition in February 1994, and Ren Xin, returned an elevated T/E ratio at the Goodwill Games, just a few weeks prior to the World's in Rome. Both swimmers were part of the "five golden flowers" who dominated the 1992 Barcelona Olympics. The other swimmers in that group were said to have retired prior to the 1994 world championships.[17]

China brought a young, though not completely inexperienced, team to the world championships. None of their swimmers at the 1994 competition had participated at the 1992 Olympics, however. Even so, several of the young swimmers held world records at the time.

China's coach, along with some of the swimmers, spoke to *The New York Times* about the use of steroids. Chen Yunpeng, China's national coach, told the *Times* that he was more interested in getting his athletes prepared for the 1996 Atlanta Olympics than in winning gold medals at the 1994 World's in Rome. Chen also pointed out that the swimmers who tested positive for banned substances came from provincial teams, rather than his national team.

"We stress time and again to the swimmers that if you take steroids, it will severely hurt your health," Chen told the *Times*, "and we often show them videos of the bad effects and they can see that they will become more like a man with more muscles and acne on their skin."

Several of Chen's swimmers agreed. One rising star on the 1994 Chinese team, Len Bin, said, "The state has banned it and once it is discovered, there can be severe punishment, and also it can do severe harm to your body."

Another Chinese swimmer, Le Jingyi—who held the world record in the 100-meter freestyle at that time—said, "The Olympic spirit is about fair competition, but by taking steroids, it means you get an unfair advantage, and you have violated the spirit of the Olympics."

Chen also blamed the amount of weight training that he required of his swimmers for causing others to be suspicious of China's success. "One of the main reasons that foreigners suspect Chinese swimmers take steroids is our weight training, which is very heavy. That's our secret."

Weight training, as well as altitude training, may have played a role in the team's success, but other factors also influenced their results. However the Chinese team came by its success in 1994, none of their swimmers tested positive at the world championships in Rome that year. In fact, the team dominated the competition, winning 12 of the 16 gold medals. At the Asian Games later that year, a different picture would emerge.[18]

On September 30, 1994, two days before the Asian Games were set to occur, an unannounced test caught the Chinese swim team by surprise. Spurred on by complaints from a number of nations, the IOC drug testers requested that 16 members of the Chinese women's swim team provide urine samples when they finished their daily workout, in Hiroshima, Japan, in preparation for the Asian Games.

According to Dr. Yoshiteru Mutoh, "They were surprised, but after about 10 minutes they cooperated." Dr. Mutoh, a Japanese physician, collected the urine samples for FINA. The results of this unannounced testing, along with results from other tests taken during the Asian Games, led to a startling discovery—the first documented evidence of widespread use of dihydrotestosterone, a banned anabolic steroid more commonly known as DHT. DHT is a metabolite of testosterone that has a stronger effect when administered to a person than other forms of testosterone.

Eleven Chinese athletes tested positive for DHT at the Asian Games in 1994. Of those, seven were swimmers. Three of the female swimmers caught were world champions. In the twenty-two years between 1972 and 1994, 22 swimmers tested positive for banned substances. Of those 22 swimmers, 13 were from China—and these athletes tested positive during the period from 1988 to 1994.

Dr. Manfred Donicke, the German chemist who often served as the IOC's expert on doping matters, told *The New York Times*, "It is my personal impression that, in swimming, the use [of DHT] was at least widespread [by Chinese athletes at the Asian Games]. Systematically, if it has been used on the order of trainers and functionaries, I cannot say. It is difficult to say what is the amount of collective criminal energy behind it."

Dr. Donicke, with the help of other scientists in the German antidoping laboratory in Cologne, pioneered the techniques for detecting steroid use. In 1978, the laboratory registered the first positive test result for steroid abuse. The Cologne lab was also instrumental in establishing the 6:1 testosterone to epitestosterone ratio, deemed to be evidence of doping with testosterone.

That ratio would be reduced to 4:1 beginning with athletic competitions occurring in 2005 and later.

In 1988, Dr. Donicke and his lab developed a set of five chemical fingerprints to identify the use of DHT. In 1992, only one athlete—a cyclist—had tested positive for DHT use prior to the Chinese athletes at the Asian Games two years later. The results caught Dr. Donicke by surprise. "I would not have expected the extent that in one nation, one swimming federation, that DHT would have been systematically used or misused," he told *The New York Times*.

At the time, DHT had been rumored to be the latest designer drug. Few of the 24 accredited antidoping labs in 1994 actually tested for DHT. But the Mitsubishi lab in Tokyo happened to be one of the few that did. The test results, however, were not released right away. In fact, the results were not released for another month, during which time the data was reviewed by both the Cologne lab and the Mitsubishi lab in Tokyo.

In the end, two Chinese world champions were caught by the surprise tests of September 30, 1994. Yang Aihua tested positive for testosterone, and Lu Bin tested positive for DHT. The third Chinese world champion swimmer to test positive at the 1994 Asian Games was Zhou Guanbin. Her test, like Lu Bin's, came out positive for the use of DHT.

As a result of the scandal, Dr. Donicke proposed more out-of-competition testing, along with detailed record-keeping of each athlete's test results. With a detailed antidoping test history, the IOC would then be able to monitor each athlete's results for suspicious changes over time. But 1994 wasn't the last time that Chinese swimmers would run afoul of the antidoping tests during the decade.[19]

When word of the positive doping tests first came out, China's Olympic Committee released a statement saying that it was "shocked and upset" by the revelations. They immediately asked for investigations by the national sports federations, and stated that any athlete found guilty should be suspended. Eventually, all 11 athletes who tested positive at the Asian Games would be suspended.[20] Several days after the athletes' suspensions were announced, the Chinese government took a hard-line stance against doping in sports, saying that the suspensions proved the government was serious about fighting the use of illegal substances in sport.[21]

Two years later, at the 1996 Olympics in Atlanta, Georgia, the Chinese swim team didn't fare as well as they did at the 1994 Asian Games. Early on in the competition, the Chinese swimmers struggled to come close to the performance of just two years prior. In the end, the team managed to win some medals, but unlike the Asian Games of 1994, they did not dominate competition. In the end, the Chinese women's swim team won five medals in Atlanta—one gold, two silver, and two bronze—a much smaller haul than the 12 of 16 possible medals at the World's in Rome in 1994.

The final chapter for the Chinese women's swim team during the 1990s was written in 1998, when swimmer Yuan Yuan was caught bringing human growth hormone (HGH) into Australia shortly before the 1998 world championships. The substance was found by Australian customs inspectors in Sydney in 13 vials, hidden inside a Thermos in Yuan's luggage. Yuan told customs officials that she was bringing the contents of the Thermos in for a friend, while coach Zhou Zewen admitted to packing the bag.

The discovery was a deep embarrassment to the Chinese athletics officials, who had been denying that a string of world-record performances had been produced through the use of performance-enhancing drugs. As a result of the discovery, Yuan, a silver medalist at the 1994 world championships in Rome, was ordered home, along with coach Zewen.

With the scandal came calls for the entire Chinese women's swim team to be banned from competition. "These kids are in a no-win situation now," John Leonard, the head of the World Swim Coaches Association, said. "If everyone wins, there will be an uproar that they are doped. If they don't, it's the no-hope, no-dope story."

Yuan was ultimately banned from competition for four years.

DIEGO MARADONA TESTS POSITIVE AT THE 1994 WORLD CUP TOURNAMENT

Just hours before a match between Argentina and Bulgaria during the 1994 World Cup Tournament, Argentine officials suspended superstar player Diego Maradona. Maradona tested positive for five variants of ephedrine after submitting to random drug tests, when he was one of two players selected at random for drug screenings following the Argentine team's previous match, a 2–1 victory, against Nigeria the previous week.

Although his teammates were told to go out and win the game for their captain, the Argentine team was unable to do so, resulting in a 2–0 loss to the Bulgarians. According to at least one news report, the decision to remove Maradona from the game was made by Argentine soccer federation officials as a way of warding off any further sanctions from FIFA, soccer's international federation. This was not the first time Maradona had run afoul of doping rules. The superstar player served a fifteen-month ban in 1991 and 1992 after testing positive for cocaine use. Maradona had not been expected to be a major factor in the tournament. However, during the 1994 World Cup series, he scored points in games against both Greece and Nigeria during the first round of tournament play.

Maradona told an Argentine television station following his removal from the lineup, "They have retired me from soccer. I don't think I want another revenge, my soul is broken."

The five variants of ephedrine reportedly found in Maradona's system were:

- Ephedrine
- Phenylpropanolamine
- Pseudoephedrine (the active ingredient in Sudafed)
- Non-pseudoephedrine, and
- Methylephedrine

Some of these substances can be found in over-the-counter allergy medications, and some are found in asthma medications. Maradona had told a team trainer that he was taking a medication for minor allergy symptoms. Ephedrine and its related drugs are often used to relieve allergy or hay fever symptoms. When taken in larger doses, ephedrine and its variants have a stimulant-like effect. It has been used in the past to increase energy and to lose weight. During the run-up to the 1994 World Cup, Maradona lost 26 pounds.

Michel d'Hooghe, a FIFA official, said at the time that no single over-the-counter medication would contain all five of these ingredients. D'Hooghe, a member of FIFA's executive committee who is also a physician, said, "Maradona must have taken a cocktail of drugs because the five identified substances are not found in one medicine. Whatever way there is of taking it, it is forbidden under the doping regulations of FIFA."[22]

Although Maradona would claim he used the drugs to lose weight at the behest of FIFA, the international soccer federation denied Maradona's claims. At a disciplinary hearing in August 1994, Maradona was handed a fifteen-month suspension that ran until September 29, 1995. He was also fined $15,400.

Following his suspension, Maradona played with Boca Juniors, one of the first teams that hired him as a young player breaking into the professional soccer ranks. He played with Boca Juniors until 1997, when he retired as a player. Following his retirement, Maradona would try his hand at coaching. Drugs, especially cocaine, continued to play a role in his life. Maradona has been in and out of rehab a number of times over the last ten years, a sad set of circumstances for a man who's often mentioned as one of the greatest soccer players of all time. In April 2007, Diego Maradona was hospitalized for two weeks due to hepatitis brought on by years of drug and alcohol abuse.[23]

IAAF BEGINS IMMEDIATE SUSPENSIONS FOR TRACK AND FIELD ATHLETES

In November 1994, the International Association of Athletics Federations (IAAF) changed the rules regarding suspension for positive antidoping tests.

The previous rule required that before an athlete could be suspended, his or her B sample tests would need to confirm a positive result for the initial A sample tests. With the new rule, athletes would be suspended immediately after a positive result came in for an athlete's A sample.

Arnie Ljunqvist, the IAAF's doping commission chairman, told the Associated Press, "Our decision is based on a wish to speed up the entire doping control procedure, as well as to cut down rumors." While the athlete would be suspended immediately, a B sample analysis could still be requested in order to contest the suspension.[24]

SWIMMING SCANDAL TORPEDOES U.S. SWIMMING'S MORAL HIGH GROUND

In the summer of 1995, only shortly after U.S. and other countries' swimming federations pushed for sanctions against Chinese swimmers who'd been doping, a fifteen-year-old American swimmer became embroiled in a doping scandal. The story of Jessica Foschi's ordeal at the hands of her own country's swimming federation, as well as knocked the U.S. women's team's reputation down a notch or two at a time when they were leading the fight against doping within the sport.

After placing third in the 1,500-meter freestyle at the US Summer Nationals in Pasadena, California, Foschi tested positive for what *The New York Times* described as "an obscure anabolic steroid from the black market." Several months later, a US Swimming review panel issued a controversial 2–1 decision granting the young, up-and-coming swimmer two years probation rather than a two-year suspension from competition.

Coaches from around the world contacted John Leonard, the executive director of the American Swimming Coaches Association, to protest Foschi's lenient punishment. "It doesn't matter how it got into her system, our rules tell us she has to be suspended for two years," Leonard told *The New York Times* in November 1994.

"If everybody who tests positive for steroids can get out of it by saying he or she didn't do it, then our whole sport's going to go down the tubes. As far as that board of review decision goes, two members chickened out."

Jill Sterkel, a four-time Olympian who was one of the review board members that voted in favor of the probation, said, "Her times from the Nationals shouldn't exist anymore, but I'm skeptical about throwing her out for two years when this could have been a one-time thing. I don't think she knowingly took it."

Sterkel and fellow panel member Bill Stapleton, a sports lawyer and agent at the time, advocated probation instead of suspension from competition after Foschi, her parents, and her coach all passed polygraph tests covering their denials of the alleged use or any connection to alleged use of the banned drug. Fellow review panel member Gerry Olsen, a former vice president of

United States Swimming (also known as US Swimming), voted to impose a suspension on Foschi.

The day the review board's decision was announced, Carol Zeleski, the president of US Swimming, appealed to FINA. In the appeal, the federation asked the international governing body to impose a suspension upon the young athlete. In lodging the appeal, Zeleski said that she was "95 percent sure" FINA would follow suit.

At the time, the majority of swimming coaches backed the national federation. Despite all of that, Foschi remained steadfast in her denial. "I have never taken any steroid or any other banned or illegal drug. Anyone who knows me knows I would never cheat, lie or do anything dishonest in or out of the pool."

Foschi, her parents, and her attorneys maintained that she was framed. They speculated that the person who framed her might be an enemy of the United States Swimming program or someone purposely trying to harm Foschi.[25] In February 1996, FINA imposed a two-year suspension.

Shortly after the ban was announced, Foschi's parents filed a lawsuit against US Swimming and the USOC, seeking to overturn their daughter's sanction. In filing the lawsuit, they asked the New York State Supreme Court to prevent US Swimming and the USOC from interfering with the girl's right to compete until her samples could be tested at an independent lab. Another case would occur in short order that forced the international governing body to reduce her penalty back down to probation.[26]

Less than three weeks after banning Jessica Foschi from competition for two years, FINA made a decision in the case of Samantha Riley, an Australian swimmer who tested positive for dextroproposyphene at the world short-course championships in early December 1995 in Brazil. Riley had accidentally ingested the banned substance when she took a headache pill given to her by her coach, Scott Volkers.

In speaking about the decision, Prince Alexandre de Merode, chairman of the IOC's medical commission, said, "I am very satisfied. I think they made a decision that is fair and just. I think it was an intelligent interpretation of the rules. This decision gives credibility to the anti-doping fight."

At the same time, to some it appeared to be inconsistent with the ruling in the Foschi case. Given the differences in punishment between the two athletes, Carol Zeleski, of US Swimming, asked FINA to look into the Foschi matter once again.

"In light of FINA's decision to give Riley a strong warning instead of a two-year suspension, I will ask FINA to review the facts of the Jessica Foschi matter," Zeleski told *The New York Times*.[27] In early March 1996, Jessica Foschi's ban from competition was repealed.

At least one athlete was not happy about the final turn of events. "I am ashamed and embarrassed to be part of an organization that can't stand up for what it believes in," Janet Evans said just before the 1996 Olympic swimming trials began in Indianapolis. "Last year, their whole thing was as soon as someone tests positive for steroids, regardless if they know it or not, they're out."[28]

AS THE SNOWBOARD TURNS

Dope and doping made sports headlines a great deal during 1998 and it started early in the year at the Olympic Games in Nagano, Japan. Snowboarding joined the Winter Olympics that year and the sport made a huge first impression. Unfortunately, part of that first impression had to do with a positive doping test. Ross Rebagliati, a Canadian athlete, became the first man to win a snowboarding gold medal in Olympic competition. He also became the first snowboarder to test positive for dope at the Olympics. Not just any dope, real dope. Marijuana. In a strange round of lab results, disciplinary hearings, appeals and counter appeals, Rebagliati lost his gold medal and then had it reinstated.

Darren Chalmers, who was Rebagliati's roommate during the Nagano Games, dubbed the affair "As the Snowboard Turns." From the time Rebagliati's gold medal was taken away as a result of his positive drug test to the time it was restored by an ad hoc Court of Arbitration for Sport arbitration panel was a scant 32 hours. Rebagliati went from winner to loser to winner again. Rebagliati told a news conference following the arbitration panel's decision, "I won the gold medal twice."

In their decision, the arbitration panel noted that "cannabis consumption is a serious matter of social concern," but they ruled that there were no legal grounds for sanctioning the Canadian athlete because both the IOC's rulebook and the International Ski Federation's (FIS) rulebook did not clearly state what sanctions should be applied to someone found guilty of using marijuana.

Carol Anne Letheren, head of the Canadian Olympic Association, voiced concern about the ruling, saying, "What we are concerned about for sure is that this could potentially send out a mixed message, but I think what's important here is that this athlete is treated fairly in this competition."

When the decision was made to strip Rebagliati of his gold medal, the snowboarding community reacted with outrage. One Canadian snowboarder, Mike Michalchuk, held up a banner protesting the decision after he finished his qualifying run in the half-pipe. Michalchuk's banner read, "Ross is the champion. Give the gold back!"

In 1998, the IOC medical code made no mention of penalties for the use of marijuana unless a sports federation had specifically outlawed its use and implemented specific punishments for those found guilty of smoking dope. FIS regulations at the time said that a penalty could be imposed for a positive test. Marc Hodler, head of the FIS, informed the arbitrators that the federation considered Rebagliati's event to be one where no marijuana testing was warranted or necessary.

Letheren said of the arbitration panel, "The FIS said marijuana was in their guidelines to help protect the health and safety of athletes who might take the drug to overcome fear in sports where that might be important. They quoted ski jumping as an example. They said they were not at any time asked if they wished to have marijuana tested for in snowboarding, and that if they had been asked, the answer would have been no because it is no advantage in giant slalom."

Letheren told *The New York Times* that "clarification early on in these Games would have certainly helped everybody." During the scandal, Rebagliati maintained that he tested positive for marijuana, but only because the tests were sensitive enough to detect trace amounts of the drug, because he had been breathing secondhand smoke at a party in his hometown of Whistler, British Columbia.

Letheren said that according to what she had been told by Canadian drug authorities, someone who smokes marijuana would have about 400 nanograms of THC (tetrahydrocannabinol) per milliliter of urine, while Rebagliati's concentration was 17.8 nanograms per milliliter. Letheren added that if Rebagliati had been "in a room with eight to 10 people [smoking marijuana] for one hour a day for six days" the reading would be 100 nanograms per milliliter.[29]

One FIS medical official, Tapio Videman of Finland's University of Jyvaskyla, allowed that Rebagliati's explanation about being exposed to secondhand marijuana smoke could be correct. "It is possible things are as he says," Videman told *The New York Times*. "So, I am glad he got his medal."

Rebagliati was being questioned by Nagano police officers when he learned of the decision to restore his gold medal. He took the medal out of his pocket and held it again after not being able to do so for several days.

Rebagliati told a reporter for *The New York Times*, "Officially, it was supposed to have been taken away from me, but it wasn't. I had it in my front pocket the whole time. I wasn't able to look at it because I didn't know if it would be mine or not. All I wanted was for it to be close to me."[30]

MARY DECKER SLANEY FALLS VICTIM TO ANTIDOPING FEVER

As a result of a test at the June 1996 Olympic Trials, Mary Decker Slaney became embroiled in a four-year drama centered around allegations that she used testosterone to boost her running performance. At the time, the only test used to determine whether an athlete used testosterone was the testosterone to epitestosterone ratio. In the 1990s, an athlete's test would be considered a positive doping test only if the ratio exceeded 6 to 1. Mary

Decker Slaney's test at the Olympic Trials in 1996 came back above the legal limit. She was not suspended from competition immediately. In fact, she was allowed to compete at the Olympics and then to continue competing afterward. Over time, USA Track & Field (USATF) conducted more tests on Slaney, both in competition and out of competition. No action was taken against Slaney until the following summer.

On June 11, 1997, the IAAF suspended Slaney from competition and demanded that USATF suspend her, too. At first, a spokesman for USATF was noncommittal about what the organization would do. Although federation spokesman Pete Cava had initially stated that USATF would "invalidate" Slaney's entry, he then backpedaled and made a statement that the American federation would allow Slaney to compete while they reviewed their options. When asked what the federation would do, Cava answered, "No one knows at this point." He indicated that a decision would occur the following day.

When word of Cava's statement reached Istvan Gyulai, the general secretary of the IAAF, Gyulai said that a refusal to suspend Slaney would be "unprecedented" and an "outrage," because the IAAF believed that Slaney had clearly been doping.

"We still expect USA Track and Field to carry out its responsibility and protect Mary's right to compete," Jim Coleman, Slaney's attorney, told *The New York Times*.[31] Slaney and her legal team didn't have to wait long to find out what the USATF would do. The following day, the track federation suspended Slaney and barred her from competing at the 1997 U.S. national track and field championships. Slaney's only hope would be to take the U.S. federation to court, which she chose not to do. Still, Slaney and her lawyers threatened to hold USATF accountable for their actions.

"We're going to hold them completely responsible," Coleman told reporters in response to USATF's ruling. "They have completely disregarded Mary's rights and treated her in a way that is disgusting. Mary's rights will be vindicated. She has suffered substantial damages. It will be her decision whether she wants to recover them. There's no doubt she will be able to."

In September 1997, the review board considered arguments from Slaney's lawyers and from USATF and issued its decision. In a brief statement, the review board accepted Slaney's arguments that the T/E ratio test discriminates against women because their levels of testosterone can be affected by the aging process, menstruation, the use of birth control pills and the consumption of alcohol. The ruling meant that Slaney would be allowed to compete again. After the ruling was announced, Richard Slaney, her husband, told reporters, "It's tough to be vindicated for something you feel you never did. I appreciate what the panel did. This part is over. But it's not over because this process has to change. Nobody should have to go through this."

And, in fact, the process wasn't over. Even though the U.S. federation had vindicated Mary Decker Slaney, she could not compete internationally unless the IAAF reversed its ban. While the IAAF's general secretary commented after learning of the U.S. federation's decision that the international federation would review the case, it was not a sure thing that the IAAF would change course.

"Our experts brought their decision [in May 1997 to suspend Slaney from competition] on what they thought was a sufficient number of tests that showed this was not a natural function of the body, but that this was a doping case," Gyulai commented. "We have to look at the arguments USA Track & Field used to reinstate her. Maybe they found new evidence. We will look at it very seriously."

At the same time, he indicated that if upon review the IAAF disagreed with the U.S. federation's ruling, they would seek arbitration to settle the matter. Slaney won this round of the fight, but the fight was far from over.

After the ruling in her favor was announced, one of Slaney's attorneys commented, "They never replaced it with another theory. They never found a prohibited substance, which was the burden they had. And they did not take into account various things known to affect the [T/E] ratio so as to exclude them as possibilities."[32] But just because the evidence wasn't good enough for the U.S. federation to find Mary Decker Slaney guilty of doping didn't mean that the IAAF wouldn't be able to convince an arbitration panel that Slaney had doped.

In April 1999, the IAAF prevailed. An arbitration panel found Slaney guilty of doping, citing her elevated T/E test from the 1996 Olympic Trials as proof. In stark contrast to the decision of the American review board, the IAAF's arbitration panel ruled that Slaney could not prove that her urine sample was affected by any of the factors cited in the ruling that reinstated her for competition in September 1997.

They imposed a retroactive two-year ban on Slaney running from June 1996 to June 1998, and voided her results from the 1997 world indoor track and field championships, where she finished second in the 1,500-meter run. Although the retroactive ban ran from June 1996 through June 1998[33], Slaney's story still wasn't over.

About two weeks before the IAAF ruled against Slaney, she and her attorneys filed a lawsuit against both the international federation and the USOC in a U.S. District Court in Indianapolis, Indiana. Jim Coleman, her attorney, said at the time that the drug test Slaney failed in 1996 was "totally dishonest." In response, the IAAF said they would defend themselves in the lawsuit, and they also announced that their arbitration panel would reconvene in ten days' time to continue looking into her case. Slaney's attorney told *The New York Times* that the IAAF's inability to take action on her case prompted the lawsuit. It may also have prompted the ruling made by the arbitrators.

Coleman had sharp words for the two organizations, saying, "Both the USOC and IAAF know that things other than doping can cause a woman's

T-E ratio to go above 6:1." He cited evidence presented during the American review board's hearing. Research at Duke University suggested that using the T/E ratio to determine testosterone doping is flawed when applied to women in their late 30's and early 40's who use birth-control pills. At the time of the 1996 Olympic Trials, Slaney was using the pill.

Coleman went on to say, "The IAAF has no other way to detect the use of testosterone. Rather than trying to find a valid way, they are willing to take the chance that they will prosecute and damage an innocent athlete."

An IAAF official took issue with the lawsuit, telling *The New York Times*, "In whichever country, civil justice does not have the right to judge sporting rules of an international federation. The IAAF cannot be under the jurisdiction of a court in Indiana. IAAF rules are enforced in 209 countries, and the rules are the same for everyone. Otherwise, there would be confusion and chaos."[34]

Mary Decker Slaney's case reached its conclusion in March 2001, when the U.S. District Court in Indianapolis ruled that it did not have jurisdiction over the lawsuit. The court's opinion stated that it was required to recognize the arbitration decision, and that even though the arbitration panel was not bound by the same rules of evidence as the District Court, the issue couldn't be relitigated. After almost five years, the Slaney case finally was over.[35]

FORMER EAST GERMAN SPORTS OFFICIALS PUT ON TRIAL

With the fall of the Berlin Wall in the late 1980s and the reunification of Germany a couple of years later, the legendary East German doping program came to an end. At first, it merely faded into the background. But a few voices, like husband and wife antidoping crusaders Werner Franke and Brigitte Berendonk, kept demanding justice. By the late 1990s, a modicum of justice was delivered.

In March 1998, more than seven years after the two Germanys became one, the first of two important trials related to the doping of East German athletes began in the state courthouse in Berlin. The information that emerged during the 1998 trial painted a picture more detailed than some had suspected: From the 1970s onward, the East German government ran a sports program fueled by anabolic steroids geared to achieve one overarching goal: To dominate Olympic sports, win more gold medals, and to prove the superiority of the communist system. For a time, the program worked.

Officials started looking into allegations of rampant doping in East Germany only a couple of years after the two countries reunited. Beginning in 1993, investigators looked into the history of East Germany's sports doping program, trying to assemble any and all documentation that had not been destroyed during the run-up to reunification in 1991. Eventually, they found approximately 60 documents that detailed various doping schemes and activities. In May 1996, state prosecutors coordinated raids of 50 homes throughout the former East Germany in a search for even more documentation regarding the state's secret doping activities. Shortly before the trials began, a treasure trove of documents was unearthed from the files of the Stasi, East Germany's feared secret police.

The information that investigators discovered provided details of the research and programs conducted by the former Communist country's secret sports doping committee. And from these records, a number of high-ranking officials involved in doping were identified. Among the documents were those detailing "State Planning Theme 14.25," which was a highly organized approach to steroid use. In almost every imaginable sport—including canoeing, swimming, and track and field—East German athletes were given steroids or other performance-enhancing drugs by their coaches and trainers. The drugs came from two sources: Jenapharm, based in the town of Jena, and VEB Arzneimittel, a pharmaceutical company based in Dresden.

The doping programs were coordinated by two East German agencies: The German College for Physical Culture, along with the Research Institute for Physical Culture and Sport. From these two organizations, the web of intrigue spread far and wide, through various local sports committees, state-sponsored research institutes, and the Stasi. The performance enhancement programs that spread throughout East Germany's sports establishment created a pool of thousands of athletes doped to the gills while competing at home and abroad.

After almost five years of investigation, charges were brought against four swimming officials: Rolf Gläser, Dieter Krause, Dieter Lindemann, and Volker Frischke. Charges were also brought against two sports physicians involved with the East German swimming program: Bernd Pansold and Dieter Binus. The six were charged with doping 19 athletes, mostly girls and young women, by forcing them to take various steroids in order to win gold in international competition. By the time the trial ended, the lid had been completely blown off the East German antidoping machine.[36]

The trials also created a great deal of friction between residents of the former East Germany and residents of the West. For a number of East Germans, the trials were the act of a group jealous of the East's athletic success. For those from the West, it was a necessary and painful step toward holding those responsible for the programs accountable for the effects doping had on the athletes.

Of the 19 female athletes who testified at the trial, many showed masculine traits, such as facial hair and deep voices. Most of the athletes who testified were minors at the time their coaches first started forcing them to take "little blue pills" of what the girls were told were vitamins, but were shown during the trial to be Oral-Turinabol. As one witness testified during the trial, there was a saying amongst the East German swimmers regarding the little blue pills: You eat the pills, or you die.[37] In other words, those who didn't go along with the program would be kicked out—and they would lose the special privileges that star athletes and their families received from the government.

But going along with the program was not without danger. The pills had powerful side effects, such as those listed above, much (if not all) of which was known as far back as the 1960s. The information could be easily found, on the product labeling and in medical reference books like the Physicians' Desk Reference (PDR).[38]

Christiane Knacke-Sommer was one of the athletes who testified against the defendants. Steven Ungerleider, in his book *Faust's Gold*, details a particularly powerful exchange between the prosecutor and Knacke-Sommer.

When the prosecutor asked her, "Did defendant Gläser or defendant Binus ever tell you the blue pills were the anabolic steroid known as Oral-Turinabol?" Knacke-Sommer replied, "They told us they were vitamin tablets, just like they served all the girls with meals."

"Did defendant Binus ever tell you the injection he gave was Depot-Turinabol?" the prosecutor asked. "Never," Knacke-Sommer said, "He said the shots were another kind of vitamin."

"He never said he was injecting you with the male hormone testosterone?"

"Neither he nor Herr Gläser ever mentioned Oral-Turinabol or Depot-Turinabol."

"Did you take these drugs voluntarily?"

"I was fifteen years old when the pills started. The training motto at the pool was, 'You eat the pills, or you die.' It was forbidden to refuse. But the pills and the shots, they destroyed me physically and emotionally."

Knacke-Sommer went on. "They destroyed my body and my mind. They gave me those pills . . . which made me crazy and ruined my body. They even poisoned my medal!" She rose from her chair and threw her bronze medal from the 1980 Olympics to the floor.

"It is tainted. Poisoned with drugs and a corrupt system. It is worthless and a terrible embarrassment to all Germans." As Ungerleider noted, the judge "gaveled a stunned courtroom to silence."[39]

At least one athlete, Heidi Krieger, testified that the drugs deepened her own sense of sexual ambivalence. So much so that in 1997 she underwent a sex change operation to become a man, now known as Andreas Krieger. Krieger, the 1986 European shot-put champion, said of the drugs given to her as a child, "I knew it wasn't clean, but I did not know it was hormones."

Other athletes told stories of being forced into having abortions because of the potential for deformities related to steroid abuse, while others—including a 1980 Olympic gold medalist in swimming—suffered liver and heart problems.[40]

Testimony in the trial occurred over a period from April until August 1998. In the end, all of those charged in the case were found guilty, and fined ninety days' wages.[41] The defendants avoided jail time by admitting during testimony that they had doped the athletes who testified against them.

More trials would occur over the next couple of years, culminating with a trial in 2000 of some very high-ranking former officials of East Germany's sports programs.

THE FESTINA SCANDAL

Just days before the 1998 Tour de France was to begin in Dublin, Ireland, an arrest was made in the France-Belgium border town of Lille that would unleash the biggest doping scandal to date in the world of professional cycling. Willy Voet, the soigneur for the Festina team, was stopped for a routine border search. What the customs agents found in Voet's car—an official car provided by the Tour de France—was a virtual treasure trove of doping substances, including amphetamines, EPO, steroids, and various masking agents.

It would be the biggest scandal to hit the Tour de France and professional cycling since the death, thirty-one years earlier, of Tommy Simpson, from a combination of heat exhaustion and excessive amphetamine usage. Ten years before the Festina scandal rocked professional cycling, Pedro Delgado (who went on to win the 1988 Tour) had tested positive for the use of a masking agent to disguise the presence of anabolic steroids in his system. But Delgado managed to avoid punishment, because the masking agent found in his system had not yet been banned by the UCI. Ten days after Delgado's test results, the UCI banned the masking agent found in his system.

When the Festina scandal struck, professional cycling was second only to soccer in terms of the sport's popularity in Europe. The impact of the Festina scandal can be felt to this day, in the developments that came as a result of the sporting world's reaction to what happened.

As the scandal began to unfold, the Festina team was allowed to compete in the Tour. With that decision, riders such as Alex Zülle and Richard Virenque—both viable contenders for the Tour victory in Paris several weeks later—were allowed to begin cycling's biggest event. Another Festina cyclist competing during the 1998 Tour, Christophe Moreau, was wrapped up in a doping controversy of his own.

Not long before the 1998 Tour, Moreau tested positive for a banned endurance booster. Even though a cloud was hanging over his head, Moreau was also allowed to race. It wouldn't be long before a number of teams would be tossed from the Tour due to connections with the Festina affair, or because someone believed they had connections of that sort. Other teams would leave the race in order to protest their treatment at the hands of the police or other law enforcement authorities.

A week after Voet's arrest, other members of the team began to come under scrutiny. Eric Ryckaert, the team's physician, and Bruno Roussel, the team's directeur sportif (i.e., coach or team manager), were being held in connection with the case. A couple of days after that, just hours after the end of the Tour's 6th stage, the entire Festina squad was banned from the rest of the race.

Within two weeks of Voet's arrest, information emerged that suggested the team's riders were expected to contribute to a doping fund. A story in the French newspaper *Le Parisien* quoted the lawyer for Eric Ryckaert as saying, "The riders were obliged to put part of their win bonuses into a 'black box' fund to buy banned substances. These products, like regular drugs, were held at Festina's headquarters in Lyon."

At least one other team was suspected of having an EPO program during the 1998 Tour. At the same time as Ryckaert's lawyer was speaking to the press, the UCI was asking the Dutch cycling federation to investigate reports that EPO had also been found in another team's (TVM) official team car.[42]

The TVM team's hotels and vehicles were searched at least twice during the 1998 Tour, once on July 23, 1998 and again on July 29, 1998. After the first search, two team officials were taken into police custody: Cees Priem, the directeur sportif, and Andre Mihailov, the team doctor. After the second search, police carted away several suitcases filled with what later turned out to be various banned substances. In addition, four cyclists and the assistant directeur sportif were taken away for questioning.

Other teams that fell under suspicion during the 1998 Tour included Spanish team ONCE, French teams Big Mat-Auber, Casino and Le Française de Jeux, and the Italian team Polti.[43]

In time, a number of Festina riders ejected from the Tour would admit to using EPO or one of the other banned substances found in Voet's car. In October 1998, Alex Zülle, Laurent Dufaux, and Armin Meier were each fined $2,164 by the Swiss Cycling Federation after having admitted to using EPO. They were also banned from competition for a period of eight months, two months more than the minimum required punishment at that time for those who confessed to doping. Similarly, the fines imposed were greater than the minimum required by the UCI. According to Remo Van Daniken, the president of the Swiss Cycling Federation's special antidoping commission, the greater punishments were imposed in order to send a signal to other riders who might be tempted to dope.[44]

Some of the riders who confessed, like Zülle, claimed that they felt pressured into using EPO. "As a rider, you feel tied into the system. It's like being on the highway. The law says there's a speed limit of 65, but everyone is driving 70 or faster. Why should I be the one who obeys the speed limit?"[45]

At one point during the 1998 Tour, the riders became so frustrated with the constant searches and arrests that they staged two sit-down strikes on the same day, refusing to continue unless the police changed tactics. With the intercession of Tour officials such as Jean-Marie LeBlanc, the police agreed to limit their aggressive approach.[46]

Bobby Julich, who would go on to finish third in the 1998 Tour, told *The New York Times*, "Guilty by association is not the correct way of doing things. Just because a friend of yours steals a car doesn't mean that you're a car thief. The problem here is being publicly ridiculed and physically violated by the police."[47]

Kevin Livingston, one of Julich's teammates, noted, "Not too many people understand what's going on, including us. But if it goes on like this, there won't be any sport. It can't go on like this."

By the time the Tour rolled into Paris three weeks after it began, less than half of the riders who started the race crossed the finish line. Mostly, the attrition was due to teams either being ejected from the Tour (such as Festina) or teams such as ONCE and Banesto dropping out of the Tour in protest over what they saw as mistreatment.

Willy Voet, the man whose arrest started the whole Festina scandal, published the book *Massacre à la Chaîne* in November 1999 (translated into English in 2002 as *Breaking the Chain: Drugs and Cycling: The True Story*), in which he described many of the doping practices he witnessed and participated in during his years in professional cycling. In the years since the Festina scandal, Voet has been unable to find a job in cycling, and has been declared persona non grata at the Tour de France.

When the organizers of the Tour de France presented the route for the 1999 Tour at a ceremony in Paris several months after the 1998 edition had ended, they promised to crack down on doping in subsequent Tours de France. Jean-Marie Leblanc announced that if the actions of any rider or team before or during the 1999 Tour threatened the race's reputation, action would be taken including expelling individual riders or entire teams.

Leblanc's position was echoed by Jean-Claude Killy, the French skiing star who headed corporate operations for the Tour at the time. "We will be absolutely hardnosed," Killy said. "The Tour will never be the symbol of doping but of the fight against doping."[48] The same day that Tour officials promised tough action against doping, the Festina cycling team parted company with Richard Virenque, who had not yet admitted to having used performance-enhancing drugs.[49]

Richard Virenque, one of Festina's star riders going into the 1998 Tour, steadfastly maintained that he had not used performance-enhancing drugs for several years, until he testified at a major doping-related trial in October 2000. During the trial that grew out of the Festina scandal, Virenque suddenly changed his story. He admitted during his testimony that he had, in fact, used various performance-boosting drugs such as EPO. "I took doping substances. I didn't have the choice," Virenque told the court in Lille, France. "I was the sheep—if they threw me out of the herd I was finished."

Virenque also told the court, "I live in a world where the rules are set up a long time in advance. I didn't cheat other riders. In the pack you never use the word doping but medical help. You are doped only when you get caught."[50]

HOW'D THAT WHISKEY GET IN THERE? MICHELLE SMITH GETS BANNED FOR TAMPERING WITH A DRUG TEST

At the 1996 Atlanta Olympics, Irish swimmer Michelle Smith was one of swimming's golden girls—literally. She won three gold medals, one in the 400-meter individual medley, another in the 400-meter freestyle and a third medal in the 200-meter individual medley. And she won a bronze in the 200-meter butterfly event. Various members of the U.S. Olympic team, including American star swimmer Janet Evans, openly voiced suspicion about Smith's achievements. Evans and others felt that Michelle Smith's improvements over the previous few years were too great to be achieved at such a late age (swimming-wise) only through hard work. Though no one could prove it, the suspicion was that Smith had been doping.

It didn't help matters that she was involved with (and eventually married) Erik de Bruin, a Dutch shot-putter and discus thrower who eventually tested positive for steroids. But throughout her swimming career, Smith never tested positive for any drugs. Both she and her husband maintained that their sporting achievements were the result of their training programs, which included weight lifting.

What tripped Michelle Smith up, and ultimately ended her swimming career, was an out-of-competition drug test in January 1998. Smith's test occurred on the same day that a Chinese swimmer was caught trying to smuggle performance-enhancing drugs into Australia before an international meet. Two drug testers showed up unannounced at Smith's home, to collect a urine sample as part of the International Swimming Federation (FINA) drug-testing program. What happened when she provided the sample is a matter of debate. Smith's sample was transported to an IOC-approved testing laboratory in Barcelona, Spain, for testing.

According to the lab's report, Smith's sample showed "unequivocal signs of adulteration." The report went on to say that the concentration of alcohol in the sample was "in no way compatible with human consumption" and that the sample had "a very strong whiskey odor." In other words, the lab's results alleged that Smith had spiked her sample with alcohol.

A second test, performed in May 1998 on Smith's B sample, yielded the same results. After a hearing in July 1998, the panel looking into Smith's case ruled that although they couldn't determine exactly how, Smith had in fact manipulated the urine sample. According to the panel's ruling, the sample was not contaminated or manipulated during transport from her home to the Barcelona lab, nor had it been contaminated during the testing process.[51]

Smith denied the charges, and fought her case vigorously, appealing the ruling to the Court of Arbitration for Sport. In June 1999, the CAS, after hearing Smith's case, ruled that she "was the only person with the motive and opportunity to manipulate the sample."

Shortly after the CAS announced its decision, Smith retired from the sport, still maintaining her innocence. In a statement to the press, she said, "I am deeply saddened by the decision of the Court of Arbitration for Sport and in particular their decision to prefer circumstantial evidence concerning the (drugs testing) manipulation charge, as distinct from direct evidence given by me at the hearing of my appeal."

In appealing her suspension, Smith and her attorneys followed a two-pronged attack on the evidence against her. First, they maintained that the sample in question did not belong to Smith. And second, the defense maintained that the manipulations to Smith's sample may have been performed by another, unknown, person. The panel, in ruling against the Irish swimming star, rejected both claims.

Smith also said, "I reaffirm that I have never used any banned substance in the course of my career, nor have I ever been charged by FINA of using any banned substance in the course of my career.

"I am proud of what I have achieved and assure those who have supported me and believe in me that my victories in Atlanta were not hollow and were achieved without the use of any illegal performance-enhancing substance."

Smith was banned from competition for four years, which meant she could not compete in the 2000 Olympics in Sydney, Australia, or at the 2001 world championships.[52] Whatever became of Michelle Smith? Over the coming years, she went back to school, completed a law degree and went on to practice as an attorney in Ireland.[53]

THE HOME RUN DERBY HAS AN EAST GERMAN ACCENT

In 1998, professional baseball was very much in need of a fix. Attendance at ball games had dropped off in the years following the 1994 Baseball Strike. With fewer fans filling the stadiums, something needed to be done to excite those who followed the sport. That something turned out to be a race for the all-time record number of home runs hit in a single season. Before 1998, the record belonged to Roger Maris, who hit 61 home runs in 1961 to beat Babe Ruth's record of 60 home runs in a single season. Maris' record stood for thirty-seven years before Mark McGwire, playing for the St. Louis Cardinals, and Sammy Sosa, playing for the Chicago Cubs, slugged home run after home run as each man pursued Maris' record during the 1998 baseball season.

According to a CBS News/*New York Times* poll in September 1998, the home run derby reversed the slide in interest. As the race between McGwire and Sosa heated up, fans came back to the stadiums in droves. News stories and sports columns were filled almost daily with stories of McGwire's or Sosa's latest homer. Headline writers and reporters breathlessly reported the latest feat of the two sluggers. But the race for the record would not be without its share of controversy.

In August 1998, a reporter saw a bottle of pills in Mark McGwire's locker that turned out to be androstenedione. Androstenedione is a precursor to testosterone, meaning that it is one of the building blocks that the body needs to manufacture the hormone. Theoretically, more building blocks mean more testosterone, which in turn may have an effect on muscle building, recovery, and athletic performance.

When the story came out in August 1998, McGwire spoke to the Associated Press, saying, "Everything I've done is natural. Everybody that I know in the game of baseball uses the same stuff I use." In addition to using androstenedione (also known as "Andro"), McGwire acknowledged that he used creatine, another supplement thought to help build muscles. McGwire, like a number of other ballplayers (including Sammy Sosa), was open about his use of creatine. He had been using creatine for the previous four years, believing that the supplement could help him recover faster from his daily weight training workouts.

Creatine and Andro were not without their downside, however. In 1998, no definitive studies had looked into the long-term effects of the use of either supplement. Dr. Gary Wadler told *The New York Times*, "There have been no studies of their safety or efficacy. And the side effects don't manifest themselves immediately. It takes months, years, sometimes generations." Wadler told the *Times* that although Andro wasn't a steroid, it could have similar side effects, including heart attacks, liver dysfunction, and some forms of cancer.[54]

Andro was not a banned substance for professional baseball players in 1998, and neither was creatine. But Andro has an interesting history. It was originally developed in East Germany in the 1970s for use in their infamous doping program. With the fall of the Berlin Wall in 1989 and the reunification of Germany, the doping experts of the former East Germany began exporting their technology. The U.S. Drug Enforcement agency became very concerned about how various synthetic hormones had made their way into the U.S. market.

In 1998, the DEA learned that two East German physicians had managed to get a patent for a nasal spray version of the drug by claiming it could be used to treat Parkinson's disease. As one official wondered in a letter to Dr. Werner Franke, "How is it that Rüdiger Häcker, a central figure in the former East German government doping program, can capitalize (i.e., be granted patents) on information gathered from the program when other scientists have been or will be tried in German court for their participation in the program?"[55]

In the days after the McGwire story broke, a number of sportswriters, columnists, and editorial writers reacted strongly, with some suggesting that McGwire's accomplishments might merit an asterisk next to his name in the record books.[56] But technically, Mark McGwire didn't break the rules. And McGwire was clear that if it had been against the rules he wouldn't be using the supplements. "If somebody tells me that it's illegal and I shouldn't be taking it, I will stop," he told *The New York Times*.[57]

In other sports at the time, however, the use of Andro—if detected—could have serious consequences. Other athletic federations had already limited or banned the use of Andro, including both the NFL and the IOC. Randy Barnes, the shot-putter, was banned by USATF and the IOC after testing positive for Andro.

In the wake of the media uproar caused by the McGwire story, Major League Baseball, along with the players' association, decided to look into the use of nutritional supplements.[58] In doing so, officials from both organizations promised to ban Andro if they were able to determine whether users suffered any serious side effects. To find out whether the "supplement" actually has a performance-enhancing effect, Major League Baseball sponsored research by two Harvard doctors. Their work would be the first full-scale study of Andro's effects on athletes, and baseball officials promised they would take action to ban the supplement should the results show that it could give an athlete a performance benefit. At the same time, however, baseball and players' union officials vowed not to be bullied into banning the substance before any proof existed one way or the other.

"Baseball's posture has been driven by a desire to understand and have a good scientific basis for what we do as opposed to having concern for any particular player and whether he uses it. Our policy will not be driven by public relations but by what the scientific information shows," baseball executive Rob Manfred said in early 1999.

Union official Gene Orza said, "Our job is to protect baseball players. If we found that Andro is bad for you, we'd have no hesitancy in saying, 'Guys, it's dangerous for you.' But right now we don't know that."[59]

For several years, the major leagues left the question of whether or not to ban the use of Andro unanswered. A ban on the supplement quietly came into being at the start of the 2004 baseball season, five years after management and the players' union started looking into the effects of Andro on otherwise healthy baseball players. At the same time, the FDA banned the sale of Andro, saying that the supplement has the same health risks as using anabolic steroids.[60]

STEROIDS ON THE TENNIS COURT

With all the scandals hitting sports in the late 1990s, tennis was no exception. In the summer of 1998, Petr Korda tested positive for steroids while competing at Wimbledon, one of the four biggest tennis tournaments in the world. Korda was not the first men's player to test positive for a banned substance—Ignacio Truyol of Spain tested positive for steroids in early 1997. In 1995, Matts Wilander and Karel Novacek tested positive for cocaine and were fined and suspended from competition. Korda's case generated controversy among his fellow professionals and set an unusual kind of first—the first decision in a doping case where the sports federation appealed their own decision to the Court of Arbitration for Sport.

In December 1998, the International Tennis Federation announced that Korda had tested positive for steroids at Wimbledon. Korda had been informed in August 1998 of the positive test, and was issued a formal notice of violation at the beginning of October. While the federation's committee looking into the matter found Korda guilty of using the performance-enhancing drugs, they ruled that due to "exceptional circumstances" no harsh sanctions would be imposed.

Korda told the committee that he and his advisers made very thorough attempts to determine how the drug nandrolone wound up in the tennis player's system, but that they could not determine the source. The ITF's committee accepted Korda's defense that he had been unaware of taking the steroid at Wimbledon. Korda would not have to serve a one-year suspension, but he was required to forfeit both the $94,529 in prize money he earned at the Grand Slam event, and he also had to forfeit the ranking points he earned.

"I am delighted that the committee has cleared my name and that I am free to carry on playing and competing," Korda told reporters following the announcement. "I would like to say that I completely support the tennis antidoping program and the efforts of the sports authorities to insure [sic] that the sport is clean."[61]

Within several weeks, Korda would again become the subject of controversy as he prepared to compete at the 1999 Australian Open. At the same time the controversy over whether Korda should be allowed to compete at the Australian Open, the ITF filed an appeal with the Court of Arbitration for Sport seeking to overrule its own committee's decision. The ITF was seeking to suspend the Czech tennis player for one year, on top of the forfeiture of prize money and his ranking points.

ITF spokesman Alun James told *The New York Times*, "We're not out to conduct a witch hunt on Petr Korda, but we believe the appeals committee misapplied the rule. We do not feel extenuating circumstances were proven by Mr. Korda, and we feel a suspension is warranted. A blanket 'I don't know how the drugs got there' is not sufficient."

"We're not after giving rewards to players who come up with the best excuses, but we believe this case sets a worrying precedent where players will feel they can hide behind a blanket 'I don't know,'" James continued. "It does look a little strange for us to go against our own appeals committee, but we need to have a clarification on the ruling, the consequence of which might be a ban to Mr. Korda."

At a press conference, Korda told reporters, "I wanted to play in Australia because I haven't done anything; why should I hide? I wish to state categorically that I am not a drugs cheat."

Players lined up both to support Korda and to demand that he be barred from playing at the Australian Open. Mark Miles, the head of the Association of Tennis Professionals (ATP), said at the time, "I don't think this is personal about Petr: I think it shows a zero tolerance for cheating. The good news is that our players are demanding a clean sport and a doping program that has real teeth." Miles went on to tell reporters that the ATP had never intended that a player should be able to escape responsibility for doping based on a simple denial, and he expressed hope that the appeal would lead to changes regarding what extenuating circumstances would warrant a reduced suspension.

Andre Agassi, who practiced with Korda before the tournament, gave his colleague some qualified support. Agassi told reporters, "I feel the need to give the benefit of the doubt to Petr, but we have certain rules, and to find out the reasons behind the decisions that are made is something the players are entitled to."

In announcing the decision to appeal their own panel's ruling, Brian Tobin, the ITF president, told reporters that they weren't trying to victimize the Czech player. Korda, however, saw things differently. "I proved my innocence in accordance with the ITF's own rules. I would like to think everyone will now respect that finding."[62]

Ultimately, the ITF won their appeal, and Korda was banned from tennis for one year. In addition, he was fined a total of $660,000, which was the amount of prize money he earned between July 1998 and September 1999, when the sanction was imposed. In effect, Korda's career as a tennis player was over. He never returned to the professional game.[63]

The other tennis doping story from the late 1990s is the story of Samantha Reeves. Reeves, in an effort to recover quicker from an ankle injury in late 1997, decided to try an over-the-counter "all natural" supplement to help her return to competition sooner. The product promised to help burn fat and build muscle. But there was a small catch: It contained a substance called Nor-Andro 19, a variation on nandrolone, the same steroid involved in the Korda case, and the same steroid that led to the downfall of Canadian sprinter Ben Johnson ten years earlier.

At a tournament in December 1997, Reeves was required to give a urine sample. When the test results came back, she became the first female tennis player to fail a drug test. After being informed of the test results, Reeves issued a statement saying that she had never knowingly done anything to harm her tennis career.

That she had never knowingly taken a steroid supplement did not absolve Reeves of responsibility in the eyes of those deciding her fate. Still, the committee looking into her doping offense decided that she would not be suspended or disciplined in any way. The ITF's James noted that "although the decision against any further punishment is arguably lenient, if caught again, she could face a life ban as a second offender."

Reeves' case was one of the first due to the use of over-the-counter nutritional supplements. As Alan Jones, a professor at the University of Mississippi told *The New York Times*, "There's tons of steroids out there, and they're not all coming from the black market." James was also a toxicology consultant to a company administering drug tests for the ITF, WTA, and ATP.

The problem with supplements like the one Reeves took is that although it's sold under the guise of being natural, some of the ingredients are not as benign as the labeling might suggest. As James also told the Times, "It's conceivable that a player could be oblivious to the fact that they're using something that contains an anabolic substance. They think: it's natural, it's pure, it's good for me. And that is an absolute fallacy."

Alan Jones characterized Nor-Andro 19 as "the new kid on the block."

"It's not a testosterone type of steroid, and the labs originally weren't testing for it," Jones said. "It's offered as a food supplement and marketed as a performance and training enhancer that increases muscle strength, mass and endurance."

News of her positive test for steroids came as a surprise to both Reeves and her parents. Before they were informed that she had tested positive for a nandrolone metabolite, Reeves and her family were asked to provide records of every type of drug or medicine that the young tennis player had taken. And then, shortly after the 1998 Wimbledon tournament, the ITF announced the results of Reeves' December 1997 test: positive for steroids.

Jack Reeves, Samantha's father, was critical of the process to which his daughter was subjected. "We thought it was good news that they'd figured out how the stuff got into her system; we thought that was the end of it. Then we were told the review board had decided to pursue the case and test a second sample. It's a kind of guilty-until-proven-innocent process where you're dealing with a lot of nameless, faceless parties. They do hold a player responsible for whatever is in their system, and they're not particularly interested in how it got there. You'd have to be a molecular biologist to know this would occur."

"It's been a very troublesome, frustrating experience," Reeves' father said in the summer of 1998. "These days, Samantha won't drink a glass of water without having it analyzed."[64]

Samantha Reeves continued playing tennis until 2005. In 2003, she achieved her highest ranking in women's tennis—75th in the world standings.[65]

THE TOUR OF REDEMPTION

If the 1998 Tour de France was the Tour of Shame, the 1999 Tour promised to be the Tour of Redemption, breathing new life into a sport that was seemingly in a great state of crisis. The Tour began with Lance

Armstrong winning the opening prologue (a short time-trial event)—a stunning comeback after having been successfully treated for testicular cancer. It was the kind of beginning that the Tour—and cycling—sorely needed after the Festina scandal of the previous year.

In the opening days of the stage race, Tour organizer Jean-Marie Leblanc couldn't be happier. When a reporter asked him if he was happy with the prologue's outcome, he said, "Yes—for me, for the Tour and for Lance above all. This is the Tour of renewal, of a return to the top level, and look at him: He incarnates that."[66]

After two very difficult years dealing with and recovering from testicular cancer—a devastating illness—1999 was the year that Lance Armstrong began his streak of seven consecutive victories in the Tour de France. But the 1999 Tour would not pass without doping accusations, including an accusation against the eventual victor. In addition, a cyclist from the Lampre team was kicked out after he informed a race doctor that he'd received a cortisone injection to treat injuries he suffered in a crash about a month before the Tour started.

The Italian cycling team sacked Ludo Dierckxsens, the reigning Belgian national champion, as a "preventive measure," claiming that the cyclist failed to inform Lampre's team doctor about receiving the medication. The story came out when Dierckxsens won the 11th stage of the Tour and had to provide a urine sample at the doping control facilities shortly after the stage's completion.

Dierckxsens told one of the race doctors about having received a shot of a drug called Synacthene. He also claimed to have given a copy of the prescription to Lampre's team doctor, but the cycling team denied that this had happened. Lampre directeur sportif Pietro Algeri was vague when talking to the media about whether Dierckxsens had been fired, or whether he had merely been withdrawn from the Tour.

Jean-Marie Leblanc, whose mood was upbeat at the beginning of the Tour, sounded less so when he spoke to reporters about the Dierckxsens situation. "There was no other choice but to expel their rider after he admitted taking drugs. Morally it was no longer acceptable for him to participate." Leblanc went on to say that if Lampre hadn't expelled the Belgian rider, the Tour organization would have. But it was unclear whether Dierckxsens broke any rules.

The UCI declined prosecuting Dierckxsens, on the grounds that he hadn't failed any drug tests. Four Lampre riders had been ejected from the Tour of Switzerland earlier in 1999, after failing blood tests. Many in cycling wondered whether Lampre would be allowed to start the 1999 Tour. But the rumored ban on the Lampre team never materialized.[67]

During his career, and even afterward, Lance Armstrong has been a frequent target of doping accusations. From the beginning of the 1999 event, rumors published in various newspapers suggested that Lance Armstrong's miraculous comeback from cancer had been powered by doping. Four days before the finish of the 1999 Tour, the American rider had a commanding lead, on course to winning the race if nothing went wrong. Armstrong again became embroiled in a doping controversy, this time fending off allegations of using corticosteroids. Armstrong apparently tested positive for the drug after using an anti-inflammatory cream to treat saddle sores during the Tour.

A French newspaper reported that Armstrong had tested positive, prompting him to hold a press conference where he acknowledged using the salve, while also denying that he had used any performance-enhancing drugs. The International Cycling Union (UCI) defended the American rider, noting that Armstrong had used a topical skin cream for which he had a prescription. In the UCI's opinion, no doping had occurred.

Armstrong told reporters at the news conference, "I made a mistake in taking something I didn't consider to be a drug." After explaining that he'd used a skin cream to treat rash associated with saddle sores, he said, "When I think of taking something, I think of pills, inhalers, injections. I didn't consider skin cream 'taking something.'"

With Armstrong's string of seven consecutive Tour victories, he became a sports hero to many noncycling fans by virtue of his amazing comeback from testicular cancer. Armstrong started his own foundation to promote cancer awareness. The ubiquitous yellow armbands worn by millions of cancer patients, relatives, and friends of cancer patients are an outgrowth of Armstrong's activism, which has now become one of the main focuses of his postcycling career.

THE WORLD ANTI-DOPING AGENCY ARRIVES ON THE SCENE

All the doping scandals that emerged in 1998 brought into focus what appeared to be a growing problem in sports. While it's not entirely clear how many athletes who were competing at the time were using the drugs, the pace of doping scandals throughout the last decade of the twentieth century seemed to constantly accelerate. As an outgrowth of such major scandals as the Festina affair at the 1998 Tour de France, the International Olympic Committee felt an increasing pressure to find a solution. In the final months of 1998 and into 1999, various discussions and investigations took place with the goal of finding a way to solve the doping problem in sports.

Even before the 1998 Tour was over, the head of the IOC weighed in on what he felt should be done to combat the problem. The problem, he said, wasn't the cyclists. Instead, it was those around the cyclists. "Doping demands an exact definition," Samaranch said, "and I have been asking for it for years." Samaranch's initial reaction to the Festina affair was to say that the number of banned drugs should be reduced. "Doping is everything that, firstly, is harmful to an athlete's health and, secondly, artificially augments his performance. If it's just the second case, for me, that's not doping. If it's the first case, it is."[68]

Samaranch's view was controversial. As the doping scandals put pressure on the IOC and the international athletic federations to do more to combat what appears to be a growing trend, the IOC had other problems not related to doping. A scandal swirled around the committee over allegations of payoffs to the members of the IOC involved in the selection of host cities for the games. Many allegations centered the awarding of the 2002 Winter Olympics to Salt Lake City. The crisis that the IOC was facing was nothing less than an attack on the organization's credibility. Adding the many doping scandals to the mix gave rise to the question of whether the IOC was still relevant, and whether it should be radically overhauled in order to restore some semblance of credibility to the committee and to the Olympic movement.

In early February 1999, the IOC held a conference that was intended to reestablish the committee's authority over doping controls and antidoping policy. While that may have been the intention, the meeting quickly turned into a forum where representatives of various countries and various athletic organizations vented their frustration at the IOC's inability to bring the doping problem under control.

General Barry R. McCaffrey, the director of drug policy during the Clinton administration, addressed his comments to Samaranch, saying, "Let me sadly but respectfully note that recent examples of alleged corruption, lack of accountability, and the failure of leadership have challenged the legitimacy of this institution. These events have tarnished the credibility of the movement."

Others, like British Sports Minister Tony Banks, told the meeting that his government expected the IOC to "clean up its act." And Denmark's Minister of Culture and Sport said that the important thing to stress was values, not who the leaders were.

But the criticism expressed at the conference was a two-way street. Jacques Rogge, a member of the IOC's executive board who would go on to become the next leader of the Olympic committee, criticized American professional sports for allowing athletes to openly use supplements that were banned by the IOC. In particular, Rogge singled out Mark McGwire, who had been using Andro in his quest for the single-season home run record.

"If you go on the moralizing and lecturing tone," he said in response to Gen. McCaffrey's comments, "you must be sure your own house is in order."

Prince Alexandre de Merode, a Belgian member of the IOC who had been involved in doping issues for several decades and was generally thought to be the person who would head the antidoping effort for a new IOC agency, remarked, "I take offense that politicians don't trust me to chair this agency. Why should I trust politicians?"

The meeting had been called, in part, to establish a new international organization to fight the problem of doping in sports. In an unusual move, attendees included representatives from various governments and various outside agencies. It was the first time that such a meeting was held, where non-Olympics officials were able to offer their input. When it ended, a new antidoping organization had not been formed. But it was on the horizon.[69]

One idea floated by Prince de Merode was that athletes serving a suspension should be allowed to compete in a number of smaller events and fund-raising events without the fear of being called to account. While arguments were made that this would not completely deny athletes the opportunity to earn a living, de Merode was trying to balance the financial needs of athletes to earn a living while not being allowed to compete. Even under de Merode's plan, athletes convicted of a doping offense would be barred from competition in the major events (such as the Olympics or other events, i.e., the Tour de France) The plan was never approved by the committee.[70]

Attempts to address the problem of doping in sports would continue throughout 1999, with the IOC leader Juan Antonio Samaranch's spear-heading efforts to create a worldwide agency within the IOC organization to fight doping. With other concerns over the ethics and integrity of the IOC, various European governments, in conjunction with the United States, rebuffed Samaranch's gambit to create and head such an agency in March 1999. Both European and American officials felt that Samaranch lacked the credibility needed to start and head such an agency.[71]

By November 1999, the IOC and its member countries settled on the creation of an independent agency, partially funded by the Olympics organization and by various countries within the Olympic movement. The person selected to head the agency was Dick Pound, a Canadian lawyer and a first vice president of the IOC whose previous assignments included negotiating broadcast rights for various Olympic games. In addition, he led the investigation into allegations of bribery surrounding the selection of Salt Lake City for the 2002 Winter Olympics.

Pound told reporters during a break at the Canadian Olympic Association's November 1999 board meeting, "I'm prepared to do it for a year or so to get it up and running. It is important and goes with the territory of being a first vice president of the International Olympic Committee."

He also noted that it was good to have a "lay person" heading up the newly created agency, instead of a scientist, as that would ensure fewer rivalries within the new organization. "My knowledge of this field is very limited," Pound said, "but what I would bring is the ability to get it organized and started and to adopt the policies that we need to adopt."

Dick Pound didn't serve just one year as the head of the new World Anti-Doping Agency. He continued in the role for a full eight years, leaving the post in December 2007. John Fahey, an Australian, was selected to lead WADA at the annual WADA conference, held in Madrid, Spain, in mid-November 2007. Less than one month before the conference, former French sports minister Jean-François Lamour suddenly withdrew from the running for Pound's job. Lamour had been considered a shoe-in for the position until Fahey managed to maneuver a spot on the ballot. Lamour had been a member of the antidoping agency for about one year when he left, and in leaving, he sharply criticized WADA and those running the agency for the lack of progress in eliminating the use of performance-enhancing drugs in sporting events. Lamour said that those in charge of WADA had "no clear and straightforward vision of its mission, and which cannot stand firm against outside pressure." He also announced intentions to set up a European antidoping agency that would be a competitor to the worldwide agency.

Dick Pound, among others, was sharply critical of Lamour's intentions, telling online newspaper *CyclingNews.com*, "The whole purpose to this international agency is to harmonize rules and policies, yet Lamour's recent proposals go counter to the entire premise behind the organization of which he was an active vice president until his resignation this week."[72]

BALCO GOES MAINSTREAM AND LEADS THE WAY TO DESIGNER STEROIDS

Victor Conte made a choice in the mid-1990s that would within a decade make the name of his company, the Bay Area Laboratory Co-operative (BALCO), synonymous with doping. Conte set up a new company, Scientific Nutrition for Advanced Conditioning, in order to move into the lucrative world of bodybuilding supplements. The company's most lucrative product, ZMA, was a combination of zinc and magnesium sold in pill form for about $30 a bottle.

As he had done before, Conte started offering testing, nutritional, and supplementation advice to a number of professional athletes, often providing these services to the pros for no charge.

Richard A. Goldman, a former employee of BALCO who once owned a bodybuilding gym, told *The New York Times* in 2003, "Victor would give away the store to top athletes. He would fly and collect samples from an entire N.F.L. team, analyze them and send 40 players a six-month supply of trace mineral supplements, all for free."[73]

One of the professional athletes Conte worked with was Bill Romanowski, who was a linebacker for the Oakland Raiders in 1996. Through Romanowski, other professional football players and athletes from other sports came into the BALCO fold. Among those people was famed Russian-born track coach Remi Korchemny, who had trained three Olympic medalists during his career.

Conte and Korchemny formed the ZMA Track Club, in part to help market ZMA and other BALCO products. Among the athletes who eventually became members of the club were Tim Montgomery and Marion Jones. At one time, Montgomery and Jones were the fastest male and female sprinters in the world.[74]

It was Conte's business relationship with Bill Romanowski that brought BALCO and its associated companies into the world of steroids. Romanowski had been using steroids for a number of years, and eventually Conte started supplying the football player with human growth hormone. Conte would go on to talk about the benefits of human growth hormone in an interview with Testosterone Nation, where he said he "didn't condone the use of anabolic steroids or growth [hormone]. However, I know a number of athletes who use growth hormone and most are reporting tremendous benefits."[75]

By the spring of 1999 Conte had obtained and was selling a steroid called norbolethone, a steroid that had been developed years earlier but never marketed due to safety concerns. Norbolethone was originally developed in the 1960s by Wyeth Pharmaceuticals as a potential treatment for children with growth problems. During testing on animals, it turned out that the drug might be toxic.[76] Wyeth Pharmaceuticals decided against bringing the drug onto the market.[77]

Norbolethone was not the first designer steroid, at least in the sense that a new chemical was created to specifically beat the antidoping drug tests. The concept behind using norbolethone—finding (or developing) steroids that the tests didn't detect—would come to play a pivotal role in doping during the first years of the twenty-first century.

Chapter 6

Is Everyone Doping? 2000–Present

DAWN OF A NEW MILLENNIUM

As the new millennium began, the pace of doping scandals quickened. In the last eight years, the scandals that have emerged touched every sport with increasing frequency, straining fans' belief in the athletic accomplishments of their heroes. The agencies charged with eliminating, or at least reducing the amount of doping occurring in sports adopted new tactics in order to keep up with, or get ahead of, the cheats. More of the accused athletes who at first denied cheating would eventually admit that, yes, they had used steroids or other drugs in order to gain an advantage over their competitors. New designer drugs would make it easier to cheat and avoid getting caught. But only temporarily. In the first years of the twenty-first century, doping stories have become so common that many believe that the use of performance-enhancing drugs is epidemic, and perhaps even endemic, among those who compete at the elite level of sport.

EPO TESTING BECOMES A REALITY

In the aftermath of the 1998 Festina scandal, the use of erythropoietin (EPO) in professional sports became impossible to ignore. But, at the time, no test existed to reliably detect the drug or its use. Researchers had already tried to develop tests, but no one had succeeded—yet. Although the initial attempts at a reliable test for EPO were unsuccessful, scientists in various parts of the world continued to work on the problem. By the year 2000, two tests would come into use that, their developers claimed, could very reliably detect the use of artificial EPO.

The development would be the culmination of a decade's worth of research by scientists around the globe. Two different types of tests actually came into use within about a year of each other. One was a blood test developed by researchers in Australia, and the other was a urine test developed by researchers at the Laboratoire National de Dépistage du Dopage, the French national antidoping laboratory often referred to by its initials, LNDD. LNDD's urine test, first approved by the International Olympic Committee in 1999, would become the subject of much controversy in the middle of the decade.

Half-way around the world, Australian researchers were spurred on in their development of blood-based EPO testing due to the looming 2000 Summer Olympics to be held in Sydney. There was a strong desire to have their EPO test developed, validated, and implemented before competition began. And with a lot of hard work, they were able to bring the test methods to fruition on time. But getting the athletic establishment to accept and use the blood-based tests was another matter.

At first, the International Olympic Committee wanted to use only the urine test as their EPO testing methodology in Sydney. But after some political wrangling during a meeting at the IOC's headquarters in Lausanne, Switzerland, the Australian researchers were able to convince the IOC to add part of the Australian methodology, known as the ON-Model, as part of their accepted testing methods. The ON-Model would be used as a confirmation technique for a positive urine EPO test, as it was developed to detect recent use of the blood-boosting drug. The other part of their methodology, the OFF-Model, was not approved for use at the Sydney Games, which was frustrating to the team.

The ON- and OFF-Models for EPO Detection

There are two forms of blood tests for EPO use, each of which has two variants. The ON-Model variants are useful for determining recent use of EPO, while the OFF-Model is useful for determining EPO use within a period of several weeks. The two models are based on biological markers that change in specifics ways due to a sudden change in the level of erythropoietin in a person's blood.

In the ON-Model, the two variants measure the following blood values:

- Hemaoglobin (Hb, h)
- Erythropoietin (E, e), and
- Soluble transferrin receptor (sTfr, s)

One variant, ON-hes, measures all three values, while the other, ON-he, measures only the first two listed above. The rationale behind the

ON-Models is that each of the blood values will be raised as a result of injecting EPO. The ON-hes model is more sensitive and specific than the ON-he model, but is also slightly more expensive to run.

For the OFF-Model, the blood values measured are:

- Hemoglobin (Hb, h)
- Reticulocytes, (r), and
- Erythropoietin, (E, e)

The two variants of the OFF-Model are OFF-hre and OFF-hr. With the OFF-Models, the hemoglobin values remain elevated, while both the levels of reticulocytes and erythropoietin in the blood drop to extremely low (and sometimes undetectable) levels. While the OFF-hre model is more specific, according to Robin Parisotto (developer of the testing protocols), the OFF-hr model is the preferred method as it is almost as sensitive and specific as the OFF-hre model, without the added expense of testing for serum erythropoietin levels.

According to Parisotto, the UCI, IAAF, and several of the Olympic winter sports use the OFF-hr model as a screening test to look for indications of blood transfusions or EPO use. Parisotto notes that the reasons for this include:

"1. Of all the models it is the best discriminator of blood doping from any other biological, physiological or medical effects. There are no other known factors (as yet) in the literature consistent with elevated OFF-hr model scores other than previous blood transfusions (or spaceflight).

2. Easy to run and requires no great technical expertise and is within the capabilities of mainstream pathology laboratories. I understand that there are moves to develop and manufacture instrument specific analyzers for use in anti-doping that would measure such parameters 'in the field.' In other words, the lab will go to the athletes.

3. It is more cost effective to collect and run hundreds of samples for screening purposes (the OFF-hr test costs about $35/sample) than to go straight to the 'top-shelf' tests like the urine EPO test (~$1500/sample) or the homologous blood doping test (~$250–$500/sample). The more expensive tests can then be limited to samples that are suspicious (high OFF-hr scores)."[1]

The IOC didn't add the OFF-Model to their testing arsenal right away because it is only an indirect indication of EPO use, and detects such use some time after the drug has been administered and has cleared an athlete's system. During the Lausanne meetings, the IOC was reluctant to adopt such indirect testing methods. Adding blood testing to the antidoping arsenal required a paradigm shift, according to Robin Parisotto, author of *Blood*

Sports: The Inside Dope on Drugs in Sport. And while that shift was slow in coming, the IOC was willing to consider making changes.

> If anything, the greatest achievement from the Lausanne meeting in 2000 was that blood testing was finally put on the agenda. It's a pity though that many sports still have not/will not consider following the IOC's lead. Despite all of the criticism heaped on the IOC over drug testing (or lack of it or mismanagement of it), at least in 2000 they went out on a limb but few have followed. The IOC cannot be blamed for the lack of take-up although everyone seems to blame them for all of the drug problems. But the IOC only has jurisdiction for two weeks every two years, so this is why the other federations need to take a stand. Despite the problems with cycling, the UCI has tried to meet the challenge head-on and is paying dearly (withdrawal of sponsors and media coverage, etc.), so in some "deluded" sense I can see why many other sports are not following.[2]

The International Cycling Union (UCI), as the IOC had initially done, declined to use the Australian methods right away, even though they are more capable of catching cheats long after they have stopped taking EPO. LNDD's test is only capable of detecting fairly recent use. The urine test has an Achilles heel. It turns out that a fairly simple trick, like dropping a soap flake into an athlete's urine sample, can beat the urine-based EPO test, causing a negative reading when that sample should instead test positive.[3]

The blood-based tests, however, are more difficult to sabotage, because between the two models (ON and OFF) five different biological markers in an athlete's blood are evaluated to determine whether or not artificial EPO has been used.

When a urine test is carried out, the results will come back negative if more than a few days have passed since an athlete injected the drug. So doping could occur almost right up to an event, and be undetected—as long as the athlete is drug-free several days before competition. Because red blood cells have a life of around 120 days, the benefits of EPO use can remain until long after whatever race, game, meet or athletic event in which the doped athlete participated.

It turns out that the ON-Model, similar to LNDD's urine test, has a relatively small window in which it is capable of detecting EPO use—smaller even than LNDD's urine test. With the ON-Model, testing needs to be conducted very quickly after a sample has been drawn, as some of the blood markers are known to be unstable. For the tests to be effective, the processing of an athlete's sample must be completed within eight hours. While it's easy to get the samples drawn, getting them to a lab with enough time for processing can be a challenge.

The story changes with the OFF-Model. This protocol is capable of detecting the use of EPO up to several weeks after an athlete has discontinued its use. When the OFF-Model is used, athletes who want to cheat have to stop their doping much earlier in order to escape detection—assuming they know in advance which form of testing is going to be performed.

It would take several years before sports governing bodies would add the Australian OFF-Model to their arsenal of drug tests. The UCI would not adopt the use of the blood tests until 2004, and in part because of a few prominent cases of suspected EPO use that had to be thrown out, on the grounds that the follow-up tests of the backup samples failed to confirm the initial results.[4]

STAND BY YOUR MAN

The 2000 Olympic Games in Sydney, Australia—like many Olympic Games during the last forty years—weren't devoid of doping incidents. In one case, two American track and field athletes were thrust into the glare of the media spotlight. C. J. Hunter, the world shot-put champion, failed four drug-screening tests for steroids prior to the 2000 Summer Games. At a press conference where Hunter faced questions about the scandal, his then-wife, Marion Jones, sat shoulder to shoulder with her husband as a public display of support. In the coming years, Jones would find herself at the center of doping allegations.

News reports mention that Hunter's nutritionist, Victor Conte (owner of the Bay Area Laboratory Co-operative, also known as BALCO), noted at the time that British runner Linford Christie and Jamaican runner Merlene Ottey had taken the same iron supplement as Hunter and had also tested positive for nandrolone. Conte said that none of the three athletes had taken steroids. Instead, he suggested that the supplement was responsible for the positive steroids test.

Three of Hunter's positive drug tests came during out-of-competition tests following the 2000 Bislett Games in Norway. The other positive test result came at a meet in Zurich, Switzerland. In all of the results, Hunter had levels of nandrolone in his system that were 1,000 times greater than the amount that would normally be present.

One International Association of Athletics Federation (IAAF) official agreed that it was possible that a nutritional supplement containing either 19-norandrostenediol or 19-norandrostenedione, or both, might have been the source of the positive test results. Arne Ljungqvist, the leader of the IAAF's medical commission, said, "I believe he could well be one of the cases [of a positive result due to] food supplements containing these precursors."

"Aside from him being an athlete and me being an athlete, he's my husband and I'm here to show support for him," Jones said to reporters at the press conference in support of Hunter. "I have full and complete respect, and believe the legal system will do what it needs to do to clear his name."[5]

Not long after news of Hunter's tests results became public, the IAAF filed a complaint against the USA Track & Field (USATF) federation, alleging that the organization had purposely withheld information about athletes who had tested positive, thus preventing the international federation from barring those who had tested positive for banned substances from international competition.

An independent commission looked into the IAAF's complaints during 2001 and ultimately issued a report that cleared the USATF of any wrongdoing, but also sharply criticized the organization for not following their own rules more closely. In their final report, the panel faulted the USATF for failing to follow its procedures "for assuring that no doping cases were ignored or suppressed." In addition, they found that the track federation applied its confidentiality rules "so restrictively that its effect was to prevent the IAAF from enforcing its own doping controls on an international level."

The IAAF's complaint against the USATF was that the American organization did not notify the international federation about athletes whose antidoping tests came back positive for one or more performance-enhancing drugs. In particular, the organization was disturbed by allegations that an unidentified American athlete who had tested positive for steroids before the 2000 Olympic Games had been allowed to compete in Sydney. And they were disturbed that they had not been informed about Hunter's results sooner.

In the case of the unidentified athlete, the commission found that a subsequent review by an appeals panel determined that a doping violation had not occurred, despite the USATF's belief that the evidence did demonstrate that a violation had occurred. The panel also noted that the USATF had not passed along any information about the case, which prevented the IAAF from reviewing the case. By preventing the review of the case by the international federation, the USATF's actions also denied the IAAF the opportunity to appeal to the CAS, in the event they disagreed with the original judgment.

The USATF also came under fire for how they handled Hunter's positive tests for nandrolone. While the commission found that the USATF had not concealed Hunter's test results from the IAAF, they did criticize the American federation for not informing the US Olympic Committee about his results. The commission criticized the USATF actions, saying that had they informed the USOC, they could have saved them the embarrassment of naming Hunter as an Olympian in the year 2000.

Due to an injury, C. J. Hunter withdrew from the Olympic Games before the competitions started. He is now retired from competition.[6]

FINNISH CROSS-COUNTRY SKIERS BUSTED FOR USING PLASMA EXPANDERS

At the 2001 FIS Nordic World Ski Championships in Lahti, Finland, six members of the home team were caught using the recently banned plasma expander hydroxy-ethyl starch (HES), a modified version of corn starch used to boost the oxygen-carrying capacity of a person's blood. Finnish athletes had long been suspected of using various blood-boosting techniques, going back as far as the early 1970s when Lasse Viren won back-to-back medals in the 5,000- and 10,000-meter track events during the 1972 Munich and 1976 Montreal Summer Olympic Games. The 2001 scandal cast a pall on Finnish cross-country skiing, and brought to light an organized doping effort within the Finnish Nordic Ski Team.

By the time the scandal had run its course, not only would the six skiers involved be suspended from competition, but the team's doctor and head coach would also suffer negative consequences for their actions. The scandal started early on in the competition, when the WADA-accredited laboratory in Helsinki determined that skier Jari Isometsä's blood sample showed the presence of the banned plasma expander HES. Shortly thereafter, another Finnish skier, Janne Immonen, tested positive for the same thing.

Three days after the championships ended, the final bombshell dropped. Four other athletes had tested positive for HES. And evidence was beginning to suggest that the ski team's head coaches and team physicians had been involved in the planning and timing of the blood-doping techniques. Isometsä told the media during a press conference that the team's physicians had given him the banned plasma expander. During the same news conference, Kari-Pekka Kyrö, the head coach of the men's team, admitted that he and fellow coach Jarmo Riski were aware of the doping going on within their team.

Kyrö spun an interesting story about how the team came to use this particular doping technique. During a press conference, he explained that during the 1999 World Championships, the Finnish team learned from some unnamed International Ski Federation (FIS) officials that several other countries' teams had used the plasma expander during that year's competition. Following that disclosure, the Finnish team decided to begin experimenting with the technique. Kyrö claimed that the team stopped experimenting with the technique once the FIS decided to ban the use of HES in 2000.

While the team had been experimenting with HES, however, several of their athletes experienced marked improvement in their performance. Kyrö also noted that the use of HES had been successful in bringing down high hemoglobin levels in various athletes.

After hearing that the antidoping labs could not actually detect the use of HES, Kyrö and his colleagues decided to try using HES during the 2001 competition in Lahti. The Finnish coach took responsibility for the decision, saying that the people involved in the scheme knew that their actions were wrong. When news of the first skier's positive test came, the men's pursuit event was already occurring. One Finnish skier withdrew from the event claiming he felt feverish. Another skier purposely broke a pole and then failed to finish the race.[7]

Initially, Jari Isometsä claimed that he had acted alone. But after Janne Immonen tested positive, the World Anti-Doping Agency staged a surprise antidoping test for the entire Finnish Nordic ski team. As a result of those tests, four other skiers were found to be positive for HES.[8]

Another bizarre twist to the case involved a mysterious medical bag that showed up at a gas station near Helsinki's airport earlier in the month. The day after Isometsä tested positive, Helsinki police received a call about a medical bag left there on the day the Finnish cross-country ski team returned from a competition in Estonia. The bag contained a number of medical products including HES, adrenaline, prednisone, solomet and depo-medrol—all of which are banned substances. Prednisone, solomet and depo-medrol are all antiasthmatic medications and are banned without a therapeutic use exemption (TUE). Along with the medications, prescriptions signed by one of the team's physicians, Juha-Pekka Turpeinen, were found in the medical bag.

Turpeinen and Pirkka Mäkelä, another FSA physician, resigned from the team after being linked to the scandal. Turpeinen claimed that he was "offended" that he had been "branded in the public debate" surrounding the Isometsä scandal. The aftermath of the scandal would be felt for some time to come. In November 2002, the FSA's managing director, Jari Piirainen, estimated that the organization suffered financial losses of approximately 3 million euros as a direct result of the scandal. Public funding for the cross-country ski team was cut by 600,000 euros for the 2003 season as compared to the budget for the 2001 season. While state funding accounted for less than 20 percent of the organization's funding, the loss of public funding meant that more money would need to be raised through sponsorship or donations.

Yet the athletic setbacks were even greater than the financial setbacks. The Finnish Nordic ski team suffered poor overall results during the 2002 season, including their worst overall performance during Olympic competition at the Salt Lake City Games.[9]

THE FIRST POSITIVE EPO TEST—OR WAS IT?

In 2001, professional cyclist Bo Hamburger became the first athlete to test positive for EPO. Or did he? At first, it appeared that Hamburger would become the first cyclist to face a penalty for EPO use, after testing positive in April 2001 during the Flèche Wallone bicycle race in Belgium. In doing so, he became the first cyclist, as well as the first athlete, to be caught by the new EPO test (the urine test developed at LNDD) that had recently been implemented by the UCI. After testing positive at the Flemish bike race, Hamburger was let go by Team CSC-Tiscali-World Online team owner Bjarne Riis, the 1996 Tour de France winner.[10]

And then something very strange happened. The results of the B samples, the backup portions saved for confirmation of an initial positive test, came back inconclusive. On the basis of those inconclusive results, the Danish Sports Board cleared Hamburger of the charges against him. Critics of the UCI's new testing method for EPO were quick to point to Hamburger's case as evidence that the new tests were flawed.

Those critics received a boost when the director of Switzerland's Laboratoire Suisse D'Analyse du Dopage in Lausanne made some critical comments about the new test to the media. Dr. Laurent Rivier, whose laboratory had actually conducted part of the analysis of Hamburger's EPO test, told Denmark's Extra Bladet newspaper, "the tests are not 100% trustworthy but I think the UCI wanted to make one step forward to get things going and to diminish the massive use of EPO that has been observed in the cycling environment."

He also told the Danish newspaper, "The UCI definitely took some risks with introducing this test but now it will be interesting to see the legal effects it will have in the case of Bo Hamburger."[11]

While Hamburger was acquitted of doping charges, the Danish Cycling Union banned him "for life" from representing Denmark on any national teams, the same penalty as any cyclist who was found guilty of doping would receive from the DCU. "The Federation's anti-doping committee acquitted Bo Hamburger on judicial grounds, but did not clear him of EPO abuse," said Peder Pedersen, head of the DCU.

In response, Hamburger told an interviewer from a Danish television network that he was "disappointed and almost embarrassed to be Danish. This is the same as clearing someone and then putting him in prison."

Danish antidoping committee spokesman Finn Mikkelsen told the European cycling publication *CyclingNews*, "In this case the problem was that there were two analytical results on the B-sample (and one was below the described screening value of 80 percent). The lab has not given any indication of why there are two results—therefore there was doubt about the B-result and thus the result from the B-sample."

Mikkelsen went on to say, "I admit this is a strange case. The decision respected the EPO-test, but they did not accept the circumstances around the B-test."[12]

The UCI appealed to the Court of Arbitration for Sport, challenging the Danish Sports Board's decision to clear Hamburger of doping charges. The cycling federation argued that because their rules only required a positive result from the urine test, Hamburger was guilty of a doping offense. In response, Hamburger's defense team argued that the urine test was flawed and had not been proven scientifically.

In January 2002, the Court of Arbitration for Sport issued their ruling, in which the CAS panel sided with Hamburger. In their written opinion, the members of the CAS panel noted that the IOC's rules required both blood and urine test results to be positive in order to declare an EPO doping violation. While the UCI's rules didn't specifically state that both tests were necessary, the panel ruled, the UCI's rule did not designate a specific level of EPO in the urine above which a positive test would be declared. Since the UCI's rule had been based on the IOC's original rule, the tribunal took the IOC's requirements into account and upheld the Danish Sports Board's original decision.[13]

Bo Hamburger continued racing as a professional until the end of the 2006 season. In late 2007, Hamburger released a book called *The Greatest Price—Confessions of a Bike Racer*. In his book, he admitted to using EPO during a period from 1995 through 1997, but claims that he was not using the medication during the 2001 season.

Hamburger told a press conference shortly after releasing his book, "Cycling was distinctively marked by doping in the 1990s. It was a little easier to look at oneself in the mirror when you knew others did the same. So I did it."

According to Hamburger, no team officials were involved in EPO use during the 1990s, but, he added, "one should have been very naive and very blind not to see what was going on." Hamburger explained to reporters that he started doping in 1995 after being injured.

"My alternative would have been to drive the bicycle in the garage and stop the career," Hamburger wrote in his book.

Brian Mikkelsen, the Danish sports minister and WADA vice president, commenting on Hamburger's statement, said, "Bo Hamburger's confession illustrates how damaged cycling was by EPO abuse in the 1990s. It is decisive that we make sure that we never go back to that time."[14]

So, while Bo Hamburger may have been the first person to test positive for EPO, and also the first person to be exonerated due to contradictory follow-up test results, the Danish rider did eventually admit to using the very same drug earlier in his career.

IT'S ALL DOWNHILL FROM HERE

At the 2002 Winter Olympics in Salt Lake City, Alain Baxter did what no Briton had ever done before. He won a bronze medal in the men's slalom event of the alpine skiing competition. Several days afterward, controversy over his medal would erupt over the presence in his urine of a mere 20-millionth of a gram of a substance related to methamphetamine. Within four weeks, the IOC would formally strip Baxter of his hard-won medal.

Baxter's troubles began when he purchased a Vicks inhaler in order to treat nasal congestion, a long-standing problem for the Scottish skier. In the United Kingdom, where Baxter lives, the Vicks inhaler contains such things as camphor, menthol, and methyl salicylate (commonly known as wintergreen), all of which have decongestant properties. The version sold in the UK contains no banned substances. Little did he know that the American version contains a trace amount of l-methamphetamine. The chemical found in the American Vicks inhaler acts as a nasal decongestant, but has little (if any) stimulant effect, unlike the related compound d-methamphetamine, which is a known stimulant.[15]

The IOC announced their decision on March 21, 2002. Baxter would be banned from competition until at least June 2002, and he would have to forfeit his medal. Craig Reedie, chairman of the British Olympic Association (BOA), told BBC News that he was, "very disappointed at the decision reached by the IOC."

Reedie went on to say, "The BOA is convinced that in no way can Alain be described as a drugs cheat. We believe the offence to be modest and the punishment very severe."[16]

Commenting on the IOC's decision, Baxter reiterated his innocence, and restated his belief that his positive test result stemmed from his purchase and use of the over-the-counter medication while competing in the 2002 Olympics. Unfortunately for Baxter, WADA's strict liability rule meant that no matter how the substance had wound up in his body, he was still responsible for it being there. On that basis, the IOC's review panel took Baxter's medal away, and imposed the ban from competition.

Baxter appealed his case to the Court of Arbitration for Sport, the last resort available to an athlete trying to clear his or her name. In August 2002, the CAS issued its ruling on the case. In their decision, the arbitration panel upheld the original ruling, but at the same time made it clear that the IOC should consider changing their rules to be more specific. In their remarks about Baxter, the arbitration panel noted that the Scottish skier was a "sincere and honest man who did not gain a competitive advantage despite the trace of lev-methamphetamine in his system."

The panel went on to suggest certain changes to the IOC's rules should be considered, saying, "The IOC may wish at some time to distinguish between the two isomers of methamphetamine and to introduce a threshold as it has done in the case of other stimulants such as caffeine."

Although the final ruling did not go completely his way, Baxter told BBC News he was pleased with one aspect of the outcome. "I'm not classed as a drugs cheat anymore." Baxter returned to competition in the 2002–2003 season and continues to compete in the men's downhill, slalom, and giant slalom events. In 2006, he competed in the Olympics Games in Sestriere, Italy, placing 16th in the slalom.[17]

DOCTOR LINKED TO NFL PLAYERS JAILED
FOR PROVIDING THEM STEROIDS

In March 2005, the CBS News program "60 Minutes Wednesday" broadcast a story linking a South Carolina doctor named James M. Shortt to allegations of doping by several members of the Carolina Panthers football team. The broadcast alleged that during the 2003–2004 season, as the Panthers made their way to the Super Bowl, Dr. Shortt prescribed various steroids to Panthers players Jeff Mitchell, Todd Steussie, and Todd Sauerbrun. Other media reports suggested that several other Panthers players may have received steroids, or prescriptions for steroids, from Dr. Shortt.

The day after the CBS broadcast, Dr. Shortt told *The Charlotte Observer* that all of the prescriptions he'd written for the athletes were for legitimate medical conditions, and that he had done nothing wrong.

"People come to me often because they're worn down, they're exhausted, or something has happened to them and they haven't recovered fully," Dr. Shortt said. The doctor also told the paper that he was careful in how he prescribed steroids. "There are folks out there, and I think it's lunacy, that are using chemically altered molecules in ridiculous unsafe quantities. I have no respect for those people, and I want to tell you right now I am 100 percent opposed to that."[18]

Despite the doctor's protestations of innocence, several weeks after the broadcast aired, a state disciplinary board suspended his license to practice medicine. In September 2005, a grand jury indicted Dr. Shortt on 29 counts of distributing steroids and human growth hormone, as well as one count of conspiracy.[19]

Not long after Dr. Shortt was indicted, NFL commissioner Paul Tagliabue told *The Washington Post* that the players involved in the scandal would be subjected to a stepped-up schedule of random drug testing. "Every player who was part of the investigation who's still in the league is being tested up to 24 times a year, which is the most important element of putting an end to this," Tagliabue told a reporter for the paper. "That's why we have not had repeat offenders. That's as important or more important than the discipline. It's testing people up to 24 times a year on a random basis." Both Tagliabue and a representative of the NFL Player's Association declined to comment on who would be subject to the testing, but one source suggested that the only players to be affected would be Mitchell, Steussie, and Sauerbrun.[20]

According to the *Post*'s story, a confidential informant claimed that the NFL's investigation into the scandal had concluded that fewer than 10 players on the Panthers football team had received steroids from Dr. Shortt between 2001 and 2004.[21]

Dr. Shortt, it turns out, not only provided steroids to players, he also provided counseling on how to beat the football league's drug-testing program. In December, a judge hearing evidence in the case listened to tapes in which the doctor advised at least one individual on how to use performance-enhancing products without testing positive.

"Now here's the key," Dr. Shortt told Wesley Wells during a February 2003 meeting. "You want to use a natural testosterone. You do not want to use testosterone or any kind of Depo (a synthetic form of testosterone that is injected) because that's how they test you. They look for the Depo."

"For somebody like you," the doctor continued, "I can triple your testosterone levels without blowing any whistles."

The tapes prosecutors played for the judge were part of 19 tapes seized under a search warrant from the doctor's office. During the hearing, prosecutors played the tapes as the judge heard a motion on whether an HBO special in which Dr. Shortt appeared could be entered as evidence. They wanted to show that what the doctor told the football players differed from what he said in the cable television special.[22]

In March 2006, the doctor pleaded guilty to charges that he had illegally distributed steroids and human growth hormone, as well as the conspiracy charge. At his sentencing in July 2006, the judge in the case sentenced Dr. Shortt to twelve months and one day in prison. The normal Federal sentencing guidelines specified zero to six months in prison. Prosecutors, however, argued for a longer sentence citing a number of factors, including the addition of Dr. Shortt's involvement in the trafficking of steroids and his prescribing steroids to a teenager for the purpose of performance enhancement. The judge agreed with the prosecutors' arguments, and also cited what he perceived to be a "lack of remorse" by the doctor as another reason for the extended sentence.

With good behavior, Dr. Shortt could be released from prison after serving ten and a half months in jail. Once he is released, he will serve an additional two years on parole.[23]

BALCO ROCKS AMERICAN ATHLETICS

The biggest doping scandal to hit American sports started out as a law enforcement investigation with simpler aspirations. When the Bay Area Laboratory Co-operative (BALCO) investigation first began in August 2002, the investigation focused on suspected money laundering and illegal distribution of steroids by BALCO and its founder, Victor Conte, rather than on suspicions of doping by any particular professional athlete. But shortly before the investigation began, a trainer within the San Francisco Giants baseball organization became concerned about the actions of Barry Bonds' personal trainer, Greg Anderson. So concerned, in fact, that he went to Giants' general manager Brian Sabean and told him that he thought Anderson was distributing steroids to some of the team's players.

Sabean was reluctant to pass the information on the major league baseball officials, in part to protect his employee from any retribution. Instead, Sabean suggested that the employee, Stan Conte (no relation to Victor Conte), contact an agent that Conte knew at the Drug Enforcement Administration (DEA) office in San Francisco. Although the connection is not definite, the timing of Conte's contact with the DEA coincides, approximately, with the agency's receiving a tip that illegal drugs were being distributed to members of the Giants team. As it turns out, that tip was passed along to an IRS agent named Jeff Novitzky who was conducting the investigation into BALCO and Conte's activities.[24]

Novitzky is known for his old-fashioned investigative methods, which include going through the trash of the person or organization he's tracking in order to find evidence of wrongdoing that will help build his case. He did much of the early work in the BALCO investigation, including rummaging through the company's trash in search of drug samples and incriminating financial statements or records. Over time, he turned up evidence linking BALCO to at least a dozen famous athletes. Novitzy's work was instrumental in the seven convictions related to the BALCO investigation.

Yet the IRS agent is not without his critics, including lawyers who've defended clients linked to the BALCO case. Those who criticize Novitzky point to the large number of charges dropped, and the relatively short sentences that were handed out as a result of convictions in the cases he helped build. The longest sentence of anyone associated with the BALCO scandal, two and a half years, was handed out to a lawyer who leaked the contents of grand jury testimony to the press. In Victor Conte's case, of the 42 original charges brought against BALCO's owner, 40 were dropped. Once convicted and sentenced, Conte served a mere four months in jail.

Some of the other names associated with the BALCO scandal include:

- James Valente, a former vice president of the company
- Track stars Tim Montgomery, Justin Gatlin, Chryste Gaines, Kelli White, and Marion Jones
- Trevor Graham, the former coach for Montgomery, Gatlin, and Jones
- Remi Korchemny, another track coach whose clients included Gaines, White, and British track star Dwight Chambers
- Barry Bonds, a baseball player for the San Francisco Giants
- Greg Anderson, Bonds' personal trainer
- Kirk Radomski, who worked in the New York Mets clubhouse and was reputed to be the biggest supplier of steroids in baseball up to the year 2005[25]

In another ironic twist, it was Graham who made the anonymous phone call that tipped antidoping authorities off about the existence of a new designer steroid in June 2003. Graham then anonymously sent a syringe filled with the designer drug tetrahydragestrinone (known as THG and "the clear") to the United States Anti-Doping Agency (USADA). USADA forwarded the syringe on to the U.S. Olympic antidoping lab at UCLA, where Don Catlin and his team of scientists identified the drug and developed a test to detect its use.[26]

In mid-February 2004, at a press conference held at the U.S. Department of Justice in Washington, DC, Attorney General John Ashcroft announced that a grand jury looking into the BALCO scandal had indicted Conte, James

Valente, Greg Anderson, and Remi Korchemny on a total of 42 counts related to the distribution of various steroids, EPO, and human growth hormone, as well as money laundering. The indictments alleged that the four men had conspired to provide a number of top amateur and professional athletes with banned substances, many of which could not be distributed legally without a prescription. Although not named in the indictments, media reports listed major league baseball players, professional football players, and track and field stars as being among the athletes who received steroids from BALCO and the men indicted.[27]

The case against the four men continued on for the better part of a year and a half. In July 2005, each of the defendants pleaded guilty to substantially fewer charges than the original counts against them. Conte and Anderson each pleaded guilty to one count of distributing steroids and a separate count of money laundering, while Valente pleaded guilty to a single count of distributing steroids. Prosecutors recommended that Anderson receive six months in prison, that Conte should receive four months in prison along with four months of home detention, and that Valente should receive probation.[28]

Two weeks later, Remi Korchemny took a plea bargain, admitting to distributing steroids illegally. When all four were finally sentenced, Conte's sentence was four months in prison followed by four months of home confinement; Anderson's sentence was three months in prison and three months in home confinement; Valente was given probation; and Remi Korchemny was also given one year's probation.[29]

Shortly after Conte, Anderson, and Valente were sentenced, the man who developed "the clear," Patrick Arnold, was charged with conspiring with Conte to distribute the designer steroid. Arnold's name had been connected to the BALCO scandal since Conte and Valente identified him as their source of the designer steroid. Arnold, a chemist at a nutritional supplement company in Illinois, specifically created the drug so that it wouldn't be detectable using the antidoping tests available before 2003. He also rediscovered desoxymethyltestosterone (DMT), another designer steroid, and manufactured norbolethone, a drug developed in the 1960s that was never marketed. Federal authorities raided his lab in late September 2005, and they also raided Arnold's home and office. In April 2006, Arnold was sentenced to three months in prison followed by three months of home confinement.[30]

The person who received the longest prison sentence in the BALCO case, in an interesting turn of events, was not one of the actual participants in the activities of the Burlingame, California company. Instead, it was an attorney who leaked information to the media about baseball player Barry Bonds' testimony and the testimony of other professional baseball players to a Federal grand jury investigating the scandal. Bonds' testimony indicated that he had used two BALCO products that contained steroids—both the cream and the clear—during the early part of the 2000s. In his testimony

to the grand jury, Bonds stated that he had not knowingly taken steroids. In fact, he said that his trainer, Greg Anderson, told him that one of the substances was "flaxseed oil." Bonds' testimony to the grand jury, like all the statements made by witnesses, was supposed to remain confidential. But somehow, the information made its way into the hands of two *San Francisco Chronicle* reporters, Mark Fainaru-Wada and Lance Williams.

The U.S. Attorney pursuing the case tried to determine who had leaked the information, pursuing a number of leads. Ultimately, he tried to force the two reporters to name their confidential source. Both reporters refused to do so, even when threatened with an eighteen-month jail sentence for contempt of court. Shortly before the two men would have been jailed, the person who leaked the information came forward. The culprit turned out to be Troy Ellerman, an attorney who at one time represented both Victor Conte and James Valente.

Ellerman admitted to providing transcripts of grand jury proceedings in 2004 for *Chronicle* reporter Mark Fainaru-Wada to view while the reporter took verbatim notes of statements by Bonds, as well as testimony by fellow baseball players Jason Giambi and Gary Sheffield. In addition, Fainaru-Wada was able to take notes of what sprinter Tim Montgomery told the grand jury. At the same time Ellerman was leaking the information to the *Chronicle*, he filed a motion to dismiss the charges against his clients, because the leaked information made a fair trial "practically impossible."

In admitting to being the leaker, Ellerman pleaded guilty to charges of obstruction of justice, making a false declaration, and two counts of contempt of court. Although the plea deal between Ellerman and the U.S. Attorney's office had set his sentence at a maximum of two years, the judge threw out the sentencing part of the deal in June 2007. In doing so, U.S. District Court Judge Jeffrey White noted that Ellerman had "corrupted the system, a system where everybody has to play by the rules," adding that "as an attorney and officer of the court, [Ellerman] should be held to a higher standard of conduct than the average citizen."

One month later, Ellerman was sentenced to two and a half years in prison for his offenses. His sentence was longer, by far, than the sentences any of the major players in the BALCO scandal faced. Ellerman's attorneys argued that their client should receive a lighter sentence, in light of President Bush's commutation of I. Lewis "Scooter" Libby's sentence for perjury in the Valerie Plame case, where Libby was being prosecuted for leaking the name of an undercover CIA operative to the media. Instead of prison time, the president changed Libby's sentence to probation.

Judge White responded to the request by saying, "If Mr. Ellerman is dissatisfied with his sentence, he should seek a commutation from the president."[31]

From the beginning, various athletes' names were connected to BALCO, a company that sold various nutritional supplements, along with supplements that either contained steroids or steroid precursors. At least one product sold by BALCO—the clear—was developed specifically to be undetectable by antidoping tests of the time. And it was, until Trevor Graham decided to send a syringe-full to USADA. Another BALCO product called "the cream" contained testosterone and epitestosterone, balanced to ensure that an athlete's testosterone to epitestosterone (T/E) ratio would appear normal. Because the screening test would yield unremarkable results, the cream enabled athletes to evade detection by the sophisticated carbon isotope ratio testing used to determine whether the testosterone in an athlete's system is natural or whether it is a synthetic. That form of testing, however, is used only when an athlete's T/E ratio exceeds a certain threshold value, currently pegged at 4:1.[32]

The BALCO case was a turning point in the pursuit of those who would cheat by chemical means, due to increased cooperation between government agencies and antidoping authorities. Cooperation on the case dated back to the original raid on the BALCO offices in September 2003, when federal agents, San Mateo county law enforcement agents, and a USADA representative descended on BALCO's Burlingame, California headquarters.[33] In May 2004, the United States Senate decided to subpoena IRS and Justice Department records and provide that material, for sixty days, to USADA to use in determining whether any antidoping cases should be pursued against athletes implicated in the investigation. This development charted new ground for both the government and USADA. And in the end, a new approach to bringing antidoping cases would be developed. Prior to the BALCO case, in order to be found guilty of a doping violation, the antidoping agency would need direct evidence—often in the form of test results—that could prove an athlete had used a banned substance.

MICHELLE COLLINS AND THE TALE OF THE FIRST "NONANALYTICAL POSITIVE"

Up to the time she was handed an eight-year ban from competition by a USADA arbitration panel, Michelle Collins never failed an in- or out-of-competition drug-screening test. But in December 2004, she was banned from competition anyway, based on a new concept in antidoping enforcement called the "nonanalytical positive."

A nonanalytical positive is a set of circumstantial evidence that an arbitration panel finds compelling enough to rule that one or more doping violations took place. In Collins' case, the evidence that USADA used against her included materials seized during the original raid of the BALCO offices in September 2003. Among that evidence were copies of email messages between Victor Conte and Collins where the track star admitted using prohibited substances. In addition, records of blood and urine test results taken in and out of competition by various IOC labs and antidoping labs were compared with records of tests performed at various medical pathology labs. BALCO's tests monitored Collins' hormone levels and the levels of the various performance-enhancing drugs.

Kelli White, another high-profile track star caught up in the BALCO scandal, also provided testimony implicating Collins. White accepted responsibility for her own actions by admitting that she used banned drugs provided by BALCO. By agreeing to cooperate with the antidoping authorities, White was able to get her own suspension from competition reduced to two years.

When the original ruling against Collins was announced, the arbitration panel handed her an eight-year suspension from competition, which would have effectively ended her career as an athlete. In May 2005, Collins' suspension was reduced to four years by USADA when she agreed to accept the shorter suspension in exchange for dropping her appeal to the Court of Arbitration for Sport.[34] According to Brian Getz, one of Collins' attorneys, the sprinter dropped her appeal due—at least in part—to injuries from which she was recovering.

"It's one thing to have a glittering career ahead and to be fighting USADA," Getz told the Associated Press. "It's another to be in a position where one can't race because of injuries and to be fighting USADA."[35]

Since she dropped her case and accepted the four-year ban, Collins has undergone a change. Travis Tygart, the head of USADA who helped prosecute the Collins case, told the Associated Press that when Collins reluctantly gave up her fight "she was a cold, rigid, angry person who you could see was clearly using these drugs from both a physical and a temperament standpoint." In the time since Collins began working with the antidoping agency to help rid sports of performance-enhancing drugs, she's had a change of heart.

"I wanted to clear my conscience. I felt like it was time to come forward and be free of this," she told Eddie Pells of the Associated Press in May 2007. In exchange for the assistance, USADA is recommending that a year be taken off of her suspension. If that happens, Collins will be able to compete in the 2008 Olympic trials. And, if she qualifies, she would be able to compete in Beijing.[36]

"Right now, I train as if I'm training for the Olympic trials and the Olympic Games. If it happens, great. If not, no big deal. But I am training," said Collins. During the time she's been serving her suspension, Collins earned her license as a massage therapist.

One interesting sidebar to the Collins decision is this: According to the WADA and USADA rules, the prosecutors of an antidoping case merely have to prove a case to the "comfortable satisfaction" of the arbitration panel. This standard is less rigorous than the normal "beyond a reasonable doubt" standard of jury trials. At the same time, it is a higher standard than typically used in most civil court cases. In the Collins decision, however, because USADA relied on "nonanalytical" evidence, the arbitration panel required antidoping authorities to prove their case beyond a reasonable doubt.[37]

TIM MONTGOMERY AND CHRYSTE GAINES: CAS UPHOLDS NONANALYTICAL POSITIVE

While Michelle Collins was the first athlete to be found guilty of doping based on a nonanalytical positive, by agreeing to drop her appeal to the Court of Arbitration for Sport, her case did not undergo the scrutiny of the final arbiters of doping disputes. Whether or not a nonanalytical positive would hold up in front of the CAS was still unknown. Once the dust settled from the cases of Tim Montgomery and Chryste Gaines, this would no longer be true. Like Collins and a number of other athletes, USADA pressed doping cases against the two athletes based on evidence garnered during BALCO investigation. And like the Collins case, USADA could not prosecute either Montgomery or Gaines for a failed doping test. And just like the Collins case, USADA was able to make an antidoping case against the two despite the fact that both had passed all the drug screenings they had ever been subjected to. Unlike Collins, however, Montgomery and Gaines decided to skip the initial arbitration round and appeal directly to the CAS.

Before all that happened, the two track stars testified in front of the BALCO grand jury in late 2003. In their testimony, Montgomery and Gaines spoke about how they became involved with Victor Conte and BALCO. Gaines also shed some light on how Marion Jones would come to be associated with BALCO. According to articles published by the *San Francisco Chronicle*, Montgomery told the grand jury that his association with Victor Conte and BALCO began shortly before the 2000 Olympics.

Montgomery was referred to the Burlingame, California company by Alvin Harrison, another sprinter. Harrison never mentioned steroids when talking about BALCO, Montgomery said, only nutritional supplements. In his testimony, he said that he spoke to Conte shortly before the Olympics while his coach, Trevor Graham, listened in. According to Montgomery's telling of the story, Graham later contacted Conte to encourage the BALCO owner not to provide supplements to Montgomery, because the sprinter was "not a big fish." Graham wanted Conte's assistance reserved for athletes who had a better chance of winning medals in Sydney.

Shortly thereafter, Conte started supplying various supplements and performance-enhancing drugs to Graham and the athletes he trained. Graham's biggest star at the time was Marion Jones, and according to Montgomery's testimony, Conte needed Chryste Gaines' permission to begin supplying products to Gaines' competitor. A deal between Conte and Gaines was apparently struck, when she told Conte that she didn't mind if he supplied Jones with products, as long as she (Gaines) got a cut of the money that

Jones paid to Conte. In his comments to the grand jury, Montgomery said, "So Chryste, from my understanding, had told Mr. Conte that: 'Whatever you charge her, if you give me a cut of it, then I don't mind.'" Montgomery indicated that he didn't know whether Gaines ever received a check from Conte.

Conte and Tim Montgomery finally met at the 2000 Olympics in Sydney, Australia. During their first meeting, Conte spoke about the clear, telling Montgomery that it was a drug that was designed to work like a steroid while not showing up on the drug-screening tests being used to catch athletes who were doping.

In his testimony, Montgomery called the clear "the magic potion." He spoke of Conte telling him to watch the performances of several athletes if he wanted to see how powerful the drug was. Among those Conte named were Chryste Gaines, Alvin Harrison and Marion Jones. Like both Gaines and Montgomery, Harrison also was charged with doping violations by USADA and eventually banned from competition.

Montgomery also spoke about other ways in which Graham acquired and distributed drugs to various athletes. Graham, Montgomery said, had a connection in Texas who got medications from a horse veterinarian in Mexico. Graham then gave or sold the drugs to his athletes.

According to Montgomery's story, Graham offered him various banned substances, but he refused to take them, in part because some of his coach's other athletes had tested positive for steroids. But just a couple of months after the 2000 Olympics, Victor Conte brought together Montgomery, Graham, Ben Johnson's former coach Charlie Francis, and a bodybuilding coach named Milos Sarcev for "Project World Record." The aim of Conte's project was simple: to turn Tim Montgomery into the world's fastest man. At the meeting, no one discussed using steroids. But not long after, Conte started giving Montgomery the clear by placing a drop under his tongue. And the BALCO owner provided Montgomery with human growth hormone, to the tune of four vials a month for eight months.

According to Montgomery, Conte also tried to get him to use EPO. Montgomery refused, telling the grand jury that he did so because, "I had heard somewhere that EPO could cause you a heart attack." There was at least one other drug that Conte wanted Montgomery to use: Insulin. Again, the sprinter refused after he discovered that such use could actually cause diabetes.

He called Conte to express his concern over the use of insulin, telling BALCO's owner, "You know what, you [sic] going to kill a lot of people." According to Montgomery's account, Conte replied, "I don't give a f—."[38]

Many athletes who have become enmeshed in the BALCO scandal have claimed that they were using flaxseed oil, or said their coaches, trainers, or others who provided them with the drug told them it was merely flaxseed oil. According to Montgomery's testimony to the grand jury, when Conte would ship the clear overseas, he would often put the substance inside a bottle marked as flaxseed oil, which is a legal supplement. For shipments to Montgomery, as with other athletes, Conte would list his name on the return address as Vince Reed.

For all the drugs and supplements that Montgomery received from Victor Conte, Montgomery told the grand jury, he didn't have to pay a cent. Instead, he received the banned substances as compensation for endorsing BALCO's ZMA supplement and doing promotional work supporting ZMA. Among other things, he did appear at various conventions and in magazine ads.

The two men had a falling out in September 2001, when they argued over money. At the time, Conte threatened to sue Montgomery. They haven't spoken since. A year after the two men parted ways, Montgomery clocked the 100-meter run in 9.78 seconds at a track meet in Paris. Although he had a tailwind during the run, it was not strong enough to nullify Montgomery's new world record. He claimed, in his testimony to the grand jury that he was not using banned substances at that time. And he also claimed that he never felt he got any benefit from using the clear.[39]

Publicly, Montgomery had been maintaining that he had never used steroids and was not guilty of the offenses USADA had charged him with. His testimony to the grand jury investigating the BALCO scandal, however, contradicted his protestations of innocence.

Originally, Montgomery's and Gaines' cases were to be argued in front of the same CAS panel during hearings in San Francisco on November 1, 2004, however, the hearings were delayed until 2005 because, as the CAS secretary general Matthieu Reeb put it, "the parties under-estimated the time needed to collect all the facts."[40] Two weeks later, the CAS announced that Montgomery's hearing would be in held June 2005, while Gaines' would occur one month later.

In finding Montgomery guilty of a doping violation, the CAS panel ruled that although the evidence against the athlete did not include any direct evidence that Montgomery had been doping (e.g., a positive result on a drug screening), there was enough indirect evidence to support such a conclusion. The evidence against Montgomery included blood test results and documents from the BALCO investigations. Ultimately, the most crucial evidence would be the testimony of Kelli White, who provided the panel with details of Montgomery's admission to her that he had used steroids from BALCO. In her testimony for the Montgomery case, White recalled a conversation between herself and Montgomery in 2001, when she says they compared the effects of the clear.

White said that the two talked about how the clear made their calves feel tight and that, although the drug wasn't mentioned by name, during the conversation it was obvious what they were discussing. In testifying about Gaines, White told the CAS panel that from 2001 to 2003 she and Gaines were training partners under track coach Remi Korchemny, who was convicted and sentenced to probation for his involvement in the BALCO scandal. She said that when she and Gaines trained together, they would talk about BALCO, BALCO founder Conte, and various performance-enhancing drugs. In addition, White told the CAS panel that at one point Gaines told her that she had spoken to the BALCO grand jury about using the clear. Neither Montgomery nor Gaines testified during the arbitration hearings.

The ruling by the CAS said that White's testimony, without any of the other evidence presented, was sufficient to prove both Montgomery's and Gaines' guilt. The panel handed each a two-year ban, running from June 2005 through June 2007, although USADA had been seeking longer bans against the two athletes for their involvement in the BALCO affair.[41]

In addition to the bans, all of Tim Montgomery's results in competitions, dating back to March 31, 2001, were erased from the record books. That includes the world record he set in September 2002 at a Paris track meet. Chryste Gaines' results dating back to November 30, 2003 were also erased from the record books.[42] One day after the CAS announced their decision in the two cases, Montgomery told the press that he was done with competition, effectively retiring from the sport one month shy of his 31st birthday.[43]

With the results of the Collins, Montgomery, and Gaines cases, antidoping prosecutors now had a powerful new weapon with which to fight doping. No longer would cases need hard, physical evidence of doping. Now doping cases could be pursued based on accusations by someone who appeared to be a credible witness.

MARION JONES

When the BALCO scandal broke, one of the many athletes whose names came to be associated with the California nutritional and supplement company was Marion Jones. Over the years, she had purchased and used a number of BALCO products, but she claimed to never have used any illicit products in order to further her athletic ambitions. Under testimony, her ex-husband, C.J. Hunter, would claim that his former wife had used steroids and other banned substances, which she received directly or indirectly from BALCO. Hunter told Federal investigators that his former wife used both human growth hormone and the clear during the Sydney Olympics, where she won five medals, including three gold medals. In speaking to IRS agents, Hunter told them that he had seen Jones inject herself, and that he had injected her with banned substances. Hunter also gave the agents details regarding who provided various performance-enhancing drugs to his ex-wife. EPO, he claimed, came from Jones' coach, Trevor Graham. Steroids came from Victor Conte, shipped via Federal Express with Conte listing the name "Victor Reed" on the return address.

Hunter's statements caused an immediate backlash from Jones' attorney. He called Hunter an embittered ex-husband who was "seeking to exact his revenge by telling lies to the government." Jones' lawyer publicly urged the government to investigate Hunter for lying to federal officials. (Ironically, a similar type of investigation would ultimately bring down Jones.) Trevor Graham's attorney also issued an immediate denial, as soon as the *San Francisco Chronicle* and other news organizations published Hunter's story.[44]

Victor Conte would claim, in a December 2004 interview with Martin Bashir for the American Broadcasting Company news program "20/20," that Jones was among his performance-enhanced clients. During the interview, Conte told Bashir that he had supplied Jones with the clear, EPO, human growth hormone, and insulin. He even went so far as to describe how he helped Jones inject herself.

"After I instructed her how to do it and dialed it up," Conte told Bashir, "she did the injection with me sitting right there next to her, right in front of me. Marion didn't like to inject in the stomach area.... She would do it in her quad. The front part of her leg."[45]

Two weeks after the interview was broadcast, Marion Jones filed a lawsuit against Conte for defamation. In the lawsuit, she claimed that the BALCO founder's remarks were part of a long-running "vendetta" that stemmed from her refusal to become a spokesperson for BALCO's ZMA supplement.

Her lawyers released a statement saying, "Jones has never taken banned performance-enhancing drugs." The attorneys also noted that Conte gave the interview in order "to curry favor with the prosecutors, garner sensationalized media attention, bolster Conte's own financial and other self-interest, and harm another individual against whom Conte has a long-standing grudge."[46]

In early 2006, Jones and Conte settled the case out of court. Terms of the settlement have not been disclosed.[47] Also in 2006, a positive result for EPO on a drug-screening test put Marion Jones squarely in the sights of the antidoping authorities. Jones' positive result came from a test after winning the 100 meters at a competition in Indianapolis in June. Her win, her 14th national title, was her first victory since 2002. Two months later, as another scandal involving Tour de France winner Floyd Landis was capturing the media's attention, Jones' results were leaked to the press. Shortly before the story broke, the American sprinter had quickly withdrawn from a meet in Zurich, Switzerland, and returned to the United States. No one knew exactly why she left the Zurich meet, except that she had received a phone call from someone in the United States and rushed back.[48]

Several days later, Jones spoke briefly to the press. "I was shocked when I was informed about the positive 'A' sample," she told a reporter for the Associated Press. "I have requested that the testing of my 'B' sample be expedited and done as soon as possible." Jones hired Howard Jacobs, a lawyer who has defended a number of prominent athletes in doping cases, to represent her. She didn't need his legal service for very long. In early September 2006, the results of her B sample test came back negative, clearing her of any wrongdoing.

"I am absolutely ecstatic. I have always maintained that I have never ever taken performance enhancing drugs," Jones said in a statement released by her attorneys. "I am pleased that a scientific process has now demonstrated that fact."[49]

"I am anxious to get back on the track," she said.

Howard Jacobs, one of Jones' attorneys, said, "I believe there are issues with that test. It's a difficult test. From what I saw on the 'A' sample, it was questionable as to whether it should've been called a positive. I can't say I was shocked that the 'B' came back negative based on what the 'A' looked like." Jacobs also commented on the apparent trend of leaking athletes' drug-screening results.

"This is perfect illustration of why this new trend of leaking 'A' positives is a horrible thing. This whole thing should have happened anonymously. Marion should've been able to keep competing and no one should have known about it."[50]

That might have been the end of the story, were it not for an investigation into a check-kiting scheme carried out by Jones' ex-boyfriend, Tim Montgomery. During the investigation, Jones made statements to Federal agents denying her involvement in the scheme, statements that were not entirely truthful. In October 2007, facing a possible prison sentence for lying to federal agents, prosecutors were able to convince Jones to plea bargain. Among the things she admitted to was that she had knowingly used steroids and other banned substances between 2000 and 2007. Over the same time period, she had been tested approximately two dozen times by the USADA. Not a single test came back positive for performance-enhancing drugs during that time, due in part to the undetectable nature of certain drugs, and her advisers' skills in knowing just when to stop taking the drugs.[51]

Ultimately, Marion Jones' undoing was her involvement in the shady dealings of her ex-boyfriend. Jeff Novitsky, who worked on the BALCO investigation, was also involved in the investigation of Tim Montgomery's check-kiting scheme. Had Marion Jones not signed her name to some of the checks that surfaced in the case, and had she not lied about doing so, Novitsky would not have had the leverage he needed to get Jones to admit that she had used steroids. As a result of her admissions, Marion Jones had to relinquish all five of the medals she won at the 2000 Summer Olympics in Sydney.

In January 2008, U.S. District Judge Kenneth Karas sentenced Jones to six months in prison for lying about her involvement in the BALCO case and two months in prison for lying about her role in Montgomery's check fraud scam. While sentencing the fallen track star, Judge Karas noted that she could serve both sentences at the same time. The judge also sentenced Jones to two years' probation, during which she will have to perform 400 hours of community service during each year.

Judge Karas, during the sentencing, noted that the community service could "take advantage of Ms. Jones-Thompson's eloquence, strength and her ability to work with kids." And he went on to suggest that Jones use the time to teach youngsters "it's wrong to cheat and to lie about the cheating."[52]

DID BARRY BONDS KNOW HE WAS JUICING?

Since the earliest days of the BALCO scandal, American baseball player Barry Bonds' name has time and again been linked to the investigation. Bonds' trainer, Greg Anderson, was one of seven people to be convicted and serve jail time in connection with the probe, raising the question of whether Anderson provided various banned substances to his client, who is also a longtime friend. Bonds' connections to BALCO have been a source of controversy over the years. With Bonds' pursuit of the home run record, arguably the most hallowed of all records in professional baseball, he became an even more controversial figure. When he finally surpassed Hank Aaron's record of 755 home runs, many people—fans, sportswriters, and pundits, as well as a number of baseball insiders—felt that Bonds' record should have an asterisk next to it, due to the controversy surrounding the player and his alleged use of steroids in pursuit of the record.

Professional baseball has been slow to adopt the stringent kinds of antidoping measures that the IOC mandates for all Olympic sports. During most of Bonds' pursuit of the home run record, baseball did not have rules governing the use of steroids, which makes the controversy surrounding his accomplishment all the more complex. Most observers of professional sports agree that the use of steroids is wrong, but what should the public's expectation and reaction be when their opinions don't match the rules set forth by a professional sports league? This is one of the key questions at the heart of the Bonds story.

In major league baseball up to the 2003 season, steroids weren't banned and the leagues weren't testing players. So the use of the cream and the clear was technically not against the rules—even if most fans and observers agree that it's a form of cheating. Starting with the 2003 season, professional baseball implemented unannounced testing for steroids, intended to catch anyone using the drugs.

According to Bonds' testimony to the grand jury investigating the BALCO case, he used various products supplied by his trainer, including the cream and the clear. But he didn't know what these products contained. Prior to the start of the 2003 season, he requested that steroid testing be carried out to ensure that he would be clean when he was tested by baseball's new drug-screening program. Bonds told the grand jury that he never saw the results of his tests, but Anderson did tell him that he was clean, implying that no steroids were in the products he had been using.

The U.S. attorneys questioning him before the grand jury repeatedly asked Bonds about various documents they found at Greg Anderson's house. Bonds denied knowing anything about the documents, which included schedules of when Bonds was given various banned substances, records of blood and urine test results, and invoices for the various products Anderson had been supplying to the slugger. When the prosecutors asked Bonds whether he knew what he was being given by his trainer, he answered that he never asked Anderson what was in the products, adding, "When he said it was flaxseed oil, I just said, 'Whatever.'"

He also told the U.S. attorneys that he had thought that the products were legal supplements to help him with fatigue and arthritis. Bonds began working with Anderson in the late 1990s, at a time when his relationship with a previous trainer was becoming strained. Bonds was dissatisfied with the training program and results, and was looking for something different. Anderson's approach to weight training was more in line with what Barry Bonds wanted to do.

As he told the grand jury, "I was getting rugged with my other trainer, you know, doing the same thing over and over . . . My other trainer was like, you do three sets of legs, three sets of this, three—you know."

"And Greg is more—16 sets of chest, more biceps, to really maximize and expand your muscle. And I liked that philosophy." The two worked together, and eventually started going to a gym close to BALCO's offices.

Sometime in 2000 or 2001, Anderson suggested to Bonds that he get his blood tested by BALCO to see what nutritional or vitamin deficiencies he might have. Conte and BALCO had an established reputation by then for being able to diagnose zinc and magnesium deficiencies, which supposedly hinders athletic performance. And BALCO's ZMA supplement is meant to address such deficiencies. Bonds told the grand jury that he agreed to the tests because he "just thought it was a neat idea."

After the test results came back, Anderson started supplying Bonds with a number of supplements, including ZMA, multivitamins, vitamin E, omega 3 fatty acids, and liver pills. Eventually, Anderson started supplying Bonds with the cream and the clear. As he told the grand jury, he started using the substances at a difficult time in his life, when he was suffering from arthritis, fatigue, and dealing with his father's terminal illness.

In his testimony, Bonds said, "I have bad arthritis. I've played 18 years, bad knees, surgeries and so on." And he was looking for something that could take away the aches and pains he felt on cold mornings, and something that could help with the fatigue he suffered.

"I'm 39 years old. I'm dealing with pain. All I want is the pain relief, you know? And you know, to recover, you know, night games to day games. That's it."

"I was battling with the problems with my father and the—just the lack of sleep, lack of everything." But the supplements did little for him, and he eventually stopped using them, Bonds told the grand jury, adding that, "If it's a steroid, it's not working."

The prosecutor, Jeff Nedrow, delved into what Anderson told him about the cream and the clear, asking, "Did he ever tell you it was a molecularly or chemically altered steroid? Did Greg ever tell you anything like that?"

Bonds answered Nedrow by saying, "No, because my other trainer, who is 50 years old, Harvey, was taking the same stuff. And he said it's flaxseed oil." Bonds was consistent in his denials when asked what he knew about the products Anderson gave him.

But Bonds' testimony was at odds with what other baseball players told the grand jury. Gary Sheffield, who trained with Bonds before the 2002 baseball season, told the grand jury that he never had direct contact with Greg Anderson. Instead, his contact was through Barry Bonds. Sheffield told the grand jury that Bonds told him, "Trust me. Do what I do."

According to Sheffield, Bonds arranged for him to get the clear, the cream and some pills called "red beans." Prosecutors identified the pills as steroids that were manufactured in Mexico. Sheffield told the grand jury that he never knew any of the products he was being given were steroids.

After Bonds' testimony was leaked to the press, his attorney, Michael Rains, expressed dismay that the confidential testimony had been leaked, but also said that he wasn't surprised that it had happened. He also pointed out that his client had not been able to see the documents that prosecutors questioned him about before the day he stepped into the witness box. Rains noted that every other athlete had been allowed to look documents over, so that they could be as helpful as possible during their testimony. Bonds' attorney took that as a sign that the government was out to get his client.

Rains told the *San Francisco Chronicle*, "That shows you what the government's attempt was and what their effort was. But it didn't work. One, because Barry testified truthfully, and they know it. And two, because the documents they showed him are so fraught with irregularities of unproven quality and character that they can't be used to secure an indictment (for perjury)."

In fact, Bonds (like a number of others called before the grand jury) testified under a grant of immunity from prosecution. Anything that he admitted to while under oath would not be prosecuted, as long as he was truthful. But with his account at odds with the testimony of others brought before the grand jury, Bonds' truthfulness came into question. And that started a whole new grand jury investigation, this time focusing on whether the slugger had committed perjury.[53]

In March 2005, Bonds' former girlfriend appeared before a grand jury looking into whether Bonds had testified truthfully about his BALCO dealings. She told the grand jury that in 2000, Bonds told her he had begun to use steroids the year before. By April 2006, the U.S. attorney handling the BALCO investigation appeared close to handing down a perjury indictment against Barry Bonds. The documents found during the 2003 raid were marked with Bonds' name, which suggested he had been using BALCO steroids and other performance-enhancing drugs supplied to him by his trainer. That information, along with testimony by a number of athletes who had been introduced to Greg Anderson through Barry Bonds, led prosecutors to be suspicious that he had not been truthful during his grand jury testimony. A tape recording of a phone call Anderson took part in, made without Anderson's knowledge, suggested that Bonds did know he was using steroids. During the conversation, Anderson stated that he had provided Bonds with an undetectable steroid in 2003 so that the baseball player could beat major league baseball's new drug-testing program.

In late April 2006, the grand jury looking into whether Bonds committed perjury subpoenaed Greg Anderson to testify. Also summoned to testify were James Valente, a former BALCO executive; Dr. Arthur Ting, Bonds' personal orthopedist; and Stan Conte, a San Francisco Giants athletic trainer. Anderson was expected to face questions about what Bonds knew and when he knew it.[54]

Anderson, however, refused to testify against his friend. In early July 2006, U.S. District Judge William Alsup found Anderson in contempt and ordered that he be incarcerated indefinitely at the Federal Correctional Institution in Dublin, California.

"Mr. Anderson, this is going to be a learning experience and probably one you won't forget for a long time," Alsup told Anderson. "The marshals will take good care of you. They're not going to punish you. The purpose is to get you to change your mind."

Although Anderson's lawyer wanted a delay in Anderson's incarceration so that he could file an appeal on his client's behalf, the judge ordered Anderson be imprisoned immediately.[55]

After more than a year and a half of investigating whether Bonds committed perjury, the grand jury indicted Bonds on November 15, 2007. In the indictment, prosecutors alleged that the baseball player lied when he denied using various banned substances, including the cream and the clear. The indictment also alleges that Bonds lied when he said that Anderson never injected him with drugs.[56] Greg Anderson was released from prison the same day that his friend was indicted.

Anderson's attorney, Mark Geragos, told reporters, "It's infuriating, when you read the indictment. Is there anything in that indictment that wasn't known a year ago? If that is the case, clearly, putting Greg in for a year was not only punitive, but was misleading the court in that (federal prosecutors) said his testimony was indispensable for the investigation."

"All of sudden, it was, 'I hope your year was therapeutic.' There has to be some kind of redress for this," Geragos continued. "The whole thing is a crock of s—. He's never said word one."[57] In early December 2007, at a preliminary hearing in a San Francisco courthouse, Bonds pleaded not guilty to the perjury and obstruction of justice charges that the grand jury's indictment contains. As of this writing, his court case is ongoing, with the next hearing scheduled for early June 2008.

As noted earlier, one of the ironies of the BALCO case is that former San Francisco Giants trainer Stan Conte tipped off a contact at the DEA in August 2002 about his concerns that Barry Bonds' personal trainer was distributing steroids to Giants players.[58] More than four years after the BALCO story first made the news, the fallout from the case continues.

FIFA SIGNS ON TO THE WADA CODE, SORT OF

At a press conference in December 2003, Sepp Blatter, the president of the International Soccer Federation (FIFA), lost his cool. Blatter, in a fit of frustration, admitted that professional soccer had a doping problem, and went on to say that the problem extended beyond the players.

"It is not just the players," Blatter declared, "but the people who employ them—the clubs, the leagues, the national associations.

"The Executive Committee has given me the mandate today to be strict, stricter than we have been before and given me the power to act.

"The situation has changed on doping. I was wrong saying there was no problem with doping. Only the stubborn don't show flexibility. As the president of FIFA I must be flexible, within the statutes.

"I thought our game was clean. It is not clean. There is now a suspicion surrounding football. I have never seen, in a doping control someone not declare their innocence. Gentlemen, let's get serious.

"If we want to have our sport clean then we have to work on that. We need decision-making in football, we need professional decisions taken by top decision-makers, not volunteers. We need those with power and knowledge."[59]

Five months later, FIFA signed on to the World Anti-Doping Code, adopting the code and its rules and procedures for antidoping tests for the world of professional soccer. At the same time, FIFA officials decided to continue their practice of determining punishment for violations of antidoping rules on a case-by-case basis. The soccer federation's policy, which they claimed fit with the WADC rules, became a point of contention between the worldwide enforcers of antidoping regulations and soccer's international governing body.

At FIFA's Centenary Conference, in May 2004, Blatter, with WADA president Dick Pound and IOC chairman Jacques Rogge present during the meeting, announced that the federation would sign on to the worldwide code of antidoping regulations.

By August 2004, WADA president Dick Pound sent a letter to Blatter and FIFA urging the organization to sign the antidoping agency's "straight-forward declaration." Blatter, according to published media reports of the time, replied to Pound's letter, saying, "We have signed."

What, exactly, each side had agreed to was unclear, as FIFA and WADA engaged in a tug-of-war over whether or not the soccer federation was in full compliance with the IOC's requirement that all Olympic sports sign on to the WADC. Because of the disagreement, the possibility existed that soccer would not be included in the 2004 Athens Olympics. Negotiations went on until the last minute, with neither side willing to budge.

At a press conference shortly before the beginning of the Athens Games, Blatter told reporters, "It is about individual case management. Everyone has the right to be analyzed individually and in FIFA that works."

Blatter also told reporters, "We have said we are going to fight doping but also that the amendments—I cannot say exceptions—which were presented by Mr. Pound are an integrated part of our signature.

"There is no problem and I don't know why a problem was brought up by the administration of WADA"[60]

The World Anti-Doping Agency saw things differently. In September 2005, FIFA contacted the CAS to determine whether the World Anti-Doping Code conformed with Swiss law, and to what extent FIFA's implementation of that code was in compliance with WADA's requirements. WADA, for their part, argued that the soccer federation's approach to doping cases was not in compliance, primarily because of the highly flexible nature of the penalties handed out. The agency stated that for a first offense, the required ban would be two years. In the year since joining WADA's code, FIFA had meted out punishments ranging from six months to two years, depending on the specifics of individual cases. In April 2006, the CAS handed down a decision, which both sides viewed as favorable to themselves.

According to a press release issued on April 24, 2006, FIFA president Sepp Blatter expressed satisfaction with the ruling. "With this legal opinion, which FIFA itself sought, CAS has laid the foundations for resolving any differences that exist with regard to the World Anti-Doping Code," Blatter said. "As an international sports federation and as a member of the International Olympic Committee, FIFA is fully aware that it is bound by the Olympic Charter. FIFA will attempt to solve any differences on its own initiative, especially as CAS jurisprudence also applies the World Anti-Doping Code in line with the principle of individual case management."[61]

According to the panel's ruling, "As an association governed by Swiss law, FIFA is free, within the limits of mandatory Swiss law, to determine such sanctions on antidoping violations as it deems appropriate." The CAS panel also added that FIFA could "establish lower minimum sanctions than provided by the WADC."[62]

WADA president Dick Pound, speaking to the media after the panel's decision was announced, noted that FIFA wasn't obligated to agree to the code. "But," Pound noted, "the IOC has modified the Olympic charter to make it mandatory for any sport that's on the Olympic program to have adopted and apply the WADC."[63]

In early June 2006, FIFA announced that they would amend their rules to make a two-year ban from competition the minimum punishment for a first doping offense. Speaking to a reporter for the Associated Press, FIFA executive committee member Chuck Blazer announced, "In principle, we agree to the two-year suspensions, which in some cases could be more or could be less. We still maintain individual case management." Several days later, the full membership of the international soccer federation ratified the arrangement.[64]

TWO GREEK TRACK STARS, A MOTORCYCLE, AND A MISSED TEST

The 2004 Athens Olympics got off to a strange start. When antidoping officials showed up at their quarters in the Olympic Village to perform an unannounced drug screening on the eve of the opening ceremonies, Greek track stars Costas Kenteris and Katerina Thanou turned up missing. Hours later, the pair showed up at a local hospital, claiming to have suffered injuries in a motorcycle accident. Both were admitted to the hospital and kept several days for observation.

It was not the first time that Kenteris and Thanou missed an antidoping test. In the months before the Athens Games, the training partners missed two other tests—one in Chicago and the other in Tel Aviv.

The missed test in Tel Aviv occurred on July 28, 2004. When drug testers arrived at the location where Kenteris and Thanou were supposed to be, neither was there. Two weeks later, on August 11, in Chicago, the drug testers once again came for them. Again, they were nowhere to be found. The athletes later explained that they had traveled to Germany. In reality, they were in the Greek town of Corinth, where people spotted the two in a restaurant.

Shortly before the Olympics began, Manolis Kolimpadis, the Greek Olympic delegation's deputy chief, saw them in the Olympic Village in Athens. When Kolimpadis greeted them, they appeared to know that the antidoping testers were looking for them. According to Kolimpadis, this was before the Greek delegation had even been notified that the two athletes were to be tested.

Kolimpadis told reporters, "They were trembling like doves. They were very frightened." About two hours later, antidoping authorities informed the Greek delegation that Kenteris and Thanou had 75 minutes to show up for an antidoping test. Officials went to test the two sprinters, but again, they could not locate them. "We didn't find them in their rooms. They were gone, but we don't know when they left."

Christos Tzekos, their coach, would later say that Kenteris and Thanou had gone to collect some clothing they had forgotten, and that they were at his house at the time the antidoping testers were looking for them, with their mobile phones turned off. In the early hours of the following morning, the pair showed up at an Athens hospital, claiming to be injured in a motorcycle accident.

From the beginning, the story of the motorcycle accident raised suspicions, both among the police and the media. Police started investigating the accident within days, and found inconsistencies in the athletes' account of what happened. The story of the motorcycle accident didn't quite add up. Kenteris and Thanou had scrapes on the right side of their bodies, but the motorcycle had scrapes on the left side. A kiosk vendor near the scene of the accident denied seeing or hearing anything. Eventually, the police focused on whether the two really had been involved in an accident at all, or whether they had filed a false police report.

For several days both Kenteris and Thanou remained out of sight, staying in the hospital recuperating from their injuries.

While in the hospital, the athletes offered to undergo drug-screening tests. Arne Ljungqvist, the IOC's medical chief, dismissed the idea, telling reporters, "It would not make any sense to test them in the hospital. You can fix things there so you don't get a positive result."

Upon leaving the hospital, Kenteris told reporters, "At this time, all those who are crucifying me are those who would come and pose for photographs after every great success. But I want to add that after crucifixion comes the resurrection." Thanou also sounded a defiant and nationalistic tone, saying, "I will continue to fight for myself and those who feel they are Greeks."[65]

Six days after the missed test and the supposed "motorcycle accident," the IOC held a hearing to look into the matter. Before the IOC could bring a case against the athletes and their coach, the athletes informed the panel that they were innocent, but they were dropping out of the Athens Olympics. At the same time, Kenteris and Thanou turned in their Olympic credentials. Because they were no longer participants at the Games, the IOC was unable to take any action against either athlete. But that didn't mean they were out of trouble.

The IOC handed the case over to the IAAF, the international federation governing track and field competition.

"With a sense of responsibility and national interest I am retiring from the Olympic Games," Kenteris told journalists as he left the hearing. "My country has waited 108 years for the Games to come home. I declared all the facts of my case, which state that I am innocent. I was never informed that I had to attend a doping test."

Thanou also spoke to reporters as she left the meeting, saying, "I want to apologize to the Greek people that I will not be at the Games, that I will not manage to race, and that is why I handed my accreditation into the IOC today. It is very hard for an athlete to withdraw from the Games, especially when those Games are at home."[66]

Up to that point, neither Kenteris nor Thanou had ever failed a test. But officials claimed that the reason that neither athlete had failed a test was because they were frequently unavailable. François Carrard, the IOC's legal adviser, told reporters, "We clearly said [to the panel investigating Kenteris and Thanou that] the antidoping violation was this pattern of unavailability, misinformation, missed information, et cetera."[67]

In mid-November 2004, Kenteris, Thanou, and Tzekos were charged with failing to appear for the drug-screening tests the day before the Olympics began, and also with faking the motorcycle accident several hours later. Tzekos, the coach, was also charged with illegally importing and distributing banned substances.

Two weeks later, on December 2, 2004, the IAAF sent letters to the Greek track and field federation (SEGAS) charging the two athletes and their coach with providing false information about Kenteris and Thanou's whereabouts, and also with missing the antidoping test in August.[68]

In March 2005, the SEGAS review panel announced their decision regarding Kenteris' and Thanou's missed test the previous August. In a surprise move, the panel acquitted the two sprinters. The IAAF's Doping Review Board immediately branded the ruling "erroneous" and appealed the case to the Court of Arbitration for Sport (CAS). The track stars were still banned from competition as they awaited the outcome of the CAS case. Tzekos, their coach, received a four-year ban from the review board for his involvement in the affair.[69]

After the IAAF appealed the ruling, the two Greek sprinters asked the CAS to lift the provisional suspension against the athletes that had been in place since late December 2004. On June 26, 2006, Kenteris and Thanou dropped their appeals after the CAS ruled that the provisional suspension would stay in place. In dropping their appeals they accepted the CAS' ruling. In addition, the Greek athletes acknowledged that they had missed three antidoping tests, which is a violation of WADA and IAAF antidoping rules.[70]

In addition to the case against them related to the 2004 Olympics, Costas Kenteris and Ekaterina Thanou were eventually linked to the ongoing BALCO investigations in the United States. Materials gathered from the BALCO investigation appeared to implicate the Kenteris, Thanou, and their coach. In late October 2007, Greek prosecutors looked into alleged links between the two athletes, their coach, and BALCO.

"The district attorney sent all evidence on the activity of the Bay Area Laboratory Co-operative (BALCO), its chairman Victor Conte and chemist Patrick Arnold related to Greek athletes and coaches," lawyer Nikos

Kollias, an attorney representing Kenteris, Thanou, and Tzekos, told a news conference.

"Greek prosecutors . . . decided that the evidence does not substantiate prosecution, let alone a trial," he continued. Tzekos, the former coach for Kenteris and Thanou, is still under investigation for illegally importing banned substances into Greece. Kenteris and Thanou will undergo trial in June 2008 on charges of perjury stemming from their 2004 account of the motorcycle accident on the eve of the Athens Olympics.[71]

RUTGER BEKE, THE KNOKKE TRIATHLON, AND EPO

Rutger Beke, a professional triathlete from Belgium, inadvertently added a page to the history of doping in sports by testing positive for EPO use at the Knokke Triathlon in September 2004. Beke won the race, and as required, provided a urine sample for analysis. Beke's sample was tested for EPO at the antidoping lab at Ghent, Belgium. He was notified about the results of his initial A sample test about three weeks after the Knokke Triathlon, according to news reports. While awaiting the test results for his B sample, Beke competed at the Ironman Hawaii, where he finished in fifth place overall.[72]

Beke's test results were leaked to the Belgian media, prompting speculation about the athlete having a high hematocrit reading, when in reality his hematocrit was not found to be high (a high hematocrit level would have led to an automatic suspension). Instead, Beke's urine test for EPO had come back positive. In a statement released in October 2004, Chris McCrary, Beke's spokesman, noted that Beke had hired a team of scientists to examine his test results and to determine how the triathlete could have tested positive without having used EPO. According to McCrary's statement, Beke also volunteered to undergo repeated testing for the blood-boosting drug in order to determine how his result could have happened.[73]

In March 2005 the Flemish Disciplinary Commission handed Beke a preliminary 18-month suspension. Beke, however, maintained his innocence and fought the case. The Flemish triathlete's team of scientists continued running tests to determine whether or not he was the victim of a false positive test result. Eventually, Beke's defense team was able to prove that he naturally excreted proteins that led to the false positive test result. With this new information, the final ruling of the Flemish Disciplinary Board concluded that there was "no evidence that [Beke] took EPO." They found Beke wasn't guilty of doping and exonerated him. The decision in his case was a landmark ruling according to *CyclingNews.com*, as it cast doubt on the rulings in all other cases where the EPO urine test was used.[74]

After the final ruling was announced, Beke commented on the case, saying, "Today is a great day for me. After 10 painful months, the appeal court

(Flemish Disciplinary Commission) has come to the conclusion that I have NOT taken EPO last year in September.

"With the help of scientists, I have proven that I can test positive on the existing WADA EPO-test without ever taking any EPO. This is what happened in Knokke and explains why I have been falsely accused. Even the director of the French Wada-lab (the lab that invented the EPO test) has admitted that I am innocent. Now that I have been fully cleared from this doping accusation, I can focus again on my job and my favorite sport. My number one objective remains to win the Ironman Hawaii one of these years."[75]

Today, Beke continues to compete as a professional triathlete. He scored his first victory in an Ironman series event by winning the Ford Ironman Arizona competition in April 2007.

"I don't think about it (the positive test) anymore," Beke told Kevin Mackinnon for an article published on *Ironman.com*. "Two years ago in 2005, that was one of my main worries when I went to Hawaii, but I have the impression that all of the guys believe me and that they don't have any problems with me. I know that there are probably some people out there who question me or doubt me, but I don't care about their opinion. The most important thing is that I know I am a clean athlete and I know most people believe that and that's the most important thing. Unfortunately, in sports these days, everybody who is a good athlete gets questioned. If you win a race there's always people who are jealous and are going to say you are taking drugs. I'm not losing any energy on that."[76]

JUVENTUS DOCTOR CONVICTED AND LATER CLEARED OF DOPING PLAYERS

A decision handed down in a Turin, Italy, courtroom in November 2004 rocked the reputation of Juventus, one of Europe's most storied professional soccer clubs. In a case over doping allegations at the club dating back to the middle of the previous decade, Dr. Ricardo Agricola, the team's physician, was found guilty of "sporting fraud" for administering EPO and other banned substances to Juventus players between 1994 and 1998. The judge presiding in the case fined Agricola €2000 (about $2600 in 2004) and sentenced the physician to twenty-two months in jail.

During the trial, Gianmartino Benzi, a university professor of pharmacology, testified for the prosecution. Benzi told the court that he saw 281 drugs of various sorts at the team's headquarters, describing the club's inventory of medications as "stocks that resembled the quantity you would find in a small hospital." Benzi was the only witness for the prosecution.

On the defense side, a number of former Juventus players testified that they had not used any banned performance-enhancing drugs during their playing days at the Turin club. Roberto Baggio, a retired player, told the court that he could not have taken some of the substances listed by Benzi, as he was allergic to the medications.

Zinédine Zidane, who was playing for Real Madrid during the 2004 season, admitted that he had taken supplements, such as creatine. At the same time, he testified that he never used any medications or supplements that were banned by FIFA. Gianluca Vialli, a talented player who retired and became a television commentator, pointed the finger at Zdenek Zeman, the man whose allegations started the whole affair. The scandal began when Zeman, a native of the Czech Republic, blew the whistle on what he called Vialli's unnaturally rapid muscular development, as well as the rapid development of another player, Alessandro Del Piero.

Despite being convicted, Agricola did not go directly to jail. Following the verdict's announcement, Agricola's attorney indicated that the appeals process would begin straight away. Defense attorney Paolo Trofino said of Agricola's conviction, "He was condemned for what was the weak point of the prosecution charges, the administration of EPO. It is a sentence that will be difficult to get through appeal." Given that no test that could definitively prove the presence of artificial EPO existed during the years being investigated, the evidence against Agricola was on shaky ground. His attorney appeared to understand that point quite well.[77]

Trofino's prediction about the ultimate outcome of the case would prove to be correct. Just over one year later, in December 2005, an Italian court in Turin overturned Agricola's conviction.[78]

TYLER HAMILTON, BLOOD DOPING, AND THE "VANISHING TWIN"

As EPO use became detectable in the early 2000s, some athletes started going back to an older method of blood doping—transfusions of blood, either their own or from a donor. Antidoping authorities and researchers recognized a need to develop a method for identifying athletes using transfused blood to boost athletic performance. In 2004, a new test came into use that could detect homologous blood doping, which is the practice of receiving a transfusion of another person's blood in order to add red blood cells capable of carrying more oxygen to an athlete's muscles. By increasing the number of red blood cells in their bodies, athletes can perform at a higher level for a longer period of time. The advantage, when two athletes are otherwise equal, could be enough to tip the scales in favor of the one who's doping.

Michael Ashenden and a team of researchers in Australia, using a similar approach to the EPO blood tests developed and partially implemented for the Sydney Olympics in 2000, developed the new test for homologous blood doping. In this new test, an athlete's blood would be analyzed for more than the typical blood types of A, B, and O. While these three main groupings are known to many, there are a number of subgroupings within each type, making for many minor variations in each person's blood. Fewer than one person in every 1,000 will match these many additional markers, so it's possible to analyze a person's blood to determine whether or not there are signs of two different cell populations within his or her body.[79] The test relies on flow cytometry, a medical diagnostic technology that has been in use for more than three decades, to separate the major blood groups into subtypes. Application to antidoping work occurred in 2002, with a study by Ashenden and others that was published in a peer-reviewed scientific journal.[80]

There are a number of ways that a person could have differing cell populations in his or her blood, including a recent transfusion during medical treatment, a bone marrow or stem cell transplant, exchanging blood in the womb with a fraternal twin, and being a chimera (a person born as a result of two embryos fusing together in the mother's womb, resulting in an individual with shared genetic information). If all of these situations can be ruled out, then a positive result from the blood screening indicates a strong probability that the athlete received a transfusion of another person's blood.

The test was first rolled out during the 2004 Tour de France, and was also implemented at the Athens Olympics shortly thereafter. The first athlete to run afoul of the homologous blood doping test was American cyclist Tyler Hamilton, who raced on the Phonak professional cycling team and who represented the United States on the U.S. Olympic cycling team. In Athens, Hamilton won gold in the men's time trial event. But not long after, his initial blood test results came back positive for homologous blood doping. Hamilton, as was his right, requested that the backup sample be tested. As it turned out, Hamilton's backup sample had been frozen, resulting in the destruction of the red blood cells crucial to the test. The B sample test could not be conducted, and thus Hamilton could not be found guilty of a doping violation.[81]

So Hamilton caught a break, because without the confirming B sample test, he could not be penalized for a doping violation. His luck, however, took a turn for the worse during the 2004 Vuelta á España (Tour of Spain), the last of cycling's three Grand Tours each year. On September 11, 2004 after winning the 8th stage of the Vuelta, Hamilton again tested positive for homologous blood doping. He was informed of the results of the Athens test and the Vuelta test two days later.[82] By the time the result was announced, Hamilton had already abandoned the Spanish stage race citing stomach problems. This time, the B sample was not frozen, and the result came back confirming the initial findings.

When news of his positive tests became public, Hamilton denied that he had engaged in homologous blood doping, claiming that the positive result came about due to a surgical procedure he had undergone in the recent past.[83] Shortly after the announcement of Hamilton's initial test results, the UCI released documents to the press which showed that Hamilton and Phonak had been informed of "irregularities" in his blood test results from the Tour of Romandie the preceding May. Among those irregularities was Hamilton's hematocrit level, which one test in May had found to be 49.7, only slightly under the UCI's cutoff for a positive EPO test result. (If Hamilton—or any rider—returned a hematocrit greater than 50, he would have been required to take a two-week "rest" from competition and undergo another hematocrit test prior to a return to action. If his level had exceeded 51, an antidoping case would have been opened.) Earlier tests of Hamilton's hematocrit levels had shown results as low at 38. The discrepancy between his readings, the UCI implied, was due to blood doping.[84]

Part of Hamilton's defense, which has been dubbed the "vanishing twin" defense, came from assistance offered from Dr. David Housman, a professor of molecular biology at the Massachusetts Institute of Technology. One morning, while reading the sports section of his newspaper, an article about Hamilton's positive test result caught his attention. Dr. Housman then contacted Hamilton's father, Bill Hamilton, to offer his assistance.

"I read it and said: 'Wait a second. I don't think the explanation they give for the blood test is the only possible explanation,'" he told Gina Kolata of *The New York Times*. According to Dr. Housman, chimeras are not unusual. Dr. Housman also told the *Times* that human stem cells turn on and off throughout an individual's life, so it is possible for a stem cell to make a small amount of "foreign" blood cells from time to time. In other words, it's possible that a person can have a miniscule amount of differing blood cells at any given time.

The question that Dr. Housman raised, since a "vanishing twin" is not uncommon, is whether or not the test used to catch Tyler Hamilton was reliable enough to detect blood doping. In her article, Kolata quotes other sources not connected to the Hamilton case that are cautious about using the test used to find Hamilton guilty of blood doping for such purposes. Dr. S. Gerald Sandler of Georgetown University Hospital said that the test was fine for research, but results from one lab to another can vary. Dr. Sandler, a professor of medicine and pathology, said that in his opinion the test "is being misapplied" when it is used in the prosecution of athletes charged with blood doping offenses.

In April 2005, an arbitration panel voted 2–1 to find Hamilton guilty of blood doping and suspended him from competition for a period of two years. The original suspension was set to run until mid-April 2007. The panel also ordered that all of Hamilton's race results following his September 11, 2004 positive test be erased, including his victory during the 8th stage of the 2004 Vuelta.

The arbitrator who dissented in the Hamilton case, Chris Campbell, took USADA and those defending the blood test at the heart of the case to task, saying that they had failed to present a compelling case against Hamilton.

Campbell criticized the World Anti-Doping Agency and the developers of the test for failing to establish the rate of false positives for the test. Campbell also made the point that while WADA could have implemented objective and verifiable standards to detect false positives, they had failed to do so. He noted that their approach to quality control was one of "I know it when I see it."

Campbell also castigated USADA and WADA for not taking into account other potential explanations for positive results, including pregnancy (which, for obvious reasons, was never raised by the Hamilton defense team) and bone marrow transplantation (also not argued by the Hamilton team). Up to and during his first arbitration hearing, Hamilton and his defense team attacked the test's accuracy and veracity.

The panel's majority didn't accept Hamilton's arguments. Despite Dr. Housman's testimony describing his scientific concerns, the majority concluded that the test used in the Hamilton case was accurate. In their opinion, the majority said, "There are no scientific studies that detect false positives in the use of the HBTT, [so] there is no need to do so because there is no suggestion in the use of the HBTT that it produces false positives."[85]

With the initial decision against him, Hamilton appealed to the Court of Arbitration for Sport. In February 2006, the CAS upheld the case against Hamilton, rejecting arguments made on his behalf. His suspension was adjusted, however, to end in September 2006, two years after the first test results came back positive and the American rider was suspended by Phonak. Shortly after Hamilton's suspension ended, he joined a new professional cycling team being formed by Russian magnate Oleg Tinkov under the Tinkoff Credit Systems banner.

Hamilton got off to a slow start during the 2007 season. Then, in May 2007, because of alleged links to the Operación Puerto scandal, Tinkoff Credit Systems suspended Hamilton, Jörg Jaksche, and Danilo Hondo from competition shortly before the beginning of the first Grand Tour of the year, the Giro d'Italia. In announcing their decision, the team said that the riders would be suspended indefinitely "until the competent authorities . . . have finally sorted out all the implication of the riders in Operación Puerto."[86] Just days before the 2007 Tour de France began, Jaksche admitted that he had worked with the Spanish doctor who was at the heart of the Operación Puerto scandal and that he had blood doped.

Although USA Cycling received information regarding Hamilton's alleged links to Operación Puerto in September 2006, so far no charges have been brought against him by USADA or any other antidoping organization for any doping violations connected to the Spanish investigation. Hamilton has not raced since April 2007, when he participated in the Tour de Georgia. After parting ways with the Tinkoff Credit Systems team, Hamilton signed with Michael Ball's Rock Racing cycling team in December 2007, and will compete on the Rock Racing squad in North American pro cycling races during the 2008 season.[87]

DID LANCE ARMSTRONG USE EPO IN 1999?

When Lance Armstrong won his seventh and final Tour de France, he gave a brief retirement speech in which he addressed the oft-repeated accusations that he could only have accomplished what he did through artificial means. "I want to send a message to people who do not believe in cycling, the cynics, skeptics. I am sorry that they do not believe in miracles, in dreams. Too bad for them," Armstrong said on July 24, 2005, immediately after being awarded his final maillot jaune (the yellow jersey, the symbol of the Tour de France leader).[88]

Just one month later, articles published in the French sports daily *L'Equipe* charged that Armstrong had used EPO when he won his first Tour in 1999. Armstrong had long been suspected of doping by various European publications, despite his firm denials, and *L'Equipe* claimed to have scientific proof that the seven-time Tour winner had used banned substances.

Armstrong quickly released a statement on his Web site vehemently denying the accusations against him. "Yet again, a European newspaper has reported that I have tested positive for performance-enhancing drugs," Armstrong's statement read. "L'Equipe, a French sports daily, is reporting that my 1999 samples were positive. Unfortunately the witch hunt continues and [their] article is nothing short of tabloid journalism.

"The paper even admits in its own article that the science in question here is faulty and that I have no way to defend myself. They state: 'There will therefore be no counter-exam nor regulatory prosecutions, in a strict sense, since defendant's rights cannot be respected.'

"I will simply restate what I have said many times: I have never taken performance enhancing drugs."[89]

Damien Ressiott, *L'Equipe*'s reporter on the doping beat, had gotten hold of documents from France's antidoping laboratory, LNDD, which purported to show that Armstrong and several other cyclists had positive test results for the blood-boosting drug EPO. The material Ressiott gathered included the results of tests conducted on old urine samples left over from the 1998 and 1999 Tours de France. LNDD claimed that the testing, performed in 2004, was research geared toward improving the urine test for the banned drug. Among the samples tested were six that appeared to belong to Armstrong, all of which—according to the documents—showed traces of synthetic EPO in his system. The revelation caused an immediate uproar.

Jean-Marie Leblanc, the director of the Tour de France, told *L'Equipe* that he felt shocked and "morally betrayed" by Armstrong, and went on to say, "It couldn't be expected, even from a controversial personality like

Lance Armstrong, who has aroused both suspicion and admiration [over the years]."[90]

In response, Chris Carmichael, Armstrong's trainer and friend for more than fifteen years, said, "There are always those who will try to destroy Lance. The attempt by *L'Equipe* being the latest example. Lance has always been one of those who has suffered most from [doping] controls. I have known Lance for the past fifteen years and he has never tested positive for the simple reason that he has never, ever used performance-enhancing drugs."[91]

Dick Pound, the head of the World Anti-Doping Agency, called the charges "serious" if the story was proven to be true. But he also noted that the events took place four months before WADA was formed, and that most likely it was the responsibility of the UCI and USA Cycling to handle the matter. Still, he said that the agency would carefully consider its options in the case. Pound added that athletes tempted to cheat should learn from the story. "It is a lesson for anyone who uses performance-enhancing drugs," the WADA chief told *L'Equipe*, "sooner or later the truth will be known."[92]

Jacques de Ceaurriz, LNDD's director told the French sports daily that the tests were done anonymously because the lab does not have any information about whose samples they are testing. He went on to say, "It was not a doping control. These tests were conducted as part of a scientific research. Our objective was to develop the test and decision criteria. But all this was part of a research program much broader, we seek to construct a mathematical model for detecting EPO. We should also remember that the samples were taken in 1999, one year before the first official use of our detection test for EPO, at the Olympic Games in Sydney. On the Tour de France, our method was applied starting in 2001."[93] De Ceaurriz went on to tell the newspaper that the lab's test was reliable, and that there was no doubt about the validity of the results.

Armstrong, however, did not trust the lab. Speaking on CNN's "Larry King Live," he said, "A guy in a Parisian laboratory opens up your sample, you know, Jean Francois so-and-so, and he tests it—nobody's there to observe, no protocol was followed—and then you get a call from a newspaper that says 'We found you to be positive six times for EPO.' Well, since when did newspapers start governing sports?"[94]

Over the coming months, various officials suggested that Armstrong be sanctioned for doping. But as the cyclist noted, and Jacques de Ceaurriz reiterated, the tests weren't carried out as doping tests. There was one other not so minor problem with respect to prosecuting the seven-time Tour winner for a doping violation. Under the WADA antidoping code, to charge an athlete with a doping offense, there must be a backup sample available for counteranalysis. This requirement exists to protect athletes from false positive results. Should the counteranalysis not confirm the initial results, there is no doping violation to prosecute.

In Armstrong's case, there was no backup sample. The samples tested by LNDD had been the backup samples from tests conducted in 1998 and 1999, which would have (and according to rules in place at the time should have) otherwise been destroyed. There was no more material to test, so the results couldn't be confirmed by another round of lab work. From a legal point of view, no disciplinary action could be taken against the seven-time Tour champion. But many continued to ask: What should be done about Armstrong's alleged positive results?

By early October 2005, the accusations and counteraccusations from various organizations reached such a fever pitch that the UCI commissioned Emile Vrijman, a lawyer who had run the Dutch antidoping agency for ten years, as an independent investigator to look into the case, including the leaks of confidential information such as Armstrong's test results. Over the next eight months, Vrijman, with assistance from Dr. Adriaan van der Veen and Paul Scholten, collected all of the UCI's information related to the case. Vrijman also requested and received information from a number of other sources during the course of their research.

While both Vrijman and Scholten are attorneys, Dr. van der Veen is an expert in the application of the International Standards Organization's ISO 17025/1999 standards to laboratories, with particular expertise in the application of this international standard to antidoping laboratories. At the end of May 2006, Vrijman and his panel released a 130-page report. In the report, he found that the retrospective testing of stored samples for the purposes of determining a doping violation was not specifically included in the World Anti-Doping Code, as written in 2003.[95] Vrijman's report also criticized LNDD and their handling of the testing, as well as noting concerns about the security of information at the lab.

In his conclusions, Vrijman indicated that while the testing of Armstrong's and the other cyclists' urine samples may have been suitable for research purposes, it was clear that the proper antidoping testing protocols and procedures had not been followed. Therefore, the results did not prove any doping violations. The report went further, saying, "Had the LNDD conducted its testing in accordance with the applicable rules and regulations and reported its findings accordingly, any discussion about the alleged use of a prohibited substance by Lance Armstrong would not have taken place. Having concluded thus, the investigator however, would like to stress that ultimately it has been WADA's improper request to the LNDD—i.e. to include 'additional information' in its report—which has triggered the chain of events leading to the publication of said allegations in *L'Equipe* and subsequently this report."[96]

The report also contains numerous criticisms of the UCI, WADA, and LNDD, including that WADA and LNDD "behaved in ways that are completely inconsistent with the rules and regulations of international anti-doping control testing." The report's authors went so far as to say that WADA's and LNDD's behavior may have also been illegal.[97]

When it became public, neither the UCI nor WADA was pleased with the result. Dick Pound, the head of WADA, said, "The Vrijman report is so lacking in professionalism and objectivity that it borders on farcical. Were the matter not so serious and the allegations it contains so irresponsible, we would be inclined to give it the complete lack of attention it deserves."[98]

Lance Armstrong, however, released a statement that said, "Although I am not surprised by the report's findings, I am pleased that they confirm what I have been saying since this witch-hunt began: Dick Pound, WADA, the French laboratory, the French Ministry of Sport, L'Equipe, and the Tour de France organizers (ASO) have been out to discredit and target me without any basis and falsely accused me of taking performance enhancing drugs in 1999. Today's comprehensive report makes it clear that there is no truth to that accusation."[99]

The report did not explain how L'Equipe's reporter Damien Ressiot received information about Armstrong's test results, and from whom he received it. In part, this may have been because both the lab and WADA refused to cooperate with the UCI's independent investigation. Vrijman suggested that a tribunal be formed to look into the matter and determine what, if any, sanctions should be levied against the organizations named in his report.

In the end, only one person connected to the scandal received any sort of reprimand or punishment. Mario Zorzoli, the UCI doctor who apparently gave copies of Armstrong's doping control forms to the French newspaper, was suspended from his duties for one month in the early part of 2006, but was subsequently reinstated. No action, to date, has been taken against any LNDD staff members for violating Armstrong's confidentiality by releasing the test results to L'Equipe's reporter.[100]

GUILLERMO CAÑAS AND THE CASE OF
THE MISTAKEN PRESCRIPTION

In February 2005, Guillermo ("Willy") Cañas, the 12-ranked player in men's professional tennis, tested positive for a diuretic classified on the World Anti-Doping Agency's Prohibited List as a masking agent. He wasn't the first tennis pro to test positive for a banned substance, but his case is among the most unusual: Cañas tested positive after receiving the wrong prescription medication in a medical mix-up.

Cañas was participating at an early-season tournament in Acapulco, Mexico, when the positive test occurred. Several days before, he had gone to see one of the tournament's physicians, and received what he thought was a prescription for medication to treat influenza. Returning to his hotel, he asked an Association of Tennis Professionals (ATP) staff member if she could get the prescription filled for him, and gave her some money to pay for the medication. A short time later, she returned to the hotel with the medicine and gave it to Cañas.

Cañas, who is said to be very careful about nutritional supplements and medications, took one of the pills, and continued to follow the instructions the tournament's physician had given him regarding the use of the drug. But he neglected to examine the label or informational material that came with the pills, assuming that everything was OK because it had been prescribed by a tournament official, and the prescription had been filled for him by an ATP staff member.

That assumption would turn out to be incorrect. Following a match on February 21, 2005, Cañas provided a urine sample for the usual antidoping tests. Accounts vary as to what happened when he gave the sample. For his part, Cañas claims that he informed the person collecting the sample that he was taking medication. In his testimony to the arbitration hearing, Cañas stated that he was told he didn't have to list it on the documents that accompany the sample to the lab where it would be tested. The person collecting the sample, however, would later claim that Cañas never told him about the medication in question.

In May 2005, Cañas received a letter telling him that the urine sample from the tournament in Acapulco had tested positive for hydrochlorothiazide (HCT), a diuretic on WADA's prohibited list because the antidoping agency believes it is used as a masking agent to hide the use of other banned substances. Yet, his sample showed no traces of any other banned substances. As he was entitled to do, the tennis player requested that his B sample be tested to verify the lab's results. Several days later, the B sample results came back confirming the original test results. Cañas was given the option of admitting to a doping infraction and receiving a two-year ban, or challenging the suspension through an arbitration hearing.

He chose to fight the charges. At the initial arbitration hearings, Cañas testified that he had met with one of the tournament's physicians. But neither of the doctors remembered seeing him during the tournament, and no records existed that showed he had visited either doctor. Cañas' defense also argued that although the test results did show the presence of HCT, had Cañas been intent on doping, a diuretic would not have been a good thing to use given the heat in which the tournament was played. Instead of providing the Argentine player with any performance benefit, by drawing liquid out of his system, the medication could actually endanger his health.

Despite the evidence provided by Cañas and his defense team, the arbitration panel felt his story lacked credibility. Although previous ATP antidoping cases made allowances for the inadvertent use of banned substances, professional tennis had recently signed on to the World Anti-Doping Code, which made no such allowances. The code, written by the World Anti-Doping Agency, is built on the concept of strict liability. Under the strict liability doctrine, no matter how a banned substance found its way into an athlete's system, the athlete is responsible for its presence. Only in very limited, exceptional circumstances can the penalties be reduced. And in Cañas' case, the arbitration panel felt that those circumstances had not been met.

So the Argentine tennis pro was handed a two-year suspension and fined an amount that totaled all his tournament prizes between the time he tested positive in February 2005 and a subsequent negative test during the French Open in June 2005. The arbitration panel, using their discretion, did not require Cañas to pay the entire amount all at once. Instead, they set up a payment plan that required him to pay approximately $11,500 each month over a period of twenty-four months.[101]

Cañas decided to appeal the decision against him to the Court of Arbitration for Sport. After looking at the evidence from the first hearing, along with new evidence presented, the CAS came to a different conclusion about Cañas' positive test. First, while the original panel discounted testimony that Cañas had actually seen one of the tournament's physicians, new evidence contradicted some of the statements from the two physicians.

It turns out that a number of athletes had seen the physicians, and that record keeping was not as thorough as the first panel had been led to believe. In a number of cases, athletes had seen one of the physicians, yet no information about the visits was properly recorded. Another player at the Acapulco tournament, Juan Monaco, came forward with an account that contradicted the doctors' contentions that the tournament had supplies of cold medication and other related drugs on hand. Monaco's testimony also bore out the contention that the record keeping was not as meticulous as the doctors described during the initial hearing. In the CAS ruling, the panel noted the fact that a record of Monaco's physician was created long after the player had sought medical assistance. Monaco's story was uncontested by the ATP, according to the CAS's final award.

But the evidence that helped persuade the CAS that Cañas had unintentionally used HCT came from Paulo Sergio Carvallo, the coach of another tennis pro. It turns out that on the same day, and at roughly the same time that Cañas asked an ATP employee to fill his prescription, Carvallo had also requested that an ATP employee have a prescription filled for him for Rofucal, a medication that contains HCT. When the medications were finally delivered to Carvallo and to Cañas, each received the other person's medication. Cañas' story about how he tested positive turned out to be true. He had accidentally been given the wrong medication.[102]

While such a development might in other circumstances lead to a complete dismissal of charges against the Argentine player, the World Anti-Doping Code does not allow such an option. Because of the strict liability doctrine, Cañas was still responsible for the fact that the medication wound up in his system. And as such, he would still be sanctioned for the use of the drug—even though no proof had ever been offered that Cañas tested positive for any other banned substance, which he might have wished to conceal by using a masking agent. Although the panel found that Cañas had "no significant fault or negligence," because the drug had been found in Cañas' urine sample, WADA's rules prevented them from granting the tennis player a complete acquittal.

In the end, Cañas was given a fifteen-month ban, three months longer than the minimum one-year ban. Because of the nature of the infraction, the CAS panel ruled that Cañas should not be fined and reversed the financial judgment against the athlete. The ATP was ordered to return any money that Cañas had already paid as a result of the fine, which amounted to about $40,000 according to the CAS ruling.

Cañas' suspension from tennis ended in September 2006. When he came back to competition, he quickly climbed back through the ranks, and in early 2007 he twice defeated world number one player Roger Federer, of Switzerland. Cañas continues to compete as a professional tennis player. The time away from competition and the events he's been forced to endure have provided him with a new outlook on the game.

"I don't know if it gave me more focus in the way I play," Cañas told *ESPN.com*'s Bonnie DeSimone. "I think the big change I made is that I enjoy a lot to go to the court.

"A lot of people supported me in the bad moment, a lot of people in my country supported me in the bad moment. The only way to say thanks to those people is to go on the court and give my 100 percent. So this, yes, I am focused to do that. It's the only thing I can be sure I'm gonna do."

The story doesn't end with the CAS decision, or with Cañas reclaiming his place in the world of professional tennis. Cañas and his attorney chose to continue fighting the charges, even though the CAS reduced the athlete's suspension and nullified the fine imposed upon him. Because the World Anti-Doping Agency is chartered in Switzerland, Cañas was able to appeal the matter in the Swiss court system.

After hearing Cañas' appeal in March 2007, a Swiss Federal Tribunal did something very unusual. They voided the judgment against Cañas, including the suspension, and ordered the CAS to reconsider the case.[103] In May 2007, the CAS panel revisited the Cañas case. After reviewing the evidence a second time, they upheld their ruling.

Cañas' attorney, Cedric Aguet, said of the ruling, "It's simply not acceptable to suspend someone who was the victim of an accidental positive control for a detrimental substance. Sanctions in doping have to be proportionate to offenses, or it distorts competition."

Aguet continues to fight for his client's rights and has filed an antitrust complaint before the European Commission. In Aguet's complaint he cites wrongdoing by the agencies involved in the Cañas case, including the ATP, WADA, and the CAS. According to Aguet, he is not asking for monetary damages in the case before the European Commission. However, he also doesn't rule out the possibility that another case might be filed to seek damages.

"That is for another lawyer," Aguet said. "I will not be the one to litigate that. My purpose and Willy's purpose is to bring justice to this process."[104]

DIETARY SUPPLEMENTS CAUSE PROBLEMS
FOR PAKISTANI CRICKETERS

To many American eyes, cricket is an almost incomprehensible cousin to baseball. Instead of four bases that players must go around to score a run in baseball, in cricket there are two wickets* that players run between in order to score runs. And while an inning in baseball can be over in a relatively short amount of time, innings in cricket can last for hours or more. Where a baseball game may be over in 2 or 3 hours, a cricket match can go for several days. And while the sport gets little coverage in the United States, cricket is not immune to the occasional doping scandal.

In the autumn of 2006, Pakistan Cricket players Shoaib Akhtar and Mohammed Asif were pulled from competition at the International Cricket Council Champions Trophy in India after testing positive for nandrolone. The Pakistan Cricket Board initially banned the two, who are star fast bowlers† on Pakistan's national cricket team, from competition in November 2006. Akhtar received a two-year ban, while Asif was given a one-year suspension. A controversial decision by an appeals panel just over a month later, however, set the players' bans aside by a 2–1 vote.

According to the panel's written opinion, because the players had not been warned that using dietary supplements could lead to positive drug screenings, the two players could not be held responsible for the traces of the banned steroid found in their systems. Fakhruddin G. Ebrahim, the chairman of the appeals panel, told reporters that under PCB rules, "this appeals committee holds that Shoaib Akhtar and Mohammed Asif cannot be deemed to have committed a doping offense."

As the written verdict stated, "[The] appeals committee by majority of two to one is of the considered view that Shoaib Akhtar and Mohammed Asif have successfully established that they held an honest and reasonable belief that the supplements ingested by them did not contain any prohibited substances."

Nasim Ashraf, the PCB chairman, told reporters that because Asif and Akhtar were tested by the cricket board's out-of-competition testing program, neither the International Cricket Council nor the World Anti-Doping Agency would be able to appeal the decision.

Dick Pound, the head of WADA in 2006, told reporters for the Associated Press that he did not agree with the panel's reasoning that the players should

---

*A wicket consists of three upright poles ("stumps") with two crosspieces ("bails") sitting on top.
†Bowlers are to cricket what pitchers are to baseball.

have been warned, saying "No, it's quite clear that if you are an international athlete, you've got to be aware of the risks. You don't get any points for saying someone forgot to warn me."

Pound also took exception to Ashraf's statement that neither the ICC nor WADA had jurisdiction in the case, and promised that his organization would confer with the ICC to determine what the next steps would be. The panelist who dissented, Danish Zaheer, took the Pakistan Cricket Board to task for the way it had handled the case. In Zaheer's opinion, the staff assigned to conduct the tests were not properly trained, and the original committee that banned the two players possessed only "very basic or no knowledge of these sensitive technicalities involved in the process of such testing."

Zaheer also called on the Pakistan Cricket Board to use WADA's anti-doping regulations, rather than the PCB's own rules. And he suggested that new tests should be conducted following WADA's rules.

The decision was a boost for the Pakistan national cricket team, according to the PCB chairman, who noted that the outcome "will strengthen our team for the World Cup."[105] WADA did appeal the ruling to the Court of Arbitration for Sport. However, because the PCB does not specifically recognize the CAS in their regulations, the CAS declined the appeal.[106]

In their written opinion, the CAS tribunal noted "with considerable regret" that CAS rules "require that a direct reference to the CAS be contained in the statutes or regulations of the body whose decision is being appealed." After two months of sitting out, Akhtar and Asif were able to return to international competition on the Pakistan cricket team.

OPERACIÓN PUERTO

A raid on a Spanish doctor's office in May 2006, reminiscent in some ways of a raid several years earlier at BALCO, set off the European equivalent of the BALCO scandal. Dubbed Operación Puerto (or "Operation Mountain Pass"), the investigation that led to the raid focused on a blood doping ring led by Dr. Eufemiano Fuentes.

During the initial raids, which included searches of several private residences, the Spanish Civil Guard arrested five individuals. Among those collared by the Civil Guard was Dr. Fuentes. Also caught up in the arrests was Manolo Saiz, the directeur sportif (manager) of the Liberty Seguros cycling team. Fuentes at one time had been the team doctor for the Kelme cycling team, with which Saiz was also involved. Fuentes had been suspected of doping athletes in the past, and with the Operación Puerto investigation, Spanish authorities finally seemed to have brought the doctor to justice. According to news reports, Fuentes was accused of doping professional cyclists and then "cleaning" their blood so that their activities would go undetected.[107]

The evidence seized during the initial raids included one thousand doses of various anabolic steroids, approximately one hundred packs of blood or blood products, as well as medical equipment used in performing blood transfusions. Initial reports about the scandal suggested that as many as 200 professional athletes were connected to Dr. Fuentes and his blood-doping work. Some stories suggested that the athletes involved included professional cyclists, soccer players, tennis players, and track and field athletes. In September 2006, former Spanish pro rider Jesus Manzano said in an interview on the France 3 television network that he had seen a number of soccer players at Dr. Fuentes' offices.

"I saw well-known footballers, but I cannot say how many," Manzano told the French television network. He added, "[Fuentes] takes care [of athletes] from all over the world." Among Manzano's comments on French television was his claim that the soccer players he saw were from Spain's top level of soccer, La Liga. And he also confirmed that Marco Pantani (the star Italian cyclist known as "Il Pirata" because of the colorful bandanas he wore) was one of Dr. Fuentes' clients. (Pantani, who was known for his strength in mountainous bicycle races, died of a cocaine overdose in 2004.[108])

Although Manzano's claims appeared to implicate a number of professional soccer players, and other reports suggested that athletes from other sports were among those involved in the scandal, in the time since the story first broke only the names of professional cyclists have been published. Shortly after the investigation became public, the Liberty Seguros team's title sponsor cancelled their contract.

The team carried on under the Astana-Würth banner, with the hopes of being able to ride the 2006 Tour de France. Astana-Würth went so far as to appeal to the Court of Arbitration for Sport just days before the Tour was scheduled to begin. Although the team received a favorable decision from the CAS, Tour organizers insisted that with five of their nine riders unable to start the race due to connections to the scandal, the team had too few riders available to race. With only four riders available to start, Astana-Würth was two riders short of the race's minimum six-man team. Alexander Vinokourov, a member of the Astana-Würth team and a prime contender for the 2006 Tour, was unable to participate despite no connections between the Kazakh rider and Dr. Fuentes. Würth pulled their sponsorship when the team was denied entry in the 2006 edition of the Tour de France and the team became known simply as Astana.[109]

Vinokourov was not the only top rider prevented from racing the 2006 Tour de France. Virtually every top contender was forced to sit out of cycling's premier event. In the days and weeks before the start of the 2006 Tour, race organizers sought to ban every rider who was suspected of working with Dr. Fuentes. Literally hours before the race was set to start, almost every rider favored to win the race was withdrawn. Jan Ullrich and his teammate Oscar Sevilla were suspended by T-Mobile on the eve of the Tour, as were Ivan Basso of Team CSC and Francisco Mancebo of AG2R-Prevoyance. Three weeks later, the T-Mobile team cancelled their contracts with both Ullrich and Sevilla. In addition, T-Mobile directeur sportif Rudy Pevenage was suspended right before the Tour began and let go by the team in early July 2006 due to his connections with Operación Puerto.[110]

As T-Mobile cycling team spokesman Stefan Wagner told *CyclingNews* after the announcement, "As soon as there were suspicions, we asked to see the files. We don't know why we didn't get them until today. The facts in the case contradict Ullrich's claims of innocence so strongly that we had to take this step, in order to follow our goal of a clean sport."

And a T-Mobile official, Christian Frommert, said in a statement about the decision, "Our stance was always unequivocal. If we are presented with evidence, which leads us to doubt the credibility of one or other of our riders, then we act upon it immediately. That is the case now."[111] While it had not been proven at that point that Ullrich and Sevilla had actually doped, nonetheless they were suspended, in part for lying to their team about involvement with Dr. Fuentes.

Several days after the 2006 Tour de France ended, the Spanish courts cleared a number of cyclists of any involvement in the scandal, including all five riders from the Astana team that had been forced to sit out the race. Among those whose names were cleared was a young Spanish cyclist named Alberto Contador, who would go on to win the 2007 Tour.[112]

In early October 2006 the Spanish courts told Spain's cycling federation (RFEC) that they would not be able to use documents from the Operación Puerto investigation in any disciplinary proceedings until after the trials of Dr. Fuentes and the others arrested in connection with the case were complete, and until the court determined exactly what had occurred in the case.[113] Three weeks later, the RFEC announced that they were dropping proceedings against the riders named in the scandal due to lack of evidence. The news came one day after Italy's cycling federation dropped their case against Ivan Basso, one of the prime contenders for the 2006 Tour before the scandal broke.[114]

By November 2006 Spanish newspaper *El Mundo* reported the antidoping lab in Barcelona tested approximately 90 of the 234 bags of blood and blood products seized during the original raids and determined that eight of the bags contained traces of EPO. None of the cyclists connected to Operación Puerto were connected to the samples.[115] The report suggested that Fuentes' program went beyond old-fashioned blood doping and included the use of modern blood-boosting medications.

According to the newspaper's story, several weeks before a major race, the doctor or his assistants would remove blood from an athlete. Shortly before the race, they would then separate the red blood cells from the plasma and reinject the athlete with the red blood cells. If the athlete's hematocrit level got to be too high, they would then reinject some of the stored plasma to bring the hematocrit level down to legal levels.

Pat McQuaid, head of the UCI, was very disappointed in the result. McQuaid told Agence France Press, "The Italians have closed the files on Basso, and he has been cleared to race. The Spanish have also closed files on riders who have been involved. To be fair to the Spanish authorities, they were proactive in trying to carry on the investigation and they contested the judge's decision."

"I am more disappointed with the Italian authorities," McQuaid added, "but I blame very much the Spanish on this. The Spanish police uncovered a doping network whose sole objective was to help get riders out of the sport who were cheating, but despite all the evidence pointing to this it has all been shelved by the Spanish judge. It's a ridiculous situation. Our hands are tied at this point."[116]

And then, in March 2007, the criminal cases being brought against Dr. Fuentes and his associates were dismissed. During the course of the scandal, Spain had enacted some tougher laws against doping in sports, but at the time of the raids, Dr. Fuentes' work did not break Spanish law. Although the authorities were able to demonstrate that blood doping had taken place, but to make the criminal case stick, they needed to show that blood doping had endangered the athletes' lives. Because the prosecutors were unable to do so, the court said, the case had to be closed. However, that didn't mean that the athletes connected to the case were completely off the hook.

If authorities in their home countries could connect the evidence seized during the May 2006 raids with specific riders, those riders could still be in legal jeopardy. One such rider was Jan Ullrich, who had repeatedly denied any connection to the case. In order to prove his innocence, Ullrich voluntarily gave a DNA sample in February 2006.[117] Two months later, when Ullrich's DNA was connected to the DNA in bags of blood products suspected of belonging to him, his denials seemed to be disproved.

Another cyclist connected to the Operación Puerto investigation is German rider Jörg Jaksche. Jaksche, who raced on the Astana-Würth team during 2006, was eventually hired by the Tinkoff Credit Systems cycling team for the 2007 season. A teammate of Tyler Hamilton during the 2007 season, he was suspended by the Tinkoff team at the same time as Hamilton, also because of his links to the ongoing Operación Puerto scandal.

Jaksche became the first rider to admit that he had worked with Dr. Fuentes when he gave an interview to the German magazine *Der Spiegel* at the end of June 2007. In the interview, Jaksche admitted to using performance-enhancing drugs beginning in 1997.

The cyclist told *Der Spiegel*, "I believe it's important for the future of the sport that someone comes out and says, 'OK, this is how it happens here.'"

Jaksche went on to tell the magazine, "It's perverse, but the doping system is just, because everyone dopes. Cycling without doping is only just when really no one is doping any longer."

Jaksche admitted to the magazine that he began working with Dr. Fuentes in 2005, and that his blood was indeed stored under the code name "Bella." (Fuentes used the names of riders' pets as their code name. Bella was Jaksche's beloved black lab.) The German cyclist's introduction to doping, he told *Der Spiegel*, came during the 1997 Tour of Switzerland, when he first used EPO. "That was my crash course. A team assistant injected me with EPO in my room," he said.

Jaksche had some strong words for those who organized and perpetuated doping in cycling, saying, "Of course, no one held my arm for the injection, but team leaders, who got rich off you in the past, who supplied the things, they are now pretending to push for a clean sport."[118] The German cyclist continues to cooperate with various authorities looking into the Operación Puerto scandal.

Another rider admitted to being involved with Dr. Fuentes, after initially denying that he had done anything wrong: Italy's Ivan Basso. At the end of April 2007, Basso abruptly resigned from the Discovery Channel cycling team, with whom he had signed a contract six months before. Up to that time, Basso was the team's big hope for both the Giro d'Italia and the Tour de France. Teammate Levi Leipheimer, who had originally been hired to fill the role of team leader only to be pushed aside when the Italian joined the team, moved back into the team leadership role.

Discovery had taken a lot of flak from the other UCI ProTour teams as well as from the press for hiring Basso after the Italian federation dropped charges against him the previous October. Many expressed concern that Basso was still tainted by the scandal and felt that the team should not have hired him. In July 2007, Basso announced that he was "Birillo" in Dr. Fuentes' records, but claimed that he had not actually doped. Basso said that he had intended to blood dope during the 2006 Tour, which is why he went to Dr. Fuentes, but that he hadn't actually used any of the blood he stored with the Spanish doctor. Basso expressed regret for his actions, but the Italian authorities did not reduce his suspension for the offense. Basso was handed a twenty-one-month ban from competition, taking into account the three months that he was forced to sit out of the 2006 Tour. Between the time he sat out in 2006 and the twenty-one months Basso will be unable to compete, he will spend a total of two years away from racing (which is WADA's required suspension for a first doping offense).

In all, approximately 60 cyclists were connected to the scandal. Although reports that surfaced shortly after the scandal broke suggested that 200 athletes from a number of sports were clients of Dr. Fuentes, no specific athletes from other sports have been linked to the case. In late July 2006,

Spanish prosecutors informed the International Association of Athletic Federations (IAAF), the governing body for track and field, that no track and field athletes were involved in the Operación Puerto scandal.[119]

The sport of soccer was also connected to Dr. Fuentes. An article appearing in the French newspaper *Le Monde* in early December 2006 suggested that several Spanish soccer clubs, including Real Madrid and FC Barcelona, as well as FC Valencia and Sevilla, were working with Dr. Fuentes in some manner. *Le Monde*'s article was based on documents it said were written by Dr. Fuentes, but that were not part of the information gathered by Spain's Civil Guard during the raids that began the scandal in May 2006. The French newspaper described the documents as handwritten doping plans for the soccer clubs FC Barcelona and Real Madrid, among others.[120]

When news of a possible soccer connection broke, WADA vice president Jean-François Lamour told the French sports daily *L'Equipe*, "All the sports possibly concerned by this form of doping should target a part of their anti-doping controls on it." He went on to say, "In June, FIFA has agreed in principle on the adoption and application of the World Anti-Doping Code. Now we wait for it to present its anti-doping program to WADA, and we will insist that it includes blood controls."

In May 2007, Sepp Blatter the head of the International Soccer Federation (FIFA) said that he wanted access to the Operación Puerto documents to determine if any professional soccer players or any clubs had been working with Dr. Fuentes. Blatter told a WADA meeting in Montreal that he would like to see what the Operación Puerto files contained, especially in regard to soccer. "It is of highest interest for the sport and for football," he told those in attendance.[121]

More than eighteen months after the first news of Dr. Fuentes arrest became public, the Operación Puerto scandal continues. Jörg Jaksche was handed a one-year suspension from competition in September 2007. In December, a court in Hamburg, Germany, ordered that Dr. Fuentes testify as part of a lawsuit between German antidoping crusader Werner Franke and Jan Ullrich. Franke is fighting an injunction that Ullrich obtained that bars him from claiming that Ullrich paid Fuentes €35,000 for his medical assistance. Lawyers for Franke were encouraged by the ruling, while Ullrich's attorneys called the ruling a slap in the face for the antidoping crusader. Marcus Hotze, one of the attorneys representing the now-retired cyclist, told reporters, "We have always said that Mr. Franke's claim was false—and that remains so."[122]

German prosecutors continue to investigate Jan Ullrich's involvement with the Spanish doctor, looking into cash withdrawls from his Swiss bank account in 2005 and 2006 that were said to coincide with medication deliveries to Ullrich by Dr. Fuentes. Prosecutors in Bonn, Germany, also noted in September 2007 that Ullrich had transferred €25,000 to Fuentes in 2004. Ullrich still claims that he had no contact with Dr. Fuentes, but at least one media outlet claims that documents exist which show that Ullrich and Rudy Pevenage traveled to Madrid on several occasions to meet with Dr. Fuentes.[123]

At the UCI World Championship road race in Stuttgart, Germany, race organizers tried to ban Alejandro Valverde, a Spanish cyclist, due to his connections to the Operación Puerto case. Organizers also tried to ban Paolo Bettini, the reigning road race champion, because he refused to sign the UCI's antidoping pledge, which includes a requirement that riders caught doping would have to forfeit one year's salary. Bettini objected to that requirement and signed a modified pledge where he had struck out the part with which he disagreed. The UCI, however, insisted that he agree to the entire unmodified pledge. Just days before the race occurred, the Court of Arbitration for Sport found in Bettini's favor. In a separate case, they found that Valverde should also be allowed to race. When the race was over, Bettini—despite the pressure and distraction of the fight to be allowed to race—crossed the finish line first.[124]

TRUTH REALLY IS STRANGER THAN FICTION—JUST ASK JEFF ADAMS

Perhaps the oddest "doping" case to occur since the year 2000 is the one involving Jeff Adams, a Canadian wheelchair athlete who has been fighting a doping charge since 2006. Adams, a wheelchair athlete who has raced in events ranging from short 200-meter sprints to full-length marathons, allegedly tested positive for a minute amount of cocaine in his system. To date, he continues to fight the suspension that Canadian athletic authorities have imposed on him for doing so.

What makes this tale so strange is not that there was cocaine in his system at the time he was tested. There wasn't. What makes Adams' story so strange is how the miniscule traces (less than three billionths of a gram) of a cocaine metabolite came to show up in a urine test following the 2006 Canadian wheelchair marathon championships. But first, the backstory. A week before the wheelchair marathon race in Ottawa, Ontario, where he reportedly tested positive for cocaine use, Adams spent part of an evening at Vatikan, a Toronto goth bar.

As Adams recounts on his Web site, "I was in a bar, sitting next to a woman who was on cocaine—I had been talking to her, and at some point, I stopped being interested in doing that. I told her that I was really tired, and didn't want to talk to her any more. She got pretty upset about that, and in her head, I think she thought that she would be helping me by giving me cocaine (I would no longer be tired). In the drug culture, people share cocaine all the time, and taking cocaine orally is quite common in public (I've learned), because all that needs to happen is for the substance to get to a mucous membrane, and taking it orally is a much less obvious way to do it. She turned to me, and put her hands up near my face—I had no idea what she was going to do, and she had been quite "touchy feely" up to that point, so I really didn't see it coming. She put her fingers in my mouth, and that's how it happened."[125]

Normally this wouldn't have been a problem. Cocaine is a substance that's banned for use in competition, but it is not banned (as far as the antidoping agencies are concerned) when used out of competition. By the time the meet occurred, the cocaine would have long ago cleared his system. Still, Adams immediately washed his mouth out, to try and minimize any possible problems.

Adams told reporters in June 2007, "My concern in all of this was, 'Get home, take care of myself, figure out whether I am in any kind of violation.' And that's what I did."

After he completed his race, Adams was asked to produce a urine sample for drug testing. He didn't think much of it. But when he went to the doping control area, the testers didn't have any clean catheters for him to use. Adams had to use a catheter he had with him. Unfortunately, it was the same catheter he used the night he visited the Vatikan club in Toronto. As it turned out, some residue in the catheter contained a minute amount of a single cocaine metabolite.

So when the test results came back, a miniscule quantity of cocaine (about three billionths of a gram) was detected and Adams was hit with a doping charge. Like all banned substances that aren't naturally produced in the human body, the rule for cocaine is one of strict liability—if it's in you, you're guilty, no matter how small the amount that's found.

The positive result meant the Canadian was staring at a two-year automatic suspension from competition, along with the loss of a $1,500 per month government subsidy. "If I had an inkling that catheter could have been contaminated, I would not have used it," Adams said in June 2007.[126]

Adams fought the charges, claiming that the drug testers should have provided him with a clean catheter and that they should also have warned him about the dangers of using a contaminated catheter prior to giving his sample. His attorney, Tim Danson, told a sports reporter for the Canadian Broadcasting Corporation, "An able-bodied athlete would never be confronted with this problem."[127]

Richard McLaren, the Canadian arbitrator who heard the antidoping case against Adams, was unmoved by his arguments. In his ruling, even though McLaren said that Adams was unwavering in his testimony during cross-examination, and even though two witnesses confirmed his story, he found that Adams' story, "strained credulity." The arbitrator also noted that Adams had used his own catheters throughout his career and that he neither expressed any concerns nor asked for a clean catheter when he was tested in Ottawa following the wheelchair marathon race.

Adams testified that due to the cost of replacing his catheters, he would use them more than once, and that he did not always thoroughly clean them after use. During the hearing, his defense had scientific experts testify that the trace amounts of the cocaine metabolite found could indeed have come from contamination in Adams' catheter. McLaren, however, concluded that on the balance of probabilities (the standard used in antidoping cases), the evidence presented in Adams' favor did not prove that contamination of his catheter led to the doping offense. In finding Adams guilty of a doping charge, McLaren ruled that the Canadian athlete would be barred from competition for a period of two years, which will end in August 2008, about one month before the Beijing Olympics.[128]

Speaking to the press after McLaren's ruling against him was announced, Jeff Adams said, "There was no cheating. There was no performance enhancing. But I'm being sanctioned in the same way as a cheater. The substance was involuntarily consumed.... It's too late for me. My career is over. The work I've done up until now is over. It's been destroyed."[129]

On his Web site, Adams says of the ruling, "If I was guilty, I would cop to it. I'm not guilty of anything except using a contaminated piece of equipment.

"If people think that based on this, that the punishment fits the crime, please tell me. If you don't, please help me clear this up."

Adams is appealing the decision to the Court of Arbitration for Sport. His case will be heard during the early part of 2008. He is also pursuing complaints filed with the Ontario and Canadian federal human rights commissions, citing violations of the Canadian Charter of Rights and Freedoms.[130]

THE ROAD TO MORZINE—AND BEYOND

When the 2006 Tour de France began, the riders favored to win the first Tour of the post-Lance Armstrong era were absent from the starting line, owing to their alleged connections with Operación Puerto. As the first stages rolled by, no clear favorite emerged. No rider dominated the peloton the way Lance Armstrong had done for the last seven editions of the biggest event in professional cycling. As the three-week stage race unfolded, Floyd Landis, the American team leader of the Swiss Phonak Hearing Systems professional cycling squad, found himself wearing the yellow jersey at the end of the 11th of 20 stages. It wasn't something he was surprised by. Landis believed that he had the capability to win the Tour, and he was determined to do so.

Landis, however, did not want to defend the yellow leader's jersey the entire rest of the race, so he and his team decided that the better strategy would be to allow another rider from a different team to take possession of the yellow jersey in order to give Landis and his team a break. On Stage 13, a breakaway group including Jens Voight and Oscar Pereiro gained some time on the peloton. The Phonak team didn't initiate a chase to reel the escapees back into the main pack—in fact they were actively trying to give the yellow jersey away. Since none of the riders in the breakaway were in a position to win the Tour, no other teams took chase, either. As the race wore on, the breakaway group kept gaining time on the main pack. Toward the end, the Rabobank team tried to mount a chase, in order to keep Landis in the yellow jersey. Landis responded with a bit of trash talk, telling Michael Boogerd, one of Rabobank's riders, that if they kept working he would make their lives miserable—and that Landis would ensure that Denis Menchov, Rabobank's team leader, would not win the Tour de France, either.

"I'll attack every single day to make sure of it. I don't care. I'll make your lives hell," Landis told Boogerd. A short time later, Rabobank stopped their efforts to reel in the breakaway.[131]

At the end of the 13th stage, the lead group finished more than 29 minutes ahead of the main pack. This vaulted Pereiro, a Spanish rider for the Caisse D'Espargne cycling team (who had been Landis' teammate a year before), not only back into contention but also into the yellow jersey. Pereiro had never finished higher than 10th overall in the Tour, and before the breakaway, he'd lost a large amount of time to the race leaders, dropping to 47th in the overall standings. Giving the yellow jersey away was a risky move on Landis' part, but he and his team were confident that they could reclaim it before the race concluded in Paris.

Pereiro held onto the leader's jersey for several days before Landis reclaimed the lead at the end of Stage 15. The following day, on Stage 16, Floyd Landis suffered something that every racing cyclist fears. He bonked. On the last major climb, try as he might, he could not hold the pace of the other cyclists around him. Landis slowly fell back, other riders passing him as he struggled to reach the finish. In the course of the last 10 kilometers of the race, Landis lost 8 minutes to the other riders in contention and fell from being the leader to eleventh place in the overall standings.

Watching the end of Stage 16, many knowledgeable cycling fans and commentators wrote off Landis' chances of winning the grueling race. As Landis recounts in his book, *Positively False*, he decided to go out for a couple of beers and a shot or two of Jack Daniels to drown his frustrations at losing the yellow jersey and finishing 10 minutes behind the stage winner. The next day, on the seventeenth stage of the 2006 Tour de France, something totally unexpected—at least by anyone not on the Phonak squad—occurred. A refreshed and rehydrated Landis launched a daring breakaway in the early kilometers of the race, attacking hard up the first major climb. Another breakaway group had already gone off the front before he and his team started working the peloton over. In short order, Landis caught up with them. After trying to encourage the riders to work with him, he finally rode off on his own, leading the race the rest of the way. At times, he was almost 10 minutes ahead of the main pack.

Unlike the day before, when Landis was unable to get enough to drink, on the road to Morzine the Phonak support car made sure that their leader had plenty of water—not only to drink but to douse himself with in order to keep cool during the heat of the day. Over the next several hours, the support car handed Landis more than 60 bottles of water. Some he drank. But most he poured over his head to keeping his body's core temperature down.

Amazingly, the other main contenders never took Landis' solo breakaway seriously. Instead, they thought he'd burn out and bonk on the final climb of the day, just like the day before. When the other teams finally mounted a serious chase on the final climb of the day, it was too late. Landis had enough of a lead that his rivals were unable to catch him. He roared into the finish line, pumped his fist in the air to celebrate the moment, and moved back into third overall in the standings. The effort set Landis up to reclaim the overall lead two days later, during the Tour's penultimate stage, which was a time trial. Because Landis is a stronger time-trialist than Pereiro, he reclaimed the yellow jersey just in time for the largely ceremonial final ride into Paris, which ends with the riders doing laps of the Champs-Élysées. Landis' heroic effort on Stage 17 seemed to be the stuff of legend. Certainly, no other rider has pulled off quite so dramatic a comeback during the past twenty-five years.

Sadly, Landis had less than 48 hours to savor the feeling of being the Tour champion. The Tuesday morning following the Tour's finish, he received word that there was a problem with one of the urine samples he'd given during the Tour—the one after his epic win on Stage 17, just days before claiming the overall crown. Rumors were already swirling around that there had been a positive drug test during the Tour. This was not the kind of publicity Tour organizers or the UCI wanted—especially in light of the Operación Puerto scandal and all the forced withdrawals, including the main contenders, in the days before the epic race began.

UCI president Pat McQuaid, when asked by reporters about the rumors that a rider had tested positive, answered by saying that "it is a worst-case scenario." Though he didn't mention Landis by name, the implication was clear: The Tour victor had doped. At least, that was the impression, based on information leaked from France's antidoping laboratory and the comments made by the UCI chief.

On the Thursday following the Tour, the Phonak cycling team confirmed that Landis was the rider who had tested positive for synthetic testosterone after winning the Stage 17, in Morzine, one week earlier. For testosterone, which is a naturally occurring hormone, the World Anti-Doping Agency specifies a screening test that measures the ratio of testosterone (T) in an athlete's system to another hormone, epitestosterone (E). As long as the T/E ratio is 4:1 or less, no further testing is done.

When the ratio exceeds WADA's threshold, however, a more sophisti-cated test called the carbon isotope ratio (CIR, also known as IRMS for isotope ratio mass spectrometry) is performed. The idea behind this test is to determine whether any synthetic testosterone is present in an athlete's system. According to rumors circulating at the time, Landis' T/E ratio was 11:1, and the excessive ratio prompted the CIR test. Based on the results of the additional testing, LNDD, France's antidoping laboratory, reported an "adverse analytical finding" for Landis' initial sample (the so-called A sample) from Stage 17.

Landis was immediately suspended from racing pending the results of a second (known as the B sample) analysis. By now, a media firestorm was in full progress. Landis, instead of being feted for his accomplishments, was tried and convicted by many of the mainstream media, long before either he or anyone else knew exactly what the results showed or how the lab in question had arrived at their conclusions.

At a press conference the following day, Landis was clearly nervous and not totally prepared for the onslaught that was about to come. He read a statement prepared by his Spanish attorneys—but it was written in Spanish. Landis had started to translate the statement into English but he had not finished the translation completely before the press conference began. When he began to read the portion he had not yet translated, some of the sentences came out a bit awkward and stilted. Over the coming days, answers he gave to various journalists' questions were reported as his latest excuses for how he tested positive.

As Landis commented in early August 2006, "I've come out in the press and tried to explain these test results, but I think that was a mistake. I was forced into this situation because of leaks from the UCI. All of these reasons that have come up, some from me, some from other people, we need to forget about them and let the experts figure out what's going on. The whisky idea was not mine and the dehydration was a theory from the lawyers I hired in Spain to represent me at the opening of the B sample. But I did not authorize them to say something like that so I'm disappointed with that."[132]

The analysis of Landis' B sample began on Thursday, August 3, 2006. Two days later, the results of the B sample analysis were announced. Although many fans had hoped the results would be negative, according to media reports, the analysis confirmed LNDD's initial findings. Phonak, being a UCI ProTour team, was obligated under the UCI's code of ethics to fire the American cyclist. And so they did, in an announcement that came so early that Landis was still asleep at the time.

The announcement of the confirmation gave no specifics about the results, except to say that the initial finding was confirmed. Landis and the defense team he assembled would not see the actual lab documentation until weeks afterward. Only then would they begin to get the full picture of the lab's findings and the case against him. Despite the lab's finding, Landis continued to maintain his innocence, and was determined to clear his name.

In early September 2006, the USADA referred the case to their "Anti-Doping Review Board," in order to determine what course of action should be taken. Landis' lawyer, Howard Jacobs, submitted a request that the case be dismissed due to problems with the lab's work. Among some of the problems with the lab's results were wide variations in the T/E screening test results. While all of the reported results exceeded WADA's 4:1 threshold, most of the T/E screening values were approximately 5:1.[‡] Only one of the four results showed the rumored 11:1 ratio. In addition, Landis' testosterone concentration, in real terms, was a low-normal reading. His epitestosterone results, however, were significantly below normal for Stage 17. Other problems included uncertainty over whose results were being reported.

Handwritten notations in the lab's documentation showed a number not assigned to Landis, but only slightly different from Landis' sample number. Later on it would emerge that the number, initially thought to be a simple mix-up, actually belonged to another rider whose samples from a different stage were also analyzed during the same period as Landis' sample from Stage 17.

Despite Jacobs' request, the review board decided that there was a case to be made that the cyclist had doped, and informed him that USADA would begin proceedings against him. In sending Landis their decision, the fax announcing the board's ruling was dated September 15, 2006—three days before the panel was actually supposed to meet and discuss the case. Whether the date on the faxed memorandum was a typographic error or something else is unknown.

Determined to clear his name, Landis chose something no other athlete had done in USADA proceedings. He exercised his right to an open hearing so that the media and any interested observers could see for themselves how each side presented its case. Maintaining his innocence, Landis set about showing that he had nothing to hide. In part, he did so by mounting what became known as the "Wiki Defense," posting all of the lab documentation and other information on the Internet so that anyone who was interested could take a look. Before posting the full documentation, Landis forwarded some of the lab documentation package to the blog Trust But Verify (http://trustbut.blogspot.com). TBV, as regular readers know it, compiles a daily list of news related to the Landis case, as well as occasional articles written by a number of contributors exploring various aspects of the case.

Before Landis' lab documentation became public, Dr. Arnie Baker, a physician who is also an elite cyclist, coach, and author of numerous books

---

[‡]Prior to 2005, WADA's T/E threshold ratio was 6:1. Any value below 6:1 would not have triggered additional testing or an adverse analytical finding. Had that threshold still been in effect, Landis' case would most likely never have occurred.

and articles about cycling, offered to look over the material. In addition to his knowledge of cycling and coaching, Baker has worked in medical quality assurance, reviewing medical records to ensure that the information is properly documented to conform to various legal, accreditation, and regulatory requirements. Baker had also been Landis' first coach when he switched from mountain biking to road racing in the late 1990s.

What Baker found when he looked at Landis' lab results appalled him. Data that should have been crossed out for corrections and initialed by the person making the changes was covered in whiteout, a violation of international lab standards. The data for the B sample results showed, by WADA's own criteria, evidence of contamination that should have stopped any further analysis. And due to inconsistencies in the record keeping, it was unclear whether some of the results reported belonged to Landis, or to someone else.

Baker started going through the documents with a fine-toothed comb, recording his observations in a PowerPoint presentation, and making notations about the many issues he uncovered. On one page of the laboratory's documentation, Baker found more than 15 errors in the documentation.

Unlike a standard court case, where the person on trial is presumed innocent until proven otherwise, in antidoping cases the accused is presumed guilty. Landis, like any other accused athlete, had to prove his innocence in order to be cleared of the charges. And unlike a standard court case, a number of avenues of defense are off limits. For example, Landis could not argue that the science behind the testing was faulty. According to WADA rules, the science of the doping tests is deemed to be valid. The only real avenue available to an accused athlete is to demonstrate that the lab work was performed incorrectly, or that the data was interpreted incorrectly. To do that, the defense team requires access to documents such as standard operating procedures, maintenance records, and so forth.

In October 2006, shortly after Landis posted information about his case on the Internet, USADA refused to provide Landis' attorneys with various documents they needed in order to prepare his defense, citing a WADA rule that states that labs aren't required to turn over any documentation beyond what was in the lab documentation package. WADA, however, doesn't specify exactly what is to be provided in the laboratory documentation package. Which means the amount of information an accused athlete receives depends on what documentation a particular lab sees fit to include. Without access to potentially exculpatory evidence, the athlete is trapped in a Catch-22 situation. The only way to prove one's innocence is to show errors on the part of the lab. But the athlete is denied access to the documentation that they need to show that such errors occurred. Because of Landis' openness about his case, the particulars of his situation played out in public view.

In November 2006, an unidentified person leaked various documents from LNDD to the press. The documents showed that the lab has a history

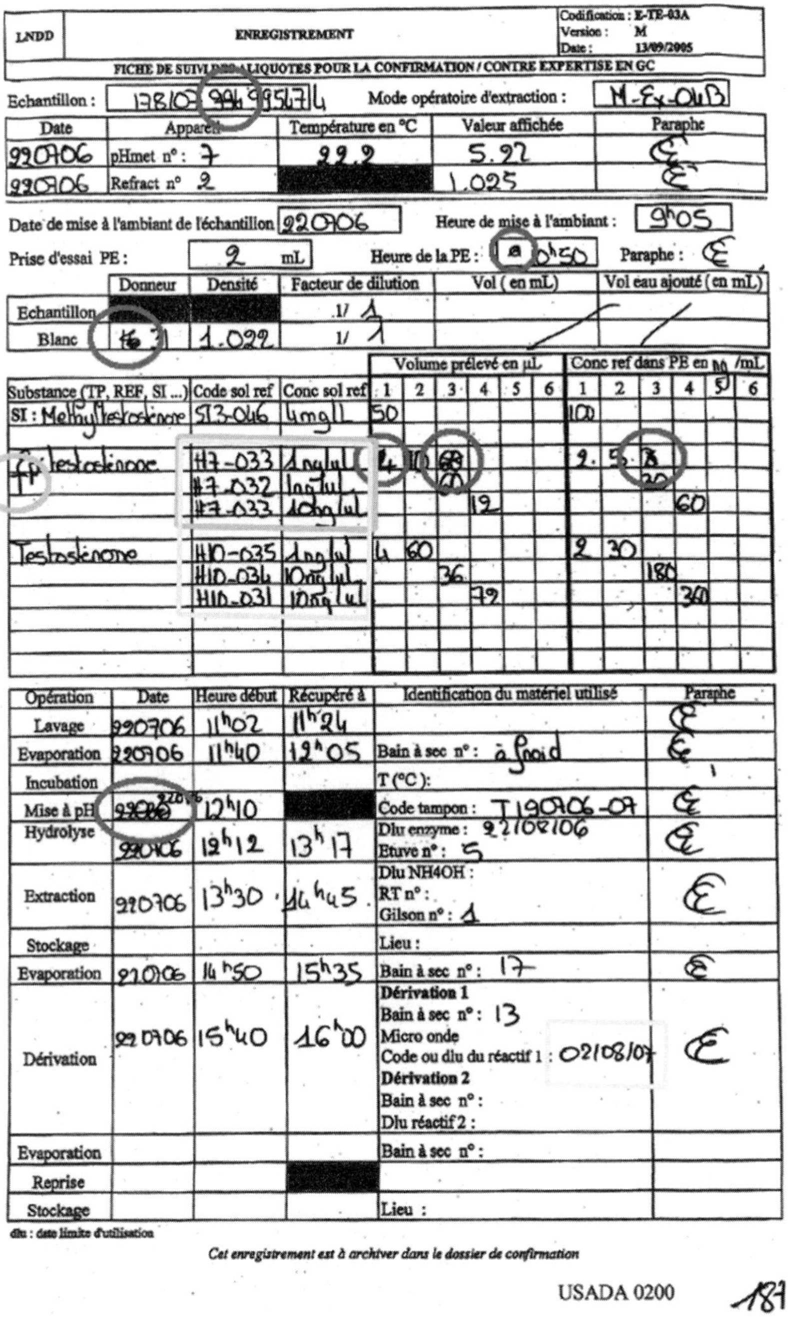

Figure 6.1 During his analysis of the laboratory documentation package that France's anti-doping lab LNDD provided to back up their adverse analytical findings in the Floyd Landis case, Dr. Arnie Baker found numerous errors. On this page there are at least 15 errors, including cross-outs and evidence that various reference solutions were not the proper concentration for the procedures being performed. (Graphic courtesy of Arnie Baker, MD. From *The Wiki Defense*, by Arnie Baker and the Wiki Defense Team, San Diego, CA: Argo Publishing, 2007, p. 53.)

of errors that were later corrected—errors that may have led to athletes being incorrectly punished for doping offenses. None of the cases in the documents leaked to the press had been as prominently covered as Landis' case. Lab officials claimed that a member of the Landis defense team hacked into LNDD's computer network, but no one has ever been identified as the source of the leak.

That same month, Landis left a comment on the Daily Peloton Forum about Greg LeMond, expressing his frustration with LeMond's continuing comments about his case. A database crash lost the full discussion thread, including Landis' comment, but part of his remarks happened to be quoted at Trust But Verify. The part that remained was as follows, "I did, as I used to do for some people, call GL privately to discuss some comments that he made about me and my situation. I used to believe that a private call was the best way to deal with public slander. I have subsequently learned that the phone call will become public and the contents thereof misconstrued into whatever fits the agenda. What Greg actualy [sic] divulged to me is what he does not want to talk about. I did not call for advice, I called to give him a chance to plead his case as to why he was speaking when he had never spoken to me nor met me in the past and in no way could be portrayed as knowing me personally.

"Unfortunately, the facts that he divulged to me in the hour which he spoke and gave no opportunity for me to do the same, would damage his character severely and I would rather not do what has been done to me. However, if he ever opens his mouth again and the word Floyd comes out, I will tell you all some things that you will wish you didn't know and unfortunately I will have entered the race to the bottom which is now in progress."[133] Unfortunately for Landis, those comments would come back to haunt him in May 2007.

During the months that followed, a lot of discussions and disagreements occurred between USADA and Landis' defense team. One issue that delayed the arbitration hearings was the selection of the three arbitrators. While both sides picked their arbitrator, the two who were picked could not agree on the third member, the arbitrator who would serve as the panel's chairman. The chairman of the panel is supposed to be a neutral party, while each side appoints an arbitrator that they hope will be an advocate for their point of view when deciding the outcome of the case.

The Landis defense team's time was also occupied by a parallel case occurring in France. While WADA's regulations provide for an athlete being prosecuted by the federation governing his or her sport in the athlete's home country, French law allowed the AFLD, France's antidoping agency, to also prosecute a doping case against Landis. In early 2007, the AFLD announced that they would hold hearings in the case. The hearings were originally scheduled for the end of January, but Maurice Suh, an attorney who joined the Landis defense effort in December 2006, was able to have the hearing postponed for two weeks. In the meantime, a deal was worked out with the AFLD, with Landis promising not to race in France during the 2007 season in exchange for a postponement of the French case until after the USADA case had been decided. The AFLD, however, reserved the right to restart the case if USADA had not taken action by the end of June.

The AFLD's move may have helped speed up the scheduling of Landis' case. Shortly after the brouhaha over the French proceedings occurred, Landis' arbitration hearings were scheduled for a period of ten days in May at the Pepperdine University School of Law in Malibu, California.

All the while, Landis' legal expenses continued to escalate. In early January 2007, the Floyd Fairness Fund (FFF) was established to help Landis raise money to carry on the effort to clear his name. In addition to raising money through donations taken in via the FFF's Web site and donations mailed in to the organization, the Floyd Fairness Fund arranged a series of barnstorming fund-raising events around the country where Landis, his spokesman Michael Henson, Dr. Arnie Baker, and others working on his case would speak. And with the help of *Bicycling Magazine* editor Loren Mooney, Landis wrote the book, *Positively False: The Real Story of How I Won the Tour de France*, which was released shortly before the 2007 edition of the Tour began.

During the pre-hearing skirmishes between USADA and the Landis defense, the antidoping agency announced that they were going to do some retrospective testing on other samples that the cyclist had provided during the Tour and that had originally turned out negative. Landis' attorneys fought back, and the Landis defense team released the information to the press.

WADA rules say that the athlete is only allowed to contest the actual positive test result. Had the Landis defense team wanted to do studies on other samples to show that he was innocent of the antidoping charges, the arbitrators deciding his case would not have to consider that evidence in making their decision. USADA, however, was looking for results that might be useful in bolstering their case, in order to counter any doubts the Landis defense team might be able to raise about the Stage 17 test. If that were the case, and USADA didn't have any backup arguments, Landis would be exonerated. In filing motions with the panel, USADA mentioned that any positive test results found during the retrospective testing would be used as evidence against the Tour de France winner.

In April 2007 LNDD performed the additional tests, with representatives of both USADA and the Landis defense team present. In addition, the panel appointed Dr. Francesco Botré, the head of the WADA-accredited Rome antidoping laboratory, as a scientific advisor to be present during the testing. But the science advisor appointed by the arbitration panel was not exactly a neutral party. As an employee of another WADA-accredited antidoping laboratory, he was bound by WADA's "good neighbor policy," which states that no member of a WADA-accredited lab is allowed to speak critically of the work performed at another lab.[134]

Botré was not always present during the testing, and Landis' representatives were barred from the testing facility during the final day of testing. The USADA representatives had left France before the testing was completed. LNDD officials, citing an alleged agreement that both sides needed to be present, locked Landis' representatives out as lab technicians finished their work unobserved. But the time spent observing the additional testing gave Landis' experts a second chance to take a close look at how the lab technicians performed their work.

Some of the results surprised them. Dr. Simon Davis, who at one time was responsible for installing and configuring the very same machinery that was in use at LNDD, found that the lab technicians did not fully understand how to operate their instruments. In one case, a green light on the equipment, which the lab technicians thought meant that everything was running correctly, indicated something entirely different. The indicator light actually meant that the machinery wasn't operating at the proper pressure.

In another instance, a different (newer) machine still had magnets used in the shipping process attached. The magnets should have been removed prior to use, and there was a possibility that their presence could adversely affect results. Many other problems came to light, including the fact that raw data from Landis' initial test results had been removed from one of the lab's computer hard drives just days before the April 2007 tests began.

Dr. Davis also found that the lab technicians had not been fully trained on the instruments. The lab didn't have a user's manual for the equipment to explain how to use the machinery or the software that was used for processing the raw data. And the software in use was written for—and being used on—a computer operating system that is no longer in use. Despite international standards that require software upgrades to be installed, LNDD had not done so over the years. At one point during the April testing, Dr. Davis had to instruct the lab technicians on how to load data into their own system for reprocessing.

As has become a pattern over the years, shortly after the April tests were completed, details about the results were leaked to the French sports daily *L'Equipe*. Among the details released was the allegation that some of the other samples tested from the 2006 Tour had shown traces of synthetic testosterone. But with the *L'Equipe* story blowing up in the media, the Landis defense team gained one unexpected benefit from the testing. With a second chance to observe how LNDD's technicians performed their work, Landis' defense team gained insights that they were able to put into use at the arbitration hearings less than a month later.

In May 2007, the Landis hearings got off to a slow start, with USADA presenting their case and the Landis team cross-examining the witnesses, including two of the lab technicians who worked on the cyclist's samples from Stage 17 and during the April tests. Although the Landis defense team had wanted to depose the lab technicians in Paris before the hearings, USADA opposed the move and the arbitration panel agreed with the antidoping agency. Cross-examining the technicians was a slow, tedious experience for Landis' attorneys. During their testimony, the two technicians painted a disturbing picture of how they were trained to perform their jobs. Neither one had been put through a formal training program to learn how to operate the machinery. Instead, they were taught how to use the equipment by coworkers, who in turn had been taught by previous coworkers. They confirmed that no manuals existed for the equipment or the software to process the data.

One of the technicians, when asked to explain why she had performed part of the data analysis a certain way answered that she was "using her scientific judgment." She was unable to offer any scientific reason, however, for why she did things the way she did. And prior to performing her part in the initial testing of Landis' samples, this same technician had only approximately six months of experience, which included her "training."

One of the more disturbing admissions to come from the technicians, though, was that as they had reprocessed Landis' original data, they overwrote the raw data files with the reprocessed data. In other words, at least some of the original data on which the adverse finding against Landis had been based had vanished into the ether. Other than taking the technician's word, there was no way for another expert to look at the original data and determine whether or not LNDD's analysis and results were, in fact, correct.

The cross-examination of the two LNDD technicians cost Landis' defense team crucial time, in a proceeding where each side has a limited amount of hours to make their case. While the Landis team appeared to score points during their cross-examinations, the early days of the hearings were nothing out of the ordinary (except, perhaps, to those following the case closely). But that changed as soon as Greg LeMond came to testify.

With LeMond's testimony came a startling revelation. The night before he testified, Will Geoghegan, Landis' close friend and business manager, placed a call to LeMond. During the call, Geoghegan made reference to something that the three-time Tour winner had told Landis the previous autumn: that he had been abused as a child. LeMond took the call to be a threat and reported the matter to the police. The next day, in the short time it took for LeMond to recount the events of the night before, the proceedings went from relatively dull, straightforward legal work to sensational news.

In an instant, a lot of hard work making Landis' case to the public that he was innocent of the charges against him was overshadowed and destroyed by LeMond's sensational revelations. Geoghegan was fired after the hearings took a short recess, and LeMond refused to answer questions from Landis' attorney Howard Jacobs when the hearings resumed.

USADA called another witness, Joe Papp, a cyclist who had also tested positive for testosterone use in 2006, to counter claims that the use of testosterone would not be of benefit to a cyclist. While not as sensational as

LeMond's testimony, USADA's strategy appeared to be to present evidence that could be used to establish a nonanalytical positive, in the case that the scientific evidence against Landis was undermined. After LeMond and Papp's testimony, the hearings returned to the scientific issues, revolving around whether or not the tests were conducted properly, and whether or not the lab properly interpreted the data.

Once the hearings adjourned, the waiting game began. Almost four months to the day after the hearings were completed, the panel finally issued their ruling. By a two to one vote, the panel found Landis guilty of using synthetic testosterone. In their ruling, the majority—in an interesting feat of legal logic—noted that the original screening test results were unreliable, but declared that the more sophisticated tests conclusively proved that Landis had doped. Arbitrator Chris Campbell, who voted against the ruling, issued a passionate dissent.

In the conclusion of his dissent, Campbell states, "As athletes have strict liability rules, the laboratories should be held strictly liable for their failure to abide by the rules and sound scientific practice.

"Because everyone assumes an athlete who is alleged to have tested positive is guilty, it is not fashionable to argue that laboratories should comply with strict rules. However, if you are going to hold athletes strictly liable with virtually no possibility of overcoming a reported alleged positive test even in the face of substantial and numerous laboratory errors, fairness and human decency dictates that strict rules be applied to laboratories as well. To do otherwise does not 'safeguard the interest of athletes.'

"WADA should be writing rules that mandate the highest scientific standards rather than writing rules for a race to the bottom of scientific reliability so convictions can be easily obtained, as this case demonstrates. Given the plethora of laboratory errors in this case, there was certainly no reliable scientific evidence introduced to find that Mr. Landis committed a doping offence."[135]

Several weeks later, Oscar Pereiro was awarded the yellow jersey during a brief ceremony in Madrid, Spain, as the newly crowned victor of the 2006 Tour de France. The day before Pereiro's coronation, Landis' lawyers filed a notice with the Court of Arbitration for Sport that they were going to appeal the case.

Meanwhile, in the autumn of 2007, the French antidoping agency AFLD reopened their case against the American cyclist. In mid-December, they announced their verdict: Landis was guilty of a doping violation under French rules. They banned him from competing in all athletic events (not just professional cycling) on French soil until January 29, 2009, the same day that USADA's sanction expires. The move by the AFLD ostensibly closed a legal loophole that might have otherwise allowed the 2006 Tour winner to compete in France during 2008 at non-UCI sanctioned events, possibly including the 2008 Tour de France. Such a move, however, ignores the fact that Landis would still need to be hired by a professional cycling team. Landis is unlikely to be employed by any team until the CAS case is decided. Only if the CAS exonerates Landis will he be able to compete during the 2008 season, and as of this writing, the outcome of his appeal is yet to be determined.

2007: DOPING SCANDALS FAST AND FURIOUS

During the course of 2007, doping scandals seemed to rock the sports world at an almost rapid-fire rate. As mentioned in the previous section, the Landis case provided a number of headlines and controversy throughout the year. Barry Bonds and Marion Jones also made headlines, as noted earlier in this chapter. But other stories abounded.

In Europe, both Operación Puerto and the Italian "Oil for Drugs" scandal continued to make headlines. In the latter case, in December 2007, Danilo Di Luca became the first athlete connected to the Oil for Drugs scandal to be sanctioned when he received a three-month suspension based on his involvement with Dr. Carlo Santuccione, the so-called Italian version of Dr. Eufemiano Fuentes. Santuccione has been banned by CONI, the Italian Olympic Committee, from working with any amateur or professional athletes for the rest of his life.[136]

During the early part of 2007, the National Football League, with the consent of the players' association, adopted tougher antidoping measures that included more frequent testing for steroids, along with adding EPO to their list of banned substances. While the changes are an improvement, a couple of prominent doping experts don't think the changes were enough. Dr. Gary Wadler, a physician and expert on doping who is also a member of WADA, told the *Baltimore Sun*, "I think there are some positives, but I don't think it goes far enough." He added that he wasn't sure why no provisions were made for blood testing or the storage of samples for use in developing future tests for such drugs as human growth hormone.

Dr. Charles Yesalis, of Penn State University, told the Baltimore paper that he didn't think much would change until an outside agency takes over the NFL's drug-testing program. "We only know about the positive tests we're allowed to know about, so it's the fox guarding the henhouse. Until that changes, I don't pay a whole lot of attention to the other moves they make."

The new provisions include using random carbon isotope testing to determine whether players are using steroids, investing $500,000 to help develop tests for human growth hormone and requiring players who test positive for banned substances to forfeit a prorated amount of the signing bonus for their current contracts. The NFL now bans players for four games for a first offense, and one year for a second offense. These penalties are shorter than the penalties in other major U.S. sports. Yesalis, however, was dismissive about the amount of money being spent on research. "It's unbelievably inadequate for the job," Yesalis told Childs Walker of the *Baltimore Sun*. "You can buy some Scotch tape and a few rubber bands with it, but that's about it."[137]

In March 2007, Australian swimming superstar Ian Thorpe was tainted by doping allegations. Damien Ressiot, who covers doping in sports for the French sports daily *L'Equipe*, published a story that claimed Thorpe had tested positive for banned substances in May 2006. Ressiot's story came out during FINA's World Championships that were being held in Australia, and Ressiot's paper made sure that he was in Australia at the time the story hit the presses.

At issue was an out-of-competition test ten months before. Thorpe had last raced in November 2005 and decided to retire afterward. But he hadn't formally retired, so he was still subject to testing. When the May 2006 test results came back, Thorpe's sample showed abnormal levels of luteinizing hormone (LH) and follicle stimulating hormone (FSH). The use of steroids can cause changes in these levels, and WADA's accredited labs routinely test for LH and FSH as part of their antidoping protocol.

As the scandal blew up, Thorpe's reputation was somewhat sullied by the press. FINA, the international federation governing swimming, demanded that Australian authorities take action against Thorpe, threatening to take the case to the CAS if necessary. However, an investigation by the Australian Sports Anti-Doping Agency (ASADA), with the input of other antidoping experts from various antidoping labs around the world, determined that Thorpe's levels were the result of natural causes. In September 2007, ASADA announced their decision not to pursue an antidoping case against Thorpe. FINA dropped their efforts to prosecute the Australian swimmer shortly afterward.

In addition to the Landis hearings, May 2007 saw several former T-Mobile riders admit to using EPO during the 1990s. Their admissions came shortly before a book by another former T-Mobile employee, Jef D'Hont, was published. In D'Hont's book, he details doping efforts within the Deutsche Telekom/T-Mobile team during the 1990s. Among the riders who spoke up was Bjarne Riis, the only Danish rider to win the Tour de France (in 1996), and Erik Zabel. Zabel continues to ride as a pro cyclist. Rumors about Riis using EPO had been around for a number of years. His reputation led to the nickname "Mr. 60 Percent," a reflection of his rumored hematocrit levels during his racing days. After Riis admitted to doping, Tour organizers made it clear that they would write him out of the event's official history, and that he would be persona non grata in France come July. Zabel, however, was allowed to participate in the 2007 Tour.

Steroids were a topic of conversation in baseball during 2007, as Barry Bonds finally surpassed Hank Aaron's home run record late in the season. Bonds ended the 2007 season with a total of 762 home runs during his professional career. Despite Bonds' new record, the San Francisco Giants decided not to renew his contract at the end of the season. With Bonds being indicted on perjury charges in November 2007, it's unclear whether any baseball team will offer the slugger a job for the 2008 season—especially given that Bonds may be spending a significant portion of 2008 in a San Francisco courtroom.

The 2007 Tour de France, despite organizers' best efforts to the contrary, suffered even more doping scandals. Two teams—Astana and Cofidis—were asked to withdraw from the race after a rider from each team tested positive for doping. Astana's team leader, Alexander Vinokourov, tested positive for blood doping after winning a time trial stage during the 2007 Tour. Cofidis rider Christian Moreni tested positive for, and subsequently admitted that he had used, synthetic testosterone. The irony of Moreni's case is that Eric Boyer, the general manager of the Cofidis team, is an outspoken opponent of doping, as is Moreni's teammate Bradley Wiggins, a Briton who is also an Olympic medalist on the velodrome.

Also during the Tour, T-Mobile rider Patrik Sinkewitz learned that he had tested positive for synthetic testosterone during a training camp in early June. Sinkewitz had withdrawn from the Tour due to injuries suffered when he crashed into a dog on his way back to the team hotel just days before his test results were announced. (The dog, according to news reports, was unharmed.) Because Sinkewitz had already withdrawn from the race, Tour organizers did not force the entire T-Mobile team to drop out. But the fallout from Sinkewitz's subsequent confession, and his cooperation with German authorities, along with continuing disclosures about the T-Mobile team's past doping history eventually cost the team their title sponsor.

In the early days after Sinkewitz tested positive, the company went out of its way to publicly state their support for the team—with the caveat that the company could pull their sponsorship in the future is circumstances warranted. In November 2007, T-Mobile dropped their sponsorship of cycling, after further revelations from the former T-Mobile rider cast ever greater suspicion about the team's past practices—and in particular the actions of the medical staff.

But doping scandals at the Tour weren't over yet. Michael Rasmussen, a climbing specialist on the Rabobank team, suffered from a doping scandal without even testing positive for any banned substances. Rasmussen missed several out-of-competition tests prior to the Tour. In part, it may have been because he was dishonest about where he planned on training in the weeks leading up to the Tour. Rasmussen claims that his team knew where he was training, and that he had filed paperwork informing the UCI of his training plans for late June. The UCI claims that they could not find the Danish rider on June 29—despite the fact that he'd faxed them the proper forms a day or two before.

But there were other missed tests, too. And a former Italian cyclist who now works as a journalist spotted Rasmussen training in the Dolomites, and then wrote an article about Rasmussen's dedication for an Italian newspaper.

But at the time, the Dane was supposed to be training in Mexico. As the scandal grew, Rabobank withdrew Rasmussen from the Tour precisely when he appeared to have clinched victory, sending him off in the middle of the night. The next day, the race started with no rider wearing the yellow jersey. Alberto Contador, a young Spanish cyclist on the Discovery team, claimed the maillot jaune at the end of the stage. Contador held onto the yellow jersey until the finish in Paris only a few days later.

Alberto Contador, too, would be touched by doping allegations. Less than a week after he won the Tour, German antidoping activist Werner Franke claimed to have documentation proving his involvement in Operación Puerto. The young Spaniard had been a part of the Astana team in 2005, and had been implicated in the case. Spanish authorities, however, had cleared Contador in late July 2006. (In fact, all five members of the Astana team who were implicated in the scandal were cleared at the same time.) The Friday after winning the Tour, Contador stood on the steps outside the Spanish Sports Ministry and proclaimed his innocence, with Discovery team directeur sportif Johan Bruyneel by his side. Also present at the time was Jaime Lissavetsky, Spain's sports minister. Later that same day, the owners of the Discovery team announced that they would shut the team down at the end of the 2007 season. Earlier in the year, a management shakeup within Discovery Communications led to a decision to discontinue sponsoring the cycling team after the 2007 season. Owner Bill Stapleton explained to reporters that the ongoing doping scandals, together with other problems within the world of cycling, had made it too difficult to bring a new sponsor on board.

Not long after the Astana team withdrew from the Tour de France, another rider on the team tested positive for blood transfusions. This time it was Andrey Kashechkin, who was tested while he was on holiday in Turkey with his family. Antidoping authorities came to his hotel after 10 P.M. one night and asked him to supply them with urine and blood samples. Kashechkin complied, but because antidoping tests aren't supposed to be conducted after 10 P.M., he was bothered by the treatment. After both the A and B samples showed evidence of blood doping, the Kazakh rider decided to challenge the results. He is currently fighting both through the antidoping appeals process and through a civil suit in Europe. In his lawsuit, Kashechkin claims that the intrusive testing is a violation of the European Union's charter on human rights, and that such testing can only be carried out by governmental agencies. Kashechkin lost his first round, but is appealing the civil case. His antidoping case is ongoing, as well.

Two major investigations by law enforcement agencies in the United States also focused on doping, but this time with the idea of identifying the people supplying the athletes. In late February 2007, a district attorney in Albany, New York, working with state narcotics agents and also with an Orlando, Florida-based federal task force, uncovered a shadowy ring of Internet pharmacies illegally supplying steroids to a number of professional athletes. The pharmacies' customers included major league baseball players, NFL football players, college and high school athletes, and bodybuilders. Among the people whose names were connected to the investigation were boxer Evander Holyfield (who ordered medications under the name "Evan Fields") and Jose Canseco, the baseball player who wrote the book *Juiced: Wild Times, Rampant 'Roids, Smash Hits, and How Baseball Got Big* about his and other players' adventures in steroid use.

One of the biggest businesses raided was the Signature Pharmacy in Orlando, Florida, a company that in 2006 was said to have done more than $36 million in business, mostly over the Internet. New York officials became involved in the investigation because Signature did approximately one-third of its business with customers in the state. In Albany County alone, Signature was believed to have done $250,000 worth of business the previous year.

Among the people caught up in the wide-ranging investigation was Richard W. Rydze, a physician for the Pittsburgh Steelers football team. Back in 1972, Rydze had been an Olympic silver medalist in platform diving. According to a story in the *Albany Times Union*, he had purchased as much as $150,000 of steroids and other medications from the Signature Pharmacy using his own credit card. Rydze told investigators a month before the raids occurred that the purchases were for his private patients.[138]

Among the other companies under investigation were Applied Pharmacy Service of Mobile, Alabama, and Cellular Nucleonics Advantage, of Sugar Land, Texas. Approximately 24 people were arrested in connection with the investigation, including six doctors and three pharmacists.[139]

In September, agents from the United States Drug Enforcement Agency arrested 124 people as part of an investigation called Operation Raw Deal. This investigation didn't just cross state boundaries. It crossed national boundaries and involved the assistance of authorities from Australia, Belgium, Canada, China, Denmark, Germany, Mexico, Sweden, and Thailand. In addition, members of both WADA and USADA worked with law enforcement agencies during the eighteen-month investigation.

Operation Raw Deal focused on companies supplying the raw materials to make steroids and other performance-enhancing drugs. The investigation uncovered an international network of Internet-based drug dealers who had stepped into the void when eight Mexican manufacturers of illegal steroids were shut down in 2005. More than 30 of the companies involved in supplying raw materials were located in China. U.S. authorities worked closely with their Chinese counterparts and were reportedly quite pleased with the assistance the Chinese officials had given them.

In the course of the investigation, a large amount of information about the customers of the various businesses was collected and stored in a database. Thousands of e-mail messages seized by federal agents connected end users to the manufacturers. John Gilbride, a special agent for the Drug Enforcement Administration in New York, told reporters, "We will be identifying all the end users." He also said that investigators had lists that they would review. While the people whose names appeared on those lists may not be prosecuted right away, he said, they would be identified.

In a separate press conference, DEA spokesman Rusty Payne said, "If we come across names, are we going to provide them to the leagues? That is going to be the decision of the Department of Justice and the United States attorney's offices that have those aspects of the case."

Payne noted that they had not turned over any names. But, he added, "we have the ability to identify individual customers, and that should send chills down the spines of athletes and high school and college students who were buying from these manufacturers. We can find you, based on our database." The initial raids netted investigators 242 kilograms of raw materials and more than 1.4 million doses of various steroids.[140]

STEROIDS AND BASEBALL IN THE NEW MILLENNIUM

Rumors of steroid use in baseball have been around for a number of years. With the 1998 competition between Mark McGwire and Sammy Sosa to beat the single-season home run record, supplements like androstenedione and creatine made news. But suspicions about steroid use existed even back in the 1980s. The BALCO case further fueled speculation, as revelations of baseball players being associated with Victor Conte and his company cast a bad light on the sport. Following the BALCO scandal and the ongoing concern over the use of the drugs in baseball, Congress got into the act with hearings in 2005. Among those testifying were Sammy Sosa and Mark McGwire, the two sluggers who battled each other for home run supremacy seven years earlier. McGwire refused to answer questions about drug use during his testimony. He did admit that, "there has been a problem with steroid use in baseball" and he told lawmakers that he was willing to assist them in the battle against steroid use in sports.

Sammy Sosa and Rafael Palmiero also testified before the committee, denying that they had used steroids. Jose Canseco, however, spoke openly about his use of steroids and told lawmakers that it would be a mistake to allow major league baseball to police itself. According to Canseco, steroids were "as acceptable in the '80s and mid-to-late '90s as a cup of coffee." He urged the committee to take strong action to address baseball's steroid problem. Ultimately, no new laws were passed, but the investigations did spur on both the owners and players to make concessions about drug testing in the sport.

The commissioner of major league baseball, Bud Selig, eventually decided that the major leagues should hire an independent investigator to determine the extent of baseball's steroid and drug problems, as well as to make recommendations on how to address those problems. Selig hired former Maine Senator George Mitchell to conduct the investigation, which began in March 2006. Mitchell and the panel he formed spent the next twenty-one months looking into the use of steroids, human growth hormone, and other performance-enhancing drugs.

When he released his report on December 13, 2007, Mitchell had amassed information from several sources, including former New York Mets clubhouse employee Kirk Radomski and former New York Yankees strength coach Brian McNamee, implicating 86 players. Those whose names appear in the report range from lesser-known athletes to some of the most famous names in baseball. While the report offers a litany of stories about alleged wrongdoing, it also contains a number of wide-ranging suggestions for how baseball could attack the doping problem. Among Mitchell's recommendations are that baseball should contract with an independent agency to conduct random, year-round testing in what the report calls a "transparent" manner. The report also suggests that the commissioner's office create an independent department of investigations, run by someone with law enforcement experience, to look into doping allegations. The Mitchell report makes a number of other recommendations, including education programs and programs geared toward clubhouse employees and management.[141]

What impact the Mitchell report will have and what changes will be made in its wake are yet to be seen.

THE ROAD AHEAD

What lies ahead? A number of new programs have been devised over the last year to address the problem of doping in sports. One of the more interesting antidoping efforts, and perhaps the most innovative is that of the Agency for Cycling Ethics (ACE). Dr. Paul Strauss and Paul Scott, a former staff member of the UCLA antidoping laboratory, created the organization as they were driving to a bike race in late 2006. Their program involves constant testing of athletes to build a biological profile of various hormone levels and other health indicators, to monitor each rider's health. Teams can hire ACE to perform the monitoring, as a kind of ad hoc doping prevention program, to keep their athletes from doping, and thus to avoid the negative publicity (and consequences) when a rider tests positive. In 2007, Team Slipstream Powered by Chipotle signed on as ACE's first client.

Under the ACE program, if an athlete has test results that may indicate doping, they conduct further testing. Additionally, they counsel the athlete about the dangers of doping. During their first year, the program turned up at least one rider who had unusual test results after training at altitude. Upon further investigation, they were able to determine that for this particular cyclist, his body reacted to the altitude and training in a specific way. The athlete wasn't doping, as it turns out.[142] The ACE program will expand during 2008, with the former T-Mobile squad, now known as Team High Road, contracting with the group to conduct their own antidoping testing program.

The International Cycling Union (UCI) embraced a similar idea when they announced that starting in 2008 they would require "biological passports" for cyclists competing at the highest levels. The specifics of how the UCI's program will be implemented have not been released at this point. Other cycling teams, like the Denmark-based Team CSC also are running antidoping programs, too.

These ad hoc programs, along with the UCI's biological passport program, may be an indication of things to come. At least in cycling, there seems to be a movement toward each team creating and administering a program designed to ensure that their athletes aren't doping. These programs will likely work in tandem with the existing testing programs. In doing so, the effort to diminish the use of performance-enhancing drugs may yet be successful. But there is a new doping technique on the horizon that may be even more difficult to detect or defeat: gene doping.

Chapter 7

Future Perfect: Genetically Modified Athletes?

DNA, GENETIC RESEARCH AND SPORTS

Over the fifty-five years since the structure and shape of DNA was first determined, extraordinary advances have taken place in terms of understanding the building blocks of life. From the earliest beginnings, when Francis Crick and James Watson first determined the double-helical structure of DNA, to more recently when researchers successfully tracked down genes responsible for such maladies as cystic fibrosis, Huntington's disease, and adult acute leukemia, to the decoding of the entire human genome, the science of DNA and genetics has undergone a massive transformation over a relatively short period of time.

Along the way, the possibility of curing diseases through gene therapy began to evolve. Although gene therapy is still in its infancy, some progress has already been made in treating rare genetic problems. The greatest success so far has been the apparent curing of about 10 individuals afflicted with what is known as "bubble boy" disease, a rare genetic disorder. Persons afflicted with the disease have little or no ability to fight off infection, and must be kept away from any infectious agents in order to survive. Promising strides have been made in treating this disease, and research is under way to develop gene therapy cures for various muscle-wasting diseases, such as muscular dystrophy. In laboratory experiments with mice, researchers have achieved some success in treating such diseases. To date, however, no gene therapy treatment of muscular dystrophy that is both reliable and safe for humans has been developed.

Research into gene therapy treatments for other types of illnesses and conditions is also under way. For example, a treatment that enables anemic patients (such as cancer patients or people with certain kidney diseases) to produce greater amounts of red blood cells could be a real lifesaver. One genetic therapy technique that is being developed to address anemia targets the genes that cause erythropoietin to be produced by the body, and genes involved in other aspects of blood cell production. Gene therapy that restores a person's ability to produce blood cells would clearly be beneficial. But gene therapy has potential for other uses, too. Unscrupulous medical practitioners could use a treatment such as the one described above as a new form of blood doping.

Athletes who are looking for any leg up on their competition keep a watchful eye on the latest medical developments. As medical science has advanced, so have the doping methods that some athletes (or their doctors or their trainers) are willing to use to improve performance on the playing field. And as the BALCO scandal illustrates, there are those who use the latest advances in science to find ways of circumventing current antidoping testing methods.

The promise that gene therapy holds no doubt tempts those who are looking for the latest and greatest edge. Better yet, so the thinking goes, it could well be undetectable. Well, maybe.

GENE THERAPY: DEFINED

So, what exactly is gene therapy? To put it simply, gene therapy is the insertion of normal DNA into a cell's DNA in order to correct a genetic defect. It is also the treatment of a disease by altering, replacing or adding DNA to a cell's genes to correct an abnormality that causes the disease.

The first successful gene therapy treatment on humans was performed by Drs. W. French Anderson, R. Michael Blaese, and Kenneth W. Culver in 1990 when Dr. Anderson and his colleagues treated a patient with genetically engineered blood cells in order to correct an immune deficiency known as adenosine deaminase deficiency.[1]

Another therapy that has demonstrated promise is a treatment for the rare disorder called X-linked severe combined immunodeficiency disorder (X-SCID). But while French researchers were able to cure nine patients, the therapy had some serious side effects. Within two years of being treated, two of the patients in the French study developed leukemia.

At least three patients have died while participating in gene therapy studies or trials. Perhaps the most well-known case that resulted in death is that of Jesse Gelsinger. The eighteen-year-old Arizona youth died in 1999, four days after being given an experimental treatment for ornithine transcarbamylase disorder (OTC) while participating in a University of Pennsylvania study of the treatment's effectiveness. OTC is a disorder that prevents the body from properly eliminating nitrogen and ammonia. Gelsinger had OTC from a young age, but was otherwise healthy. With a properly managed diet and a carefully followed drug regimen (reportedly more than 30 pills a day), he would have been able to live a normal life.

Shortly after Gelsinger's death, the study was discontinued and James Wilson, the doctor heading the program, resigned his post at the University of Pennsylvania. In a follow-up investigation, the US Food and Drug Administration determined that it was the gene therapy, itself, that caused the teenager's death. As a result of their investigation, the FDA also banned Wilson from participating in any human research.[2]

In the time since Jesse Gelsinger died, new gene therapy studies have been conducted. But the techniques are still experimental, and safety is still an issue. As recently as July 2007, the U.S. government shut down a gene therapy study after a patient died. The study, conducted by a Seattle company, was of an experimental treatment for advanced arthritis.[3]

HOW IS GENE THERAPY PERFORMED?

Most gene therapy experiments have used a modified virus in order to insert a piece of DNA into the genetic material inside cells. Scientists remove the harmful DNA in a virus and replace it with the DNA sequence designed to correct a genetic defect. Viruses are used to deliver DNA because of their ability to sneak inside a cell. Once inside a cell, the viruses then insert the DNA into the cell's DNA. Every time the modified cell reproduces, the new DNA is incorporated into the new cells.

One gene therapy study in the late 1990s was of particular interest to those interested in finding new ways of building muscle strength. Researchers looking for possible cures for muscle-wasting diseases ran an experiment to see if genes could be modified to promote muscle growth. In the study, mice were treated with a gene therapy technique that resulted in greater muscle strength and less loss of strength as the animals aged. Because of their increased muscle strength and muscle development, these animals eventually became known as "Schwarzenegger mice." In the study, a modified virus that has the ability to invade muscle cells was used to insert genes into the mice's muscle tissue.[4]

One goal for gene therapy is to be able to target specific cells within the body. In this manner, treatment can be administered where it's most effective. With techniques like the one used to create the Schwarzenegger mice, this hope for gene therapy goes from the theoretical to the practical. While the original idea was to repair a damaged gene or insert a missing gene, scientists took the technique a step further by targeting specific cells for therapy.

In the study that Jesse Gelsinger participated in, the target cells were located in his liver. For other diseases, such as muscular dystrophy, the target cells are those that make up the muscles. Potentially, gene therapy can be even more specific. Muscles are made up of so-called fast-twitch and slow-twitch fibers. In theory, a therapy could target just fast-twitch fibers (crucial to athletes who need explosive power, like weight lifters or sprinters on the track). Alternatively, it could target slow-twitch fibers, crucial to endurance athletes like marathoners or Tour de France cyclists.

Having succeeded at targeting specific cells for gene therapy, researchers may one day be able to develop treatments that strengthen or fortify muscles, other tissues in the body, or even bones.[5] But some of the treatments developed may not be used as originally intended.

GENE DOPING: DEFINED

When gene therapy becomes a viable medical treatment, performing such a treatment on an otherwise healthy athlete with the sole intention of making him or her perform better in a given sport would constitute gene doping. The kinds of gene therapy techniques that are most likely to be used would be those that confer greater strength, speed, or endurance than an athlete would otherwise have. As University of Pennsylvania physiology professor H. Lee Sweeney observed, "The sorts of things you'd want to do to help make muscle stronger or repair itself better in a diseased or old person would also make a healthy young person's muscles stronger and repair faster."

So, for instance, when gene therapy is able to correct muscle-wasting disorders, then those who seek a competitive edge via medicine may try to find ways to use those same techniques with an eye toward improving strength. But even though a therapy hasn't been fully developed, for some competitors the desire to get an edge is so strong that they are willing to act as guinea pigs for experiments if the payoff is an improvement in their performance on the playing field. In 1998, Professor Sweeney found out just how strong that motivation is, after the media reported his success in using genetic techniques to create the Schwarzenegger mice.

Shortly after stories about his work appeared in various newspapers and magazines, Sweeney started receiving calls and e-mails from athletes and coaches interested in treatment—even though the technique had not been proven safe for use on human subjects. His original goal had been to help treat muscular dystrophy and the loss of muscle that comes with aging. But he found out quickly that others had an interest, too, for entirely different reasons.

By 2004, Sweeney had developed a standard response to use whenever athletes or their coaches contacted him. "I basically say this is experimental," Sweeney told *Science News Online*. "It's in animals, and even if I had it available to give to humans, it has to go through clinical trials to make sure it's safe."[6]

HAS THE ERA OF GENE DOPING ALREADY ARRIVED?

Whether or not athletes are currently attempting gene doping is unclear. Once the antidoping agencies have workable and reliable tests, they may find that some stored drug screening samples from the current time or the recent past show evidence of its use. In February 2006, one court case in Germany certainly added to the speculation as to whether the age of gene doping has arrived. Thomas Springstein, a track coach, was put on trial for distributing steroids and injecting steroids into several German athletes without their knowledge, including Anne-Kathrin Elbe (one of Germany's best hurdlers), who was sixteen when Springstein gave her injections of what he called "vitamins."

Elbe told *The New York Times* that when she found out what he had actually given her, "I was taken aback and speechless. He said that they were vitamins."[7]

During Springstein's trial, some of the evidence presented against him included e-mail messages found on a laptop computer confiscated as evidence during a raid on his home. Among those messages was one where he made the remark that "[t]he new [genetic treatment] Repoxygen is hard to get. Please give me new instructions soon so that I can order the product before Christmas."[8]

When the passage above, from Springstein's message to a Dutch speed-skating coach, was read in court, Repoxygen went from an obscure gene therapy treatment developed by Oxford Biomedica of Oxford, England, to the face of the latest threat to sporting integrity. What is Repoxygen? In short, it's a genetic treatment to treat anemia that uses a virus to insert a gene that produces and regulates the production of EPO, the hormone that promotes the creation of red blood cells. The gene is placed into muscle cells so that the cells will manufacture EPO. Unlike other potential treatments for anemia, Repoxygen has a mechanism that only produces additional EPO when a low oxygen level is detected in the blood stream. Once oxygen levels return to normal, the gene switches off and becomes dormant—until the next time it's needed.

Repoxygen has only been tested in mice, but never on humans. So whether it is safe and effective for humans is unknown. Oxford Biomedica shelved the product when they determined that it would not be profitable, especially when synthetic EPO is relatively easy to come by and widely accepted.

"We didn't develop it any further," Oxford Biomedica's chief executive Alan Kingsman, a professor at Oxford, told Owen Slot of *The Times Online*. "So it simply remains in the fridge. And we maintain very close controls, so I'd be extremely surprised if anything we made got on to the black market."[9]

It's possible that Springstein obtained the "drug" from one of the various Web sites that advertise Repoxygen. Oxford Biomedica applied for a patent on the therapy, and in their patent application they may have provided enough detail so that a lab with the right equipment and experience could replicate the treatment.

"It would take a fairly advanced lab to make it," Kingsman told *The Times Online*. Kingsman also said, "But it would be very irresponsible for a number of reasons. For a start, we only went as far as testing it on mice. To use it in the human body would be playing with fire."

From the evidence German authorities found in Springstein's home, it appears that the track coach may not have succeeded in acquiring the treatment for his athletes. And whether it's really available through various unscrupulous Internet sites is unclear. Olivier Rabin, the medical director of the World Anti-Doping Agency, ordered some supposed Repoxygen from some Web sites in order to see what he would get. As it turns out, he received ordinary synthetic EPO. The prospect of false advertising doesn't seem to stop people who are looking for Repoxygen. As Rabin noted, "No one ever said the people willing to use gene doping will be great minds or careful scientists."[10]

Robin Parisotto, author of *Blood Sports*, in speaking to journalist Rupert Guinness, warned that "[g]ene technology is all well and good in theory, but there are some big problems with it. They have been trying to cure certain diseases but by doing so they have stimulated other diseases. A lot of people have died after being treated by gene technology."[11]

DETECTING GENE DOPING

At some point in the future, certain doctors or researchers may be able and willing to assist athletes with gene therapy. If (or when) that happens, will it be possible to detect which athletes have gene doped and which haven't? In some instances, it actually may be possible. A 2004 study by Françoise Lasne and Philippe Moullier of France's Laboratoire National de Dépistage du Dopage (LNDD) suggests that it may be possible to develop tests that detect certain types of gene doping. The study, which involved injecting the gene for EPO into the muscles of monkeys, found that the EPO made by the monkeys' muscles was slightly different in structure than the monkeys' normal EPO. If such structural differences are consistent, these might become the basis for a future gene-doping test to determine whether an athlete has used a genetic approach to blood doping.[12]

With gene doping aimed at building stronger or faster muscles, however, its use may be harder to detect than gene doping to produce more EPO within an athlete's body. Detecting gene doping for stronger or faster muscles could require a muscle biopsy. From the biopsy, technicians in a medical pathology lab would determine whether an athlete's DNA had been altered in order to determine whether doping occurred. In terms of testing on the day of competition, however, taking such biopsies is very likely to be met with resistance. Even if the procedure isn't painful, athletes might well fear that their performance would suffer as a result.

Whatever tests might be developed to detect gene doping will need to be tempered with the knowledge that genetic variation occurs within the human race, and that sometimes the variation or mutation may actually give an athlete an advantage. A case in point is the Finnish cross-country skier Eero Mäntyranta. Mäntyranta was a very successful competitor in the 1960s who some suspected of blood doping, due to the higher than normal hemoglobin levels in his blood. But, as it turns out, his family has a rare genetic mutation called autosomal dominant benign erythrocytosis (ADBE), which caused the high hemoglobin test results.

ADBE is a condition where a person's body lacks the braking mechanism that regulates the use of erythropoietin, the hormone involved in the production of red blood cells. In other words, the body creates more red blood cells than normal. This, in turn, raises an individual's hemoglobin and hematocrit values. And higher hemoglobin and hematocrit levels are a big help to endurance athletes because more red blood cells and more hemoglobin means that more oxygen can be delivered to hard-working muscles. Consequently, an athlete is able to perform at a higher rate for a longer period of time.

Even though Mäntyranta's genetic mutation is rare among the general population, the Finnish skier was far from alone. Twenty-nine of his living relatives in 1995 also carried the trait.[13] In determining whether an athlete has gene doped or not, it may therefore become necessary to compare his or her DNA against the DNA of other family members. This means that not only would an athlete be subject to antidoping tests, but his or her family may be as well.

At that point in the future when gene doping becomes a reality, and tests are able to detect that an athlete's DNA has been manipulated, how would an athlete accused of gene doping be able to prove his or her innocence? One way, for an athlete like Eero Mäntyranta, would be to demonstrate that the trait runs in his family. But what if the trait is the result of a random mutation in the athlete's genetic material? One that just happens to be a benefit in competition? And what if that mutation shows up as a positive result on some future anti-gene-doping tests? These are some of the many issues that will need to be ironed out.

WHERE DO WE GO FROM HERE?

When gene doping becomes a reality, one of the questions with which athletes and athletic federations will have to wrestle will be whether it's fair to allow someone with a genetic mutation such as Mäntyranta's to compete alongside others who aren't as fortunate. And if one of the less fortunate was able to "level the playing field" through genetic modification, will this be ethically allowable? Even though gene doping is merely on the horizon today, under current World Anti-Doping Agency regulations it is already banned. Will that always be the case? Or will changing technologies force changes in how we look at what is and isn't considered doping in sports?

Before the first athlete gets sanctioned for gene doping, however, it will need to step out of the theoretical world and into the practical world. While that may happen in the not-too-distant future, the current state of gene therapy doesn't appear to be quite ready to safely treat patients in need, much less athletes looking for a way to edge out their competitors. But technology has a sneaky way of making rapid advances when we least expect it. Will an athlete who's been treated with gene therapy to improve athletic performance be competing in the near future? Time will tell. The indications are that the development of a safe and reliable gene therapy technique has quite a way to go before the theory becomes a reality. But that doesn't mean that somewhere out there people aren't experimenting with gene therapy and gene doping outside of the scientific establishment.

As Thomas Friedmann, one of the world's leading experts in gene doping, told *USA Today*, "The sad fact is that if someone in this field wants to do it, they are not going to worry about all the quality control and the ethical aspects of manipulating people genetically."

"There are many labs, thousands of labs in the world that could do the work," Friedmann adds. "We know that there is a tremendous amount of money in sport. And where there is money and a will to do it, some people are going to do it."[14]

Eventually, someone may figure out a way to perform gene doping. As medical research and technology continues to advance, that day is drawing closer and closer.

Afterword

As I write this, it is several months before *Dope* will be available for sale. With the fast pace of doping stories in the sports world, more will have happened by the time you're reading this. In the interest of completeness, instead of including a full afterword here, I'm making this part of the book available for download from my Web site: http://rant-your-head-off.com/dopethebook/afterword.pdf.

Timeline

Date	Incident	Athlete(s)	Location
1865	Stimulants used in competition	Dutch canal swimmers	Amsterdam
1887	Alpamethyletthylamine (commonly known as amphetamine) first synthesized		
1896	Bordeaux-Paris race winner dies less than two months after victory—rumored cause: "trimethyl," actual cause: typhoid fever	Arthur Linton	Aberaman, Wales
1897	Cycling manager banned from tracks in Great Britain allegedly due to doping his riders	Choppy Warburton	Great Britain
1903	English Jockey Club bans doping of racehorses		Great Britain
1904	Runner barely survives the Olympic marathon event in St. Louis, after using a mix of strychnine, raw eggs, and brandy administered by a trainer	Thomas Hicks	St. Louis, Missouri
1910	Saliva tests for cocaine and heroin—two common doping drugs for racehorses—introduced		
1912	First recorded positive result using the saliva tests		Austria

Date	Incident	Athlete(s)	Location
1919	Methamphetamine first crystallized, making it easier to administer		Japan
1926	Male sex hormone—later dubbed testosterone—first isolated		Chicago, Illinois
1928	International Association of Athletics Federations bans doping during track and field competition		
1930	Doping tests during all races sanctioned by the International Horseracing Federation		
1935	Testosterone first synthesized		Germany
1939–1945	Amphetamines used by militaries on both side of World War II		Europe, Asia
1950	Rowers use "hormone pills" during competition.	Danish rowers	Milan, Italy
1952	Amphetamines make speed skaters ill during Winter Olympics		Oslo, Norway
1954	A Soviet sports physician tells American Dr. John Ziegler about the USSR's weightlifters' use of testosterone		Vienna, Austria
1956	Amphetamines used during swimming events at Summer Olympics	Australian swimmers	Melbourne, Australia
1957	Dr. Herbert Berger stirs up controversy claiming that the four-minute mile was achieved through the use of amphetamines		New York
1957	Football player tells *The New York Times* members of the San Francisco 49ers used amphetamines before games		

Date	Incident	Athlete(s)	Location
1958	Dianabol, a synthetic steroid, developed by Ciba Pharmaceutical		United States
1959	American Medical Association publishes first scientific studies on the effects of amphetamines on athletic performance		
1960	A Danish cyclist dies during the team time trial at the Summer Olympics. Although amphetamines were implicated in the death, the official autopsy lists heatstroke as the cause.	Knud Enemark Jensen	Rome, Italy
1961–1965	Bill March, of the York Barbell Club, wins U.S. Senior Nationals and other competitions using dianabol while being trained by Dr. John Ziegler	Bill March	United States
1962	Members of Italian soccer team suspected of doping during World Cup competition	Italian National Team	Chile
1963	Members of the San Diego Chargers use steroids during their American Football League championship season		San Diego, California
1966	The International Cycling Union (UCI) and the International Football (Soccer) Federation (FIFA) ban drug use during championship events		
1967	English cyclist dies of heatstroke near the summit of Mont Ventoux, aggravated by the use of amphetamines during 13th stage of the Tour de France.	Tommy Simpson	Mont Ventoux, France

Date	Incident	Athlete(s)	Location
1967	International Olympic Committee bans performance-enhancing drug use during Olympic competition		
1968	First Olympic athlete, a Swedish competitor in the modern pentathlon, tests positive for drug use (alcohol).	Hans-Gunnar Liljenwall	Mexico City, Mexico
1969	First recorded use of steroids in baseball	Tom House	Santa Monica, California
1970–1975	Six-time Mr. Olympia wins bodybuilding contests with "tissue-building" drugs (steroids)	Arnold Schwarzenegger	
1972	U.S. Olympic swimmer tests positive for asthma drug, relinquishes gold medal	Rick DeMont	Munich, Germany
1972	Torino soccer club drugged during Union of European Football Associations (UEFA) Cup match		
1972	Blood doping, also known as blood boosting and blood packing, pioneered by Dr. Bjorn Ekblöm		Sweden
1975	Canadian track and field athlete banned from competition after testing positive for a cold medication at the Pan American Games	Joan Wenzel	Mexico City, Mexico
1975, 1977	Tour de France winner uses testosterone during the three-week stage race. In 1977, the same rider tests positive for doping during the Paris-Nice stage race	Bernard Thevenet	France (various locations)

Date	Incident	Athlete(s)	Location
1976	After being banned in 1974, IOC introduces steroid testing during the Summer Olympics		Montreal, Canada
1976	East German women's swim team wins 11 of 13 medals possible, in part due to regimen of steroid use		Montreal, Canada
1977	East German swimmer tests positive for doping, disqualified from competition	Ilona Slupianek	
1978	Cyclist leading the Tour de France is expelled after he was caught trying to fool drug testers	Michel Pollentier	L'Alpe d'Huez, France
1979	Various professional football players, including members of the "Super Steelers" use steroids		
1984	Finnish runner tests positive for primobolan during the Summer Olympics	Martti Vainio	Los Angeles, California
1984	Members of the U.S. cycling team use blood doping during Summer Olympics. Blood doping was not specifically outlawed at the time		Los Angeles, California
1984	Human growth hormone emerges as a potential performance-enhancing drug		
1985	US Cycling Federation (now USA Cycling) outlaws the use of blood doping. Shortly afterward, the US Olympic Committee follows suit		
1985	Major league baseball implements drug-testing program for minor-league players		
1986	IOC bans blood doping		
1987	Swiss runner tests positive for traces of methyltestosterone. In an ironic twist, the lab loses its accreditation shortly after case is decided.	Sandra Gasser	Rome, Italy

Date	Incident	Athlete(s)	Location
1987	An American skier competing in the 1987 Nordic Combined event during the World Championships blood-dopes	Kerry Lynch	Oberstdorf, Germany
1987–1990	Approximately 20 professional cyclists die from suspected EPO abuse		
1988	Canadian sprinter Ben Johnson tests positive for stanozolol at the Summer Olympics	Ben Johnson	Seoul, South Korea
1988	Weight lifters from various East Bloc countries test positive for steroid use	Hunganrian and Bulgarian athletes	Seoul, South Korea
1988	In November 1988, the distribution of steroids for nonmedical uses was outlawed in the United States.		United States
1991	Dr. George Zaharian, 3rd, convicted for illegally distributing steroids to professional wrestlers		United States
1991	Ben Johnson returns to competition. His return would be short-lived. After testing positive for testosterone at a meet in Montreal in early 1993, Johnson was handed a lifetime ban from competition.	Ben Johnson	Canada
1992	Various athletes test positive for the asthma medication clenbuterol at the Summer Olympics	Jud Logan, Katrina Krabbe, Grite Breur, and Bonnie Dasse	Barcelona, Spain

Date	Incident	Athlete(s)	Location
1994	Eleven Chinese athletes, including seven swimmers on their women's team test positive for dihydrotestosterone (DHT) just days before the Asian Games		Hiroshima, Japan
1994	Star soccer player tests positive for five different variants of ephedrine prior to World Cup competition	Diego Maradona	Argentina
1995	American swimmer receives probation after she tests positive for a banned substance	Jessica Foschi	Pasadena, California
1997	Mary Decker Slaney suspended from competition after allegedly testing positive for testosterone in June 1996. Reinstated later that year, the IAAF pursued an appeal and ultimately prevailed, causing her results from meets in 1997 to be erased. Slaney filed suit in Federal court, but in 2001, the court ruled that they did not have jurisdiction.	Mary Decker Slaney	United States
1997	Female tennis professional tests positive for metabolite of nandrolone, due to use of a "natural supplement."	Samantha Reeves	
1998	Irish swimmer's out-of-competition urine test contaminated with whisky, she is accused of tampering with the sample and sanctioned.	Michelle Smith	Kellsgrange, Ireland
1998	Canadian snowboarder tests positive for marijuana use. His gold medal is taken away, and then reinstated 32 hours later, by the Court of Arbitration for Sport.	Ross Rebagliati	Nagano, Japan
1998	Chinese swimmer Yuan Yuan caught carrying human growth hormone by customs officials as she entered Australia for the World Championships		Sydney, Australia

Date	Incident	Athlete(s)	Location
1998	Former East German sports officials tried and convicted for their role in doping athletes.		Berlin, Germany
1998	Festina scandal erupts just days before the Tour de France begins.		Lille, France
1998	Baseball player in a race for the single-season home run record accused of using performance-enhancing drugs. He admits to using an over-the-counter supplement called androstenedione and creatine, which another player in the home run race also admits to using	Mark McGwire (androstenedione and creatine), Sammy Sosa (creatine)	St. Louis, Missouri
1998	Tennis professional tests positive for nandronlone, ultimately handed a one-year ban.	Petr Korda	Wimbledon, England
1999	Lance Armstrong, on his way to his first Tour de France victory, becomes embroiled in a doping scandal when he uses a cortisone cream to treat saddle sores.	Lance Armstrong	France
1999	In November, a new antidoping agency comes into existence: The World Anti-Doping Agency. Their mission is to harmonize antidoping practices around the globe.		Montreal, Canada
Late 1990s	Bay Area Laboratory Co-operative starts distributing various steroids to professional athletes		Burlingame, California
1999	French antidoping laboratory LNDD develops urine test for EPO		Châtenay-Malabry, France

Date	Incident	Athlete(s)	Location
2000	Australian researchers develop blood test to detect EPO use		
2000	American track and field athlete tests positive for nandrolone four times prior to Summer Olympics, bows out of competition in Sydney while proclaiming his innocence	C.J. Hunter	Sydney, Australia
2000	Following the Olympics in Sydney, Australia, WADA assumes responsibility for the oversight of antidoping efforts in future Olympic competitions.		
2001	Finnish cross-country skiers caught using banned plasma expander at Nordic World Ski Championships	Jari Isometsä, Janne Immonen, and four others	Lahti, Finland
2001	Danish cyclist first athlete to test positive for EPO at the Flèche Wallone bicycle race. B sample test fails to confirm initial result, however, so he is not sanctioned.	Bo Hamburger	Belgium
2002	British skier wins bronze medal in Salt Lake City, has to relinquish medal due to traces of an isomer of methamphetamine in an American version of the Vicks nasal inhaler. The UK version doesn't contain the isomer.	Alain Baxter	Salt Lake City, Utah
2003–2005	Dr. James Shortt implicated in providing steroids to Carolina Panthers football team. He pleads guilty in March 2006.		Charlotte, South Carolina
2003	BALCO scandal erupts, implicating a large number of athletes		Burlingame, California

Date	Incident	Athlete(s)	Location
2003	Runner tests positive for EPO at World Championships and then is cleared 5 weeks later, after the B sample fails to confirm the original result.	Bernard Lagat	Paris, France
2004	FIFA (the International Soccer Federation) signs on to the World Anti-Doping Code		
2004	Test for homologous blood doping, developed by Australian researchers is introduced. First during the Tour de France, and later at the Athens Olympics.		France, also Athens, Greece
2004	Two Greek track stars turn up missing when antidoping officials appear for random test; they later check into an Athens hospital for injuries due to a motorcycle accident. They withdraw from competition several days later.	Costas Kenteris, Katerina Thanou	Athens, Greece
2004	Cyclist becomes first athlete to test positive due to homologous blood doping during Olympic competition and also the Vuelta a España	Tyler Hamilton	Athens, Greece and Spain
2004	Dutch triathlete tests positive for EPO. On subsequent investigation, his defense shows that he produces proteins naturally that cause a false positive test result.	Rutger Beke	Knokke, Flanders
2004	First athlete sanctioned based on a "non-analytical positive" based on connections to the BALCO scandal	Michelle Collins	
2005	Two more athletes connected to BALCO are sanctioned based on "non-analytical positives."	Tim Montgomery, Chryste Gaines	

Date	Incident	Athlete(s)	Location
2005	Lance Armstrong wins seventh Tour de France, one month later a French newspaper reports that tests on his remaining samples from the 1999 Tour show traces of EPO. An independent report issued in May 2006 clears Armstrong of any wrongdoing.	Lance Armstrong	France
2005	Argentine tennis professional sanctioned after being given wrong prescription medication at a tournament in Acapulco. The CAS subsequently rules that the offense occurred accidentally.	Guillermo Cañas	Acapulco, Mexico
2006	At an arbitration hearing on the eve of the Winter Olympics, an American skeleton racer is banned from the 2006 Olympic Games and handed a one-year suspension after testing positive for finasteride two months earlier. Finasteride, used in hair replacement medications, was added to the list of banned substances for 2005. The drug is believed to be a masking agent,	Zach Lund	Calgary, Alberta and Torino, Italy
2006	At the Kansas Relays in April 2006, one of the United States' top sprinters tests positive for synthetic testosterone. Word of the positive result leaks to the press in July 2006, just two days after the Floyd Landis scandal breaks (see below). Gatlin contends that a disgruntled masseuse sabotaged him, but the arbitration panel deciding his case voted 2–1 to find him guilty. Gatlin's case is on appeal to the Court of Arbitration for Sport.	Justin Gatlin	Lawrence, Kansas

Date	Incident	Athlete(s)	Location
2006	In May 2006, as a result of the Operación Puerto investigation, raids are conducted on a Spanish doctor's office and the offices and residences of others. Up to 200 athletes are reported to be involved. Ultimately, only about 60 professional cyclists will be named in connection to the scandal.		Madrid, Spain
2006	Canadian paralymic athlete tests positive for a minute trace of a cocaine metabolite. The initial ruling in 2007 found Adams guilty. The case is on appeal to the CAS.	Jeff Adams	Ottawa, Ontario
2006	At a track meet in Belgium, an athlete coached by Trevor Graham tests positive for nandrolone.	LaTasha Jenkins	Belgium
2006	Tour de France winner allegedly tests positive for testosterone. In a first, his arbitration hearings are open to the public. In September 2007, after four months of deliberations, the arbitrators vote 2–1 to find Landis guilty. The case is currently on appeal to the CAS.	Floyd Landis	Morzine, France
2006	Pakistani cricket players suspended for nandrolone use, then reinstated. Appeal to the CAS fails, because the Pakistan Cricket Board does not specifically recognize the court's authority in their charter.	Shoaib Akhtar, Mohammed Asif	Pakistan
2007	NFL adopts tougher antidoping testing policy		
2007	Australian swimmer rumored to have tested positive for banned substances. Ultimately, he is cleared.	Ian Thorpe	Australia

Date	Incident	Athlete(s)	Location
2007	American law enforcement officials raid a number of pharmacies said to be illegally supplying steroids to professional and amateur athletes		Various locations in the United States
2007	Barry Bonds sets home run record. Then, in November he is indicted on perjury charges related to his testimony in the BALCO case	Barry Bonds	San Francisco, California
2007	Marion Jones admits to using banned substances in connection with BALCO, after being caught lying to Federal agents in a different, but related investigation.	Marion Jones	New York City, New York
2007	Two former T-Mobile riders, including the 1996 Tour de France winner, admit to using EPO during the 1990s. Erik Zabel, who is still actively racing, allowed to compete at 2007 Tour. Bjarne Riis, owner of the CSC team, declared persona non grata at the Tour.	Bjarne Riis (1996 Tour de France winner) and Erik Zabel	
2007	Two teams forced to leave Tour de France after a rider on each team tests positive for doping.	Alexander Vinokourov (Astana), Christian Moreni (Cofidis)	France
2007	Rider leading the Tour de France withdrawn and subsequently fired by his team after problems related to missed antidoping tests are uncovered. For at least one of the missed tests, in June, Rasmussen may have filed proper paperwork. But still, he may have lied about his whereabouts to both his team and the UCI.	Michael Rasmussen (Rabobank)	France

Date	Incident	Athlete(s)	Location
2007	Operation Raw Deal sparks police raids around the world that breaks open a shadowy network of companies supplying the raw materials to make illegal steroids. Additionally, 1.4 million doses of various banned substances seized.		United States, Australia, Belgium, Canada, China, Denmark, Germany, Mexico, Sweden, and Thailand
2007	In mid-December 2007, USADA loses an antidoping case for the first time. The case, involving allegations of nandrolone use, fails due to violations of international standards by the testing labs.	LaTasha Jenkins	United States
2007	The Mitchell Report, after a 21-month investigation into the use of performance-enhancing drugs in major-league baseball, is released, naming 86 players who may have used steroids and other drugs. Included in the report are recommendations on how the sport can deal with players' use of performance-enhancing drugs.		United States

Notes

PREFACE

1. Eugen Tomiuc (March 26, 2004), "World: Doping—Performance Enhancement Drugs a Threat to Health and Ethics (Part 1)," Radio Free Europe/Radio Liberty Web site, retrieved from http://www.rferl.org/ on December 24, 2007.

2. José Banaug (2006), "A History of Doping," United Nations Education, Scientific and Cultural Organization Web site citing the World Anti-Doping Agency and the Concise Oxford Dictionary of English Etymology, 1996, retrieved from http://typo38.unesco.org/ on March 10, 2007.

3. Robert Daley, "Survival of the Fastest, In Fierce Competitive Cycling Grind, Scandals Over Drugs Are Not New," *The New York Times* (August 30, 1960) (online edition), retrieved from http://www.nytimes.com on April 20, 2007.

CHAPTER 1

1. John T. Powell, *Origins and Aspects of Olympism* (Champaign, IL: Stipes Publishing Company, 1994), p. 110.

2. Charles E. Yesalis and Michael S. Bahrke (December 2005), "Anabolic Steroid and Stimulant Use in North American Sport between 1850 and 1980," *Sport in History*, Volume 25, Issue 3, pp. 443 and 444.

3. Podofdonny (October 1, 2005), "Magnus Goes for Record—History of the Derny Paced Hour," *Daily Peloton* Web site, retrieved from http://www. dailypeloton.com/ on March 30, 2007. Also Gary I. Wadler and Brian Hainline, *Drugs and the Athlete* (Philadelphia: F. A. Davis Company, 1989), p. 4. Also Rhondda Cynon Taf Library Service, "Aberaman," retrieved from http:// webapps.rhondda-cynon-taf.gov.uk/ on April 2, 2007.

4. Podofdonny (October 1, 2005), "Magnus Goes for Record—History of the Derny Paced Hour," *Daily Peloton*, retrieved from http://www.dailypeloton.com/ on March 30, 2007.

5. Professional Cycling Palmarès Site—Races: Bordeaux–Paris, retrieved from http://homepage.ntlworld.com/veloarchive/races/bordeauxparis.htm#notes on April 2, 2007. Also, Casglu'r Tlysau/Gathering the Jewels, The Web site for Welsh cultural history, "Bust of Arthur Linton, Aberdare," retrieved from http://www.gtj.org.uk/en/item1/2800 on April 3, 2007.

6. Podofdonny (October 1, 2005), "Magnus Goes for Record—History of the Derny Paced Hour," *Daily Peloton*, retrieved from http://www.dailypeloton.com/ on March 30, 2007.

7. Ray Minovi (Autumn 2005), "Arthur Linton's Death," *The Veteran Leaguer*, p. 16, retrieved from http://www.lvrc.org/documents/veteran_leaguer/2005/2005_autumn.pdf on March 17, 2007.

8. Ibid. Also, Podofdonny (October 1, 2005), "Magnus Goes for Record—History of the Derny Paced Hour," *Daily Peloton*, retrieved from http://www.dailypeloton.com/ on March 30, 2007.

9. Les Woodland, *The Crooked Path to Victory: Drugs and Cheating in Professional Bicycle Racing* (San Francisco: Cycle Publishing, 2003), pp. 17–19.

10. Rhondda Cynon Taf Library Service, "Aberaman," retrieved from http://webapps.rhondda-cynon-taf.gov.uk/ on April 2, 2007.

11. Rhondda Cynon Taf Library Service, "Professional Cycling. Michael v. Linton's, An Open Challenge," retrieved from http://webapps.rhondda-cynon-taf.gov.uk/ on April 2, 2007.

12. Jay Pridmore and Jim Hurd, *Schwinn Bicycles* (St. Paul, MN: MBI, 2001), pp. 30, 31. Also, Les Woodland, *The Crooked Path to Victory: Drugs and Cheating in Professional Bicycle Racing* (San Francisco: Cycle Publishing, 2003), p. 19.

13. Les Woodland, *The Crooked Path to Victory: Drugs and Cheating in Professional Bicycle Racing* (San Francisco: Cycle Publishing, 2003), p. 18.

14. Cottontown.org, "Choppy Warburton," retrieved from http://cottontown.org/ on April 2, 2007. Also, Les Woodland, *The Crooked Path to Victory: Drugs and Cheating in Professional Bicycle Racing* (San Francisco: Cycle Publishing, 2003), pp. 9, 10.

15. Les Woodland, *The Crooked Path to Victory: Drugs and Cheating in Professional Bicycle Racing* (San Francisco: Cycle Publishing, 2003), pp. 10–20.

16. Tim Moore, *French Revolutions: Cycling the Tour de France* (New York: St. Martin's Press, 2002), p. 142.

17. Jay Pridmore and Jim Hurd, *Schwinn Bicycles* (St. Paul, MN: MBI, 2001), pp. 30, 31.

18. Stephanie Pain (August 7, 2004), "Marathon Madness," *New Scientist* (online edition), retrieved from http://www.newscientist.com/ on April 5, 2007.

19. Eileen P. Duggan (July/August 2004), "The Marathon from Hell," *Marathon & Beyond* (online edition), retrieved from http://www.marathonandbeyond.com/ on April 7, 2007.

20. Ibid.

21. Ibid.

22. Gary I. Wadler and Brian Hainline, *Drugs and the Athlete* (Philadelphia: F. A. Davis Company, 1989), p. 93.

23. Charles J. P. Lucas, *The Olympic Games, 1904* (St. Louis, MO: Woodward and Tieran Printing Co., 1905).

24. Justracing.com.au (May 31, 2005), "The History of Drugs in Racing," retrieved from http://www.justracing.com.au/ on March 31, 2007.

25. Hans Brandenberger and Robert A. A. Maes, *Analytical Toxicology for Clinical, Forensic and Pharmaceutical Chemists*, article 1.4 by D. de Boer, T. J. A. Seppenwoolde-Waasdorp, and R. A. A. Maes (Berlin: Walter de Gruyter, 1997), p. 43.

26. Ruud Stokvis (November 2003), "Moral Entrepreneurship and Doping Cultures in Sport," Amsterdam School for Social Science Research working paper 03/04, retrieved from http://www2.fmg.uva.nl/assr/workingpapers/, p. 6, citing A. de Schaepdrijver and H. Hebbelink, *Doping* (London: Pergamon Press, 1965), p. 67, Information about saliva test from: David R. Mottram, *Drugs in Sport* (London: Routledge, 2003), p. 19.

27. Cornell Richardson and Bert Randolph Sugar, *Horse Sense: An Inside Look at the Sport of Kings* (Hoboken, NJ: John Wiley and Sons, 2003), p. 139. Also, Courtenay's Blog (February 6, 2007), Man O'War vs. Sir Barton, retrieved from http://cour10ay.blogspot.com/2007/02/man-o-war-vs-sir-barton.html on April 13, 2007.

28. Sal Ruibal (September 9, 2004), "Tackling Longtime Issue of Drugs No. 2 on Sports Changes Wish List," *USA Today* (online edition), retrieved from http://www.usatoday.com/ on April 17, 2007.

29. Dr. Frances Quirk, "Performance Enhancement in Sport: Mixed Methodology Research and the Development of the Performance Enhancement Attitudes Questionnaire (PEAQ)," paper presented at the Australian Consortium for Social and Political Research Incorporated conference, December 2006, p. 6.

30. Simon Cotton, "Methamhpetamine (and Its Isomers)," Molecule of the Month Web site, retrieved from http://www.chm.bris.ac.uk/motm/ on April 6, 2007.

31. Amina Ali, June Chua and Martin O'Malley (January 14, 2003), "Go-pills, Bombs & Friendly Fire," Canadian Broadcasting Corporation News, retrieved from http://www.crystalrecovery.com/ on April 7, 2007.

32. Yu-Hsuan Lee, "Performance-Enhancing Drugs: History, Medical Effects & Policy," retrieved from http://leda.law.harvard.edu/leda/data/780/LeeY06.rtf on April 4, 2007.

33. William N. Taylor, *Macho Medicine: A History of the Anabolic Steroid Epidemic*, (Jefferson, NC and London: McFarland & Company, Inc., 1991), p. 20.

34. Charles E. Yesalis (editor), Stephen P. Courson and James Wright, "History of Anabolic Steroids in Sports and Exercise," *Anabolic Steroids in Sports and Exercise* (Champaign, IL: Human Kinetics, 1993), p. 38.

35. Charles E. Yesalis and Michael S. Bahrke (December 2005), "Anabolic Steroid and Stimulant Use in North American Sport Between 1850 and 1980," *Sport in History*, Volume 25, Issue 3, p. 438.

36. Charles E. Yesalis (editor), Stephen P. Courson, and James Wright, "History of Anabolic Steroids in Sports and Exercise," *Anabolic Steroids in Sports and Exercise* (Champaign, IL: Human Kinetics, 1993), p. 38.

37. Ibid.

38. Gary I. Wadler and Brian Hainline, *Drugs and the Athlete* (Philadelphia, PA: F. A. Davis Company, 1989), p. 56, citing from B. Goldman, *Death in the Locker Room: Steroids, Cocaine & Sports* (Tucson, AZ: The Body Press, 1987).

39. John Hoberman, *Testosterone Dreams: Rejuvenation, Aphrodisia, Doping* (Berkeley: University of California Press, 2005), p.189.

40. Ibid., p. 189.

41. Ibid., p. 186.

42. *The New York Times* (June 8, 1957), "Athletes Report Use Of 'Pep Pills,'" retrieved from http://www.nytimes.com on April 1, 2007.

43. Compilation of mile record times attributed to Runner's World, retrieved from http://www.stat.colostate.edu/~jah/teach/st540/data/mile.info on May 29, 2007.

44. *Time Magazine* (June 17, 1957), "Souped-up Athletes?" retrieved from http://www.time.com on April 4, 2007.

45. John Hoberman (June 2006), "Amphetamine and the Four-Minute Mile," *Sport in History*, Volume 26, Issue 2, pp. 289–304.

46. Wikipedia, "World Record Progression for the Mile Run," citing Runner's World data listed above, retrieved from http://en.wikipedia.org/ April 15, 2007.

47. *The New York Times* (June 8, 1957), "Drug Use Charge Denied By Milers," retrieved from http://www.nytimes.com on April 1, 2007.

48. John Hoberman (April 25, 2004), "After 'Unbreakable' Barriers Fall, Doping Questions and Denials," *The New York Times* (online edition), retrieved from http://www.nytimes.com on May 1, 2007.

49. *Time Magazine* (June 17, 1957), "Souped-up Athletes?" retrieved from http://www.time.com on April 4, 2007.

50. John Bale, *Roger Bannister and the Four-Minute Mile: Sports Myth and Sports History* (Abingdon, UK and New York: Routledge, 2005), p. 114.

51. *The New York Times* (June 8, 1957), "Athletes Report Use Of 'Pep Pills,'" retrieved from http://www.nytimes.com on April 1, 2007.

52. Ibid.

53. John Hoberman, *Testosterone Dreams: Rejuvenation, Aphrodisia, Doping* (Berkeley: University of California Press, 2005), p. 187.

54. John Bale, *Roger Bannister and the Four-Minute Mile: Sports Myth and Sports History* (Abingdon, UK: Routledge, 2005), p. 47.

55. Robert K. Plumb (June 6, 1957), "A.M.A to Study Drugs in Sports; Use in Four-Minute Mile Hinted," *The New York Times* (online edition), retrieved from http://www.nytimes.com on April 1, 2007.

56. Gary I. Wadler and Brian Hainline, *Drugs and the Athlete* (Philadelphia, PA: F. A. Davis Company, 1989), pp. 82 and 83.

CHAPTER 2

1. *Time Magazine* (September 5, 1960), "Zamechaltelno!" retrieved from http://www.time.com on April 13, 2007.

2. Famielen Sørensen Hjemmside, "Min verdenhistorie 1960–1969," retrieved from http://www.aerenlund.dk/idag/historie.asp?periode=19 on April 13, 2007.

3. David A. Martin and Roger W. H. Gynn, *The Olympic Marathon* (Champaign, IL: Human Kinetics Publishers, 2000), p. 228

4. Kirsten Harkjær Larsen (September 27, 2001) "Sundhed, sejr og samvær," Danske Gymnastik- & Indræstforeninger, retrieved from http://www.dgi.dk/redaktionen/dui/27-2001/sundhed.aspx on April 12, 2007.

5. The Associated Press (August 28, 1960), "Inquiry to Last Several Weeks, Use of Roniacol Is Blamed for Death of Knud Jensen in Olympic Bicycle Race," *The New York Times* (online edition), retrieved from http://www.nytimes.com on April 21, 2007.

6. Robert Daley (August 30, 1960), "Survival of the Fastest, in Fierce Competitive Cycling Grind, Scandals Over Drugs Are Not New," *The New York Times* (online edition), retrieved from http://www.nytimes.com on April 20, 2007.

7. Verner Møller (December 2005), "Knud Enemark Jensen's Death during the 1960 Rome Olympics: A Search for Truth?" *Sport In History*, Volume 25, Issue 3, pp. 452–471.

8. The Associated Press (March 26, 1961), "Danish Cyclist Died of Heat, Not Drug," *The New York Times* (online edition), retrieved from http://www.nytimes.com on April 16, 2007.

9. The Associated Press (August 27, 1960), "Steps to Protect Athletes Taken," *The New York Times* (on-line edition), retrieved from http://www.nytimes.com on April 22, 2007.

10. Hans Blomhøj, "Historisk Begivenhed, Olypiaden I Rom 1960," Hanses Bog Web site, retrieved from http://www.blomhoej.dk/hanses_bog/1956-60/ on April 11, 2007. Also, John Hoberman, *Testosterone Dreams: Rejuvenation, Aphrodisia, Doping*, Berkeley and Los Angeles: University of California Press, 2005, p. 183. A portrait of Knud Enemark Jensen can be found at http://www.cyclingstars.dk/enemark.htm.

11. Geoffrey Wheatcroft (November 26, 2006), "Pain Then Shame on the Road to Glory," *The Observer* (online edition), retrieved from http://observer.guardian.co.uk on April 10, 2007.

12. The Association of International Marathon and Distance Races Web site, quoting Jones, Hugh, *The Expert's Guide to Marathon Training* (London: Carlton Books Ltd, 2003). Retrieved from http://www.aims-association.org/marathon_history.htm on April 29, 2007.

13. Jeff Frantz (December 24, 2006), "Pecs, Pink Pills and Power: How York Played a Role in the Steroid Controversy," *York Daily Record* (online edition), retrieved from http://www.ydr.com/ on May 14, 2007.

14. Robert Dvorchak (October 4, 2005), "Keeping steroids out of sports no easy task," *Pittsburgh Post-Gazette* (online edition), retrieved from http://www.post-gazette.com/ on March 31, 2007.

15. Ibid.

16. Ibid.

17. Robert Dvorchak (October 2, 2005), "Never Enough/Steroids in Sports: Experiment Turns Epidemic," *Pittsburgh Post-Gazette* (online edition), retrieved from http://www.post-gazette.com/ on May 24, 2007.

18. Jeff Frantz (December 24, 2006), "Pecs, Pink pills and Power: How York Played a Role in the Steroid Controversy," *York Daily Record* (online edition), retrieved from http://www.ydr.com/ on May 14, 2007.

19. International Cycling Union (July 2001), "40 Years of Fighting Against Doping," p. 5.

20. *Hartford Courant* (June 5, 1962), "Doping Rears Ugly Head in Soccer," retrieved from http://www.courant.com on May 13, 2007.

21. The Associated Press (June 2, 1964), "Italian Soccer Spot Checks Clubs for Doping; Inter, Bologna Tied," *Hartford Courant* (online edition), retrieved from http://www.courant.com on May 13, 2007.

22. *The New York Times* (March 5, 1967), "Soccer Players Acquitted," retrieved from http://www.nytimes.com on April 14, 2007.

23. Wikipedia, "Mont Ventoux," retrieved from http://wikipedia.org on April 15, 2007.

24. Podofdonny (July 20, 2002), "Tour Hero: Tom Simpson," *Daily Peloton*, retrieved from http://www.dailypeloton.com/ on March 21, 2007.

25. Ramin Minovi (2001), "Tom Simpson Lives," Association of British Cycling Coaches Web site, retrieved from http://www.abcc.co.uk/ on March 20, 2007; Michael J. Dooris, "Review: French Revolutions: Cycling the Tour de France," Bookreporter.com, retrieved from http://www.bookreporter.com/ on April 2, 2007; Matt Seaton (July 20, 2002), "Wheels within Wheels," Guardian Unlimited (*The Guardian* online edition), retrieved from http://books.guardian.co.uk/reviews/ on April 1, 2007; Also, a comment by "Cyclo200" regarding Harry Hall and Tommy Simpson at Hidden Glasgow Forums and Chat, retrieved from http://www.hiddenglasgow.com/forums/viewtopic.php?p=118092&sid=bc75b872ffa930b072b529b1063c3fb6 on May 2, 2007.

26. Podofdonny (July 20, 2002), "Tour Hero: Tom Simpson," citing *Cycling Weekly* (July 13, 1967), "The Simpson Tragedy," *Daily Peloton*, retrieved from http://www.dailypeloton.com/ on March 21, 2007.

27. Les Woodland, *The Crooked Path to Victory: Drugs and Cheating in Professional Bike Racing* (San Francisco, CA: Cycle Publishing, 2003), p. 123. More information can also be found in William Fotheringham, *Put Me Back on My Bike: In Search of Tom Simpson*, New Ed Edition (London: Yellow Jersey Press, 2007).

28. Max Jones (December 2002), "Futility and Hypocrisy in Sport Drug Testing," Coaching Science Abstracts, retrieved from http://coachsci.sdsu.edu/ on May 16, 2007.

29. IOC Medical Commission meeting minutes, December 20, 1967, translated by Marc Cogan, June 29, 2007.

30. Ruud Stokvis, "Moral Entrepreneurship and Doping Cultures in Sport," Amsterdam School for Social Science Research, ASSR Working paper 03/04 (November 2003). Also, Cynthia Crossen (August 7, 2006), "Using Drugs in Sports Used to Be Considered Just Part of the Game," *WSJ Online*, retrieved from http://online.wsj.com/ on May 9, 2007.

31. Terry Todd, "Anabolic Steroids: The Gremlins of Sport," *Journal of Sports History*, vol. 14, no. 1 (Spring 1987).

32. Ibid.

33. Tom House, as told to Tim Kurkjian, "The House Experiment," *ESPN The Magazine Special Report* (online edition), retrieved from http://sports.espn.go.com/ on May 2, 2007.

34. Ron Kroichick (May 3, 2005), "House a 'failed experiment' with Steroids," *San Francisco Chronicle* (online edition), retrieved from http://www.sfgate.com/ on May 2, 2007. Also, The Associated Press, "Former Pitcher Tom House Describes Past Steroid Use," retrieved from http://www.usatoday.com/sports/baseball/ on May 1, 2007.

35. Jack Scott (November 17, 1971), "It's Not How You Play the Game, But What Pill You Take," *The New York Times* (online edition), retrieved from http://www.nytimes.com on February 10, 2007.

CHAPTER 3

1. Yuri Brokhin (May 29, 1977), "The Big Red Machine," *The New York Times* (online edition), retrieved from http://www.nytimes.com on March 24, 2007.

2. Jack Scott (November 17, 1971), "It's Not How You Play the Game, But What Pill You Take," *The New York Times* (online edition), retrieved from http://www.nytimes.com on February 10, 2007.

3. databaseOlympics.com, "Weightlifting results for the 1972 Summer Olympics," retrieved from http://www.databaseolympics.com/ on June 18, 2007.

4. "Arnold Schwarzenegger and Steroids" retrieved from http://hjem.get2net.dk/JamesBond/www/artikler/steroidemisbrug/arnoldandsteroids.htm on July 4, 2007.

5. Steve Sailer (August 15, 2003), "What's Unique About Arnold Schwarzenegger?" United Press International.

6. Ibid., quoting Nigel Andrews' book *True Myths: The Life and Times of Arnold Schwarzenegger* (New York: Bloomsbury, revised 2003).

7. Answers.com, "Arnold Schwarzenegger: Biography and Much More," retrieved from http://www.answers.com/ on July 4, 2007.

8. Chris Schramm (March 12, 1999), "Back to Hogan's Darker Days," *SLAM! Sports*, retrieved from http://www.canoe.ca/ on May 31, 2007.

9. Steven Pegram, "Rick DeMont: First Man since Jim Thorpe to Be Stripped of Gold, usolympicteam.com, retrieved from http://www.usoc.org/ on June 8, 2007.

10. *The New York Times* (September 7, 1972), "DeMont Told to Return Medal; Alexeyev Takes Lifting Crown," retrieved from http://www.nytimes.com on June 9, 2007. Also, Alan Abrahamson, "High Performance: Thirty Years after Munich, IOC Battle against Doping Is Far From Over," Associated Press Sports Editors Web site, retrieved from http://apse.dallasnews.com/contest/2002/ on June 7, 2007.

11. Abrahamson story, above.

12. Steven Pegram, "Rick DeMont: First Man since Jim Thorpe to Be Stripped of Gold, usolympicteam.com, retrieved from http://www.usoc.org/ on June 8, 2007.

13. Ibid.

14. *The New York Times* (February 6, 2001), "Demont Recognition Is Turned Down," retrieved from http://www.nytimes.com/ on June 7, 2007.

15. United Press International (October 3, 1972), "Soccer Club Charges Doping," retrieved from http://www.nytimes.com on June 6, 2007.

16. United Press International (April 9, 1975), "Beware of Greeks Bearing Pills," retrieved from http://www.nytimes.com on June 5, 2007.

17. *The New York Times* (November 27, 1975), "Canadian Runner Banned For Life After Drug Test," retrieved from http://www.nytimes.com on June 7, 2007.

18. Cecil Smith (February 2007), "Canadian Championships Medallists 1900–2006," retrieved from http://www.athletics.ca/ on June 7, 2007.

19. Steven Ungerleider, *Faust's Gold: Inside The East German Doping Machine* (New York: Thomas Dunne Books, 2001), p. 88.

20. Eddie Driscoll (March 24, 2005), "I'm Shocked—Shocked! Super Steelers on Steroids," quoting the book *God's Coach* (by Skip Bayless), retrieved from http://eddriscoll.com/archives/006884.php on June 25, 2007.

21. Ed Bouchette (March 24, 2005), "Haslett Admits to Using Steroids," *Pittsburgh Post-Gazette*, retrieved from http://www.post-gazette.com on June 27, 2007.

22. Ibid.

23. Ibid.

24. The Associated Press (March 24, 2005), "Haslett Apologizes for Implicating Steelers," retrieved from http://sports.espn.go.com on June 28, 2007.

25. Ibid.

26. Chuck Finder (November 7, 2004), "Former Steeler Courson at Heart of Big Turnaround," *Pittsburgh Post-Gazette* (online edition), retrieved from http://www.post-gazette.com on June 27, 2007.

27. Joe Bendel (November 11, 2005), "Courson Turned His Life Around," *Pittsburgh Tribune-Review* (online edition), retrieved from http://www.pittsburghlive.com/ on June 28, 2007.

28. Bill Lauris, "Steelers of the 70's and 'roids: Let the Fire Burn," Sportpgh.com, retrieved from http://www.sportspgh.com/ on June 3, 2007.

29. Jamey Kearney (July 10, 2007), "Former Tour de France Champion Thevenet Defends His Doping Past," The Associated Press, retrieved from http://www.usatoday.com/sports/cycling/ on July 16, 2007.

30. Ibid.

31. Les Woodland, *The Crooked Path to Victory: Drugs and Cheating in Professional Bicycle Racing* (San Francisco, CA: Cycle Publishing, 2003), pp. 131–133.

32. Ungerleider, *Faust's Gold*, p. 186.

33. Ibid., p 45.

34. Ibid., p. 10.

35. Ibid., p. 10.

36. Ibid., p. 11.

37. Ibid., p. 89.

38. Ibid., pp. 87–95.

39. Ibid., p. 95.

40. *Time Magazine* (December 24, 1973), "New Blood for Athletes?" retrieved from http://www.time.com/ on June 8, 2007. Lasse Viren controversy.

41. James Raia (August 30, 1984), "An Interview with Olympic Champion Lasse Viren," RunnersWeb.com, retrieved from http://www.runnersweb.com/ on June 8, 2007. Also, John Jerome, *The Sweet Spot in Time: The Search for Athletic Perfection* (New York: Breakaway Books, 1998), p. 254. Biographical detail at *The Times Online*, Lasse Viren, retrieved from http://www.times-olympics.co.uk/historyheroes/lvire.html on June 8, 2007.

CHAPTER 4

1. Bill Pennington (November 1, 2003), "Former Musician Rocks World of Track," *The New York Times* (online edition), retrieved from http://www.nytimes.com/ on July 24, 2007.

2. Ellis Cashmore, *Making Sense of Sports*, 3rd ed. (New York: Routledge, 2000), p. 201. Also, Daniel Yi (July–August 2005), "The Inside Dope: Holding Countries

Accountable for Their Athletes Could End the Steroid Scourge," *Legal Affairs* (online edition), retrieved from http://www.legalaffairs.org/ on July 19, 2007.

3. United Press International (August 13, 1984), "Finn Disqualified; 11 Fail Drug Tests," *The New York Times* (online edition), retrieved from http://www.nytimes.com/ on July 19, 2007. Also, The Associated Press (September 27, 1984), *The New York Times* (online edition), retrieved from http://www.nytimes.com/ on July 19, 2007.

4. Daniel Yi (July–August 2005), "The Inside Dope: Holding Countries Accountable for Their Athletes Could End the Steroid Scourge," *Legal Affairs* (on-line edition), retrieved from http://www.legalaffairs.org/ on July 19, 2007.

5. Information on medal count in1912 from Parisotto, Robin, *Blood Sports: The Inside Dope on Drugs in Sport* (Pharan, Victoria, Australia: Hardie Grant Books, 2006), p. 32.

6. George Vescey (July 31, 1984), "First Things First," *The New York Times* (online edition), retrieved from http://www.nytimes.com/ on July 21, 2007.

7. Robert McG. Thomas, Jr. (January 10, 1985), "USOC Checking Use Of Transfusions," *The New York Times* (online edition), retrievd from http://www.nytimes.com on July 5, 2007.

8. Les Earnest (August 1988), "Vampirism at the Olympics," originally published in *Cyclops USA,* retrieved from http://www.stanford.edu/~learnest/cyclops/dopes.htm on July 4, 2007.

9. Ibid.

10. *The New York Times* (January 11, 1985), "US Cyclists Tested Caffeine As an Aid," retrieved from http://www.nytimes.com on July 4, 2007.

11. Untitled sidebar article to *The New York Times* (January 11, 1985), "US Cyclists Tested Caffeine As an Aid," retrieved from http://www.nytimes.com on July 4, 2007.

12. *The New York Times* (January 19, 1985), "Cycle Group Bans Use of Blood Doping," retrieved from http://www.nytimes.com on July 4, 2007.

13. Robert McG. Thomas, Jr. (May 6, 1985), "Ueberroth Orders Wide Testing for Drug Use in Baseball," *The New York Times* (online edition), retrieved from http://www.nytimes.com on July 5, 2007.

14. Michael Goodwin (June 19, 1985), "Baseball Drug Tests Are Set," *The New York Times* (online edition), retrieved from http://www.nytimes.com on July 6, 2007.

15. John Hoberman, *Mortal Engines: The Science of Performance and the Dehumanization of Sport* (New York: The Free Press, 1992), p. 230.

16. *The New York Times* (September 30, 1987), "Sports People: Runner Banned," retrieved from http://www.nytimes.com on July 9, 2007.

17. *The New York Times* (October 25, 1987), "Sports People: Swiss Runner Suit," retrieved from http://www.nytimes.com/ on July 9, 2007.

18. Hoberman, *Mortal Engines*, p. 231.

19. *The New York Times* (November 28, 1987), "Sports People: Runner Appeals," retrieved from http://www.nytimes.com on July 9, 2007.

20. Hoberman, *Mortal Engines*, pp. 230 and 232.

21. Ibid., p. 231.

22. Ibid., pp. 232, 233.

23. Ibid., p. 233.

24. Coaches titles and information about bans: John Hoberman (May 7, 1999), presentation to the Duke University Conference on Doping; Lynch suspension, page rescinded information from *The New York Times* (January 20, 1988), "Nordic Skier Is Barred," retrieved from http://www.nytimes.com on July 10, 2007; Other information from Christie Aschwanden (September 10, 2000), "Cheat? I'd Rather Get Beat, But It's No Mystery Why Doping Has Such Great Appeal," *The Washington Post*, p. B01, retrieved from http://www.washingtonpost.com/ on July 28, 2007.

25. Michael Janofsky (September 25, 1988), "The Seoul Olympics, The Best in The World, Fastest Runs Even Faster," *The New York Times* (online edition), retrieved from http://www.nytimes.com on July 19, 2007.

26. Dick Pound, *Inside The Olympics* (Toronto: John Wiley & Sons Canada Ltd, 2004), p. 175.

27. Michael Sokolove (January 7, 2007), The Scold, *The New York Times Sunday Magazine* (online edition), retrieved from http://www.nytimes.com on January 7, 2007.

28. Michael Janofsky (September 27, 1988), "The Seoul Olympics: Johnson Loses Gold To Lewis After Drug Test," *The New York Times* (online edition), retrieved from http://www.nytimes.com on March 12, 2007.

29. *The New York Times* (October 8, 1988), "More Trouble for Johnson," retrieved from http://www.nytimes.com on July 14, 2007.

30. *The New York Times* (October 12, 1988), "Sports People; Johnson Charged," retrieved from http://www.nytimes.com on July 14, 2007.

31. Laurie Mifflin (September 27, 1988), "The Seoul Olympics; Johnson's Testing Leaves Questions," *The New York Times* (online edition), retrieved from http://www.nytimes.com on July 14, 2007.

32. *The New York Times* (June 13, 1989), "Johnson Recants and Tells Inquiry That He Did Use Drugs," retrieved from http://www.nytimes.com on July 14, 2007.

33. Ibid.

34. Ibid.

35. Michael Janofsky (March 15, 1989), "Johnson Aware of Drug Use, Inquiry Told," *The New York Times* (online edition), retrieved from http://www.nytimes.com on July 14, 2007.

36. Michael Janofsky (September 8, 1989), "IOC Criticizes Federation Steroids Rule," *The New York Times* (online edition), retrieved from http://www.nytimes.com on July 15, 2007.

37. Michael Janofsky (June 14, 1989), "Johnson Admits Lying About Drugs, Asks For Reinstatement," *The New York Times* (online edition), retrieved from http://www.nytimes.com on July 16, 2007.

38. The Associated Press (September 29, 1988), "Weightlifter Used Drugs," *The New York Times* (online edition), retrieved from http://www.nytimes.com on July 19, 2007.

39. The Associated Press (October 1, 1988), "Christie Can Keep Medal," *The New York Times* (online edition), retrieved from http://www.nytimes.com on July 21, 2007.

40. The Associated Press (November 20, 1988), "Anti Drug Talks Begin," *The New York Times* (online edition), retrieved from http://www.nytimes.com on July 21, 2007.

41. Lawrence M. Fisher (May 19, 1991), "Stamina-Building Drug Linked To Athletes' Deaths," *The New York Times* (online edition), retrieved from http://www.nytimes.com on July 21, 2007).

42. Richard D. Lyons (June 14, 1984), "Athletes Warned on Hormone," *The New York Times* (online edition), retrieved from http://www.nytimes.com on July 13, 2007.

43. William N. Taylor, *Macho Medicine: A History of the Anabolic Steroid Epidemic* (Jefferson, North Carolina and London: McFarland & Company, 1991), p. 36.

44. Ibid. p. 95.

45. Ibid., p. 7.

CHAPTER 5

1. Search for the term "doping" on August 1, 2007, *The New York Times* (online edition), http://www.nytimes.com.

2. Lawrence M. Fisher (May 19, 1991), "Stamina-Building Drug Linked to Athletes' Deaths," *The New York Times* (online edition), retrieved from http://www.nytimes.com on August 14, 2007.

3. *The New York Times* (June 25, 1991), "Trial Opens for Physician in Steroid Case," retrieved from http://www.nytimes.com on August 14, 2007.

4. Chris Schramm (March 12, 1999), "Back to Hogan's darker days," retrieved from http://www.canoe.ca on May 31, 2007.

5. *The New York Times* (July 5, 1994), "Hulk Hogan, on Witness Stand, Tells of Steroid Use in Wrestling," retrieved from http://www.nytimes.com on June 1, 2007.

6. Michael Janofsky (July 24, 1990), "Return of Johnson Welcomed," *The New York Times* (online edition), retrieved from http://www.nytimes.com on June 10, 2007.

7. *The New York Times* (March 6, 1993), "Johnson Banned for Life," retrieved from http://www.nytimes.com on July 16, 2007.

8. Dave Anderson (July 1, 1991), "The Alzado Alarms On Steroids," *The New York Times* (online edition), retrieved from http://www.nytimes.com on May 24, 2007.

9. Mike Puma (no date given), "Not the Size of the Dog in the Fight," *ESPN* (online edition), retrieved from http://espn.go.com/classic/biography/ on September 16, 2007.

10. Robert McG. Thomas, Jr. (May 15, 1992), "Lyle Alzado, 43, Fierce Lineman Who Turned Steroid Foe, Is Dead," *The New York Times* (online edition), retrieved from http://www.nytimes.com on May 31, 2007.

11. Dave Anderson (July 1, 1991), "The Alzado Alarms On Steroids," *The New York Times* (online edition), retrieved from http://www.nytimes.com on May 24, 2007.

12. Robert Lipsyte (July 12, 1991), "The Cancer in Football and Pro Wrestling," *The New York Times* (online edition), retrieved from http://www.nytimes.com on May 28, 2007.

13. Ibid.

14. Michael Janofsky (August 7, 1992), "Banned American Explains Use of Drug," *The New York Times* (online edition), retrieved from http://www.nytimes.com on August 12, 2007.

15. Michael Janofsky (August 9, 1992), "US Female Shot-Putter Banned After Drug Test," *The New York Times* (online edition), retrieved from http://www.nytimes.com on September 5, 2007.

16. Filip Bondy (July 31, 1992), "Too Good? Too Fast? Drug Rumors Stalk Chinese," *The New York Times* (online edition), retrieved from http://www.nytimes.com on October 17, 2007.

17. Patrick E. Tyler (August 30, 1994), "China Is Getting Ready For Another Big Splash," *The New York Times* (online edition), retrieved from http://www.nytimes.com on October 14, 2007.

18. Ibid.

19. Jere Longman (December 18, 1994), "Drug Sleuths' Surprise Produces a Breakthrough," *The New York Times* (online edition), retrieved from http://www.nytimes.com on July 14, 2007.

20. *The New York Times* (December 1, 1994), "China to Investigate Doping," retrieved from http://www.nytimes.com on July 14, 2007.

21. *The New York Times* (December 22, 1994), "China Takes a Hard Line," retrieved from http://www.nytimes.com on July 14, 2007.

22. Sam Howe Verhovek (July 1, 1994), "World Cup '94: After Second Test, Maradona Is Out of World Cup," *The New York Times* (online edition), retrieved from http://www.nytimes.com on July 14, 2007.

23. The Associated Press (April 12, 2004), "Champions League Semis Have an English Accent," retrieved from http://www.nytimes.com on July 22, 2007.

24. The Associated Press (November 29, 1994), "IAAF Speeds Up Drug Bans," retrieved from http://www.nytimes.com on July 22, 2007.

25. *The New York Times* (November 15, 1995), "Ripples from a Positive Test," retrieved from http://www.nytimes.com on June 27, 2007.

26. The Associated Press (February 6, 1996) "Foschi's Parents Challenge Ban."

27. The Associated Press (February 22, 1996), "Warning Draws Praise From Medical Chief," published in *The New York Times* (online edition), retrieved from http://www.nytimes.com on August 20, 2007.

28. *The New York Times* (March 6, 1996), "Evans is Critical of Foschi Decision," retrieved from http://www.nytimes.com on May 27, 2007.

29. George Vecsey (February 13, 1998), "Snowboard Dude Says: No Big Deal," *The New York Times* (online edition), retrieved from http://www.nytimes.com on October 27, 2007.

30. Christopher Clarey (February 13, 1998), "The XVIII Winter Games: Snowboarding; Canadian Gets His Gold Medal Back," *The New York Times* (online edition), retrieved from http://www.nytimes.com on October 27, 2007.

31. Jere Longman (June 11, 1997), "Ordered to Ban Slaney, U.S. Reviews Its Options," *The New York Times* (online edition), retrieved from http://www.nytimes.com on October 29, 2007.

32. Jere Longman (September 17, 1998), "U.S. Federation Clears Slaney in Doping Case," *The New York Times* (online edition), retrieved from http://www.nytimes.com on October 21, 2007.

33. Jere Longman (April 27, 1999), "Slaney Found Guilty By the IAAF," *The New York Times* (online edition), retrieved from http://www.nytimes.com on October 23, 2007.

34. Frank Litsky (April 14, 1999), "Slaney Suing the IAAF in Dispute Over a Drug Test," *The New York Times* (online edition), retrieved from http://www.nytimes.com on October 23, 2007.

35. Donald A. Berry and LeeAnn Chastain (2004), "Inferences about Testosterone Abuse among Athletes," *Chance*, Volume 17, Issue 2pp. 5–8.

36. Alan Cowell (April 5, 1998), "In a Cold War Hangover, Germany Confronts a Legacy of Steroids," *The New York Times* (online edition), retrieved from http://www.nytimes.com on June 15, 2007.

37. Steven Ungerleider, *Faust's Gold: Inside the East German Doping Machine* (New York: Thomas Dunne Books, 2001), p. 7

38. Ibid.

39. Ibid., pp. 7–8.

40. Alan Cowell (April 5, 1998), "In a Cold War Hangover, Germany Confronts a Legacy of Steroids," *The New York Times* (online edition), retrieved from http://www.nytimes.com on June 15, 2007.

41. Ungerleider, *Faust's Gold*, p. 128.

42. CNN/SI.com (July 22, 1998), "Will Drug Scandal Scare Off Sponsors?" *CNN/Sports Illustrated* (online edition), retrieved from http://sportsillustrated.cnn.com/cycling/ on October 22, 2007.

43. Sam Abt (July 31, 1998), "Paris or Bust: 101 Riders Say Race Must Go On," *The New York Times* (online edition), retrieved from http://www.nytimes.com on October 24, 2007.

44. *The New York Times* (October 1, 1998), "Federation Bans and Fines 3 Riders," retrieved from http://www.nytimes.com on October 17, 2007.

45. Christopher Clary and Samuel Abt (July 3, 1999), "The Tainted Tour, A Special Report; Drug Scandals Dampen Cycling's Top Event," *The New York Times* (online edition), retrieved from http://www.nytimes.com on October 23, 2007.

46. Sam Abt (July 31, 1998), "Paris or Bust: 101 Riders Say Race Must Go On," *The New York Times* (online edition), retrieved from http://www.nytimes.com on October 24, 2007.

47. Sam Abt (July 31, 1998), "Paris or Bust: 101 Riders Say Race Must Go On," *The New York Times* (on-line edition), retrieved from http://www.nytimes.com on October 24, 2007.

48. Sam Abt (November 6, 1999), "Cycling: Notebook," *The New York Times* (online edition), retrieved from http://www.nytimes.com on November 1, 2007.

49. The Associated Press (November 6, 1999), retrieved from http://www.nytimes.com on October 31, 2007.

50. BBC Sport (October 24, 2000), "Virenque Admits Taking Banned Drugs," BBC.com, retrieved from http://news.bbc.co.uk/ on October 22, 2007.

51. Jere Longman (August 7, 1998), "Olympic Swimming Star Banned; Tampering With Drug Test Cited," *The New York Times* (online edition), retrieved from http://www.nytimes.com on October 5, 2007.

52. BBC Sport (June 8, 1999), "Defiant de Bruin Quits Swimming," BBC.co.uk, retrieved from http://news.bbc.co.uk/ on October 15, 2007.

53. Kevin Mitchell (April 16, 2004), "Dismantling of an Irish legend," TheAge.com.au, retrieved from http://www.theage.com.au/ on October 15, 2007.

54. Joe Drape (August 22, 1998), "McGwire Admits Taking Controversial Substance," *The New York Times* (online edition), retrieved from http://www.nytimes.com on October 16, 2007.

55. Ungerleider, *Faust's Gold*, pp. 176–177.

56. *The New York Times* (August 27, 1998), "Mark McGwire's Pep Pills," retrieved from http://www.nytimes.com/ on October 12, 2007.

57. Joe Drape (August 22, 1998), "McGwire Admits Taking Controversial Substance," *The New York Times* (on-line edition), retrieved from http://www.nytimes.com on October 16, 2007.

58. Ibid.

59. Murray Chass (February 6, 1999), "Science, Not Outcry, To Drive Baseball's Decision on Andro," *The New York Times* (online edition), retrieved from http://www.nytimes.com on October 14, 2007.

60. Ronald Blum (June 25, 2004), "Baseball Bans Steroidlike Substance Andro," The Associated Press, retrieved from The Home Run Guys web site, http://www.thehomerunguys.com/ on October 14, 2007.

61. *The New York Times* (December 23, 1998), "Korda Penalized for Steroids," retrieved from http://www.nytimes.com on October 12, 2007.

62. Robin Finn (January 15, 1999), "On Tennis; Sport Fighting to Toss Out Korda," *The New York Times* (online edition), retrieved from http://www.nytimes.com on October 15, 2007.

63. Selena Roberts (September 1, 1999), "Korda Must Pay Up," *The New York Times* (online edition), retrieved from http://www.nytimes.com on October 15, 2007.

64. Robin Finn (August 19, 1998), "A Hidden Threat in Tennis; A Teen-Ager's Case Points Out Over-the-Counter Access to Steroids," *The New York Times* (online edition) retrieved from http://www.nytimes.com on October 8, 2007.

65. Samantha Reeves player biography, Sony Ericsson World Tennis Association Tour Web site, retrieved from http://www.sonyericssonwtatour.com/ on October 19, 2007.

66. Sam Abt (July 5, 1998), "The Past is Prologue for Armstrong," *The New York Times* (online edition), retrieved from http://www.nytimes.com on October 24, 2007.

67. Sam Abt (July 20, 1999), "Rider for an Italian Team Is Ousted for Using Drugs," *The New York Times* (online edition), retrieved from http://www.nytimes.com on October 24, 2007.

68. *The New York Times* (July 27, 1998), "A Call for Doping Changes," retrieved from http://www.nytimes.com on October 20, 2007.

69. Paul L. Montgomery (February 3, 1998), "IOC Credibility Questioned as IOC Meeting Starts," *The New York Times* (online edition), retrieved from http://www.nytimes.com on October 25, 2007.

70. Paul L. Montgomery (February 5, 1999), "IOC Falters In Doping Bid As Summit Ends," *The New York Times* (online edition), retrieved from http://www.nytimes.com on October 22, 2007. Also, Jere Longman (January 29, 1999), "IOC Drug Chief Calls for A Shift in Bans," *The New York Times* (online edition), retrieved from http://www.nytimes.com on October 23, 2007.

71. Jere Longman (March 19, 1999), "IOC Makes Changes, But Trust Becomes Issue," *The New York Times* (online edition), retrieved from http://www.nytimes.com on October 19, 2007.

72. Laura Weislo (October 20, 2007), "WADA President Responds to Lamour," CyclingNews.com, retrieved from http://www.cyclingnews.com/ on October 28, 2007.

73. Bill Pennington (November 1, 2003), "Former Musician Rocks World of Track," *The New York Times* (online edition), retrieved from http://www.nytimes.com on August 1, 2007.

74. Mark Fainaru-Wada and Lance Williams (December 25, 2003), "Barry Bonds: Anatomy of a Scandal," *Seattle Post-Intelligencer* (originally published in the *San Francisco Chronicle*), retrieved from http://seattlepi.nwsource.com on October 21, 2007.

75. Mark Fainaru-Wada and Lance Williams, *Game of Shadows: Barry Bonds, BALCO, and the Steroids Scandal that Rocked Professional Sports* (New York: Gotham Books, 2006), p. 55

76. Ibid., p.52

77. Ibid., p. 56

CHAPTER 6

1. Personal correspondence from Robin Parisotto, author of *Blood Sport: The inside dope on drugs in sport*, December 5, 2007.

2. Ibid.

3. Alex Duff (October 29, 2007), "Athletes Fool Test of Banned Drug by Using Soap, Scientist Says," *Bloomberg.com*, retrieved from http://www.bloomberg.com/ on December 2, 2007.

4. Robin Parisotto, *Blood Sports: The Inside Dope on Drugs in Sport* (Pahran, Victoria, Australia: Hardie Grant Books, 2006), pp. 110–123.

5. The Associated Press (September 25, 2000), "IOC Chief Says Hunter Failed Four Drug Tests," ESPN.com, retrieved from http://espn.go.com/ on August 30, 2007.

6. Frank Litsky (July 12, 2001), "Track Body Criticized But Cleared," *The New York Times* (online edition), retrieved from http://www.nytimes.com on December 26, 2007.

7. Helsingin Sanomat International Edition (March 1, 2001), "Finns Numbed by Shocking Revelations of Finnish Ski Association," retrieved from http://www2.hs.fi/english/ on November 20, 2007.

8. Helsingin Sanomat International Edition (February 26, 2001), "Drugs Found in FSA Medical Bag as Lahti Doping Scandal Escalates," retrieved from http://www2.hs.fi/english/ on November 20, 2007.

9. Helsingin Sanomat International edition (November 7, 2002), "Lahti Doping Scandal Has Cost Finnish Ski Association Over Three Million Euros," retrieved from http://www2.hs.fi/english/ on November 20, 2007.

10. BBC.com (May 10, 2001), "Hamburger Tests Positive," retrieved from http://news.bbc.co.uk/ on November 20, 2007.

11. BBC.com (August 10, 2001), "New Doubts Over EPO Test," retrieved from http://news.bbc.co.uk/ on November 20, 2007.

12. Cyclingnews.com (September 7, 2001), "Hamburger Gets 'Life Ban' from DCU," retrieved from http://www.cyclingnews.com/ on November 20, 2007.

13. Richard H. McLaren (November 13, 2002), "National or International Obligation! Which to Follow?" Playthegame.org, retrieved from http://www.playthegame.org/ on November 20, 2007.

14. Jan M. Olsen (November 7, 2007), "Danish Cyclist Bo Hamburger Admits Using EPO in Mid-1990s," The Associated Press, retrieved from the International Herald Tribune (online edition) http://iht.com on December 26, 2007.

15. Simon Cotton (2007), "Methamphetamine (and Its Isomers)," Molecule of the Month Web site, retrieved from http://www.chm.bris.ac.uk/motm/methamphetamine/methc.htm on April 6, 2007.

16. BBC.com (March 21, 2002), "British Skier Stripped of Bronze Medal," retrieved from http://news.bbc.co.uk/ on November 20, 2007.

17. BBC.com (October 18, 2002), "Baxter Hails Moral Victory," retrieved from http://news.bbc.co.uk/ on November 20, 2007. List of results for Alain Baxter, International Ski Federation (FIS) Web site, retrieved from http://www.fis-ski.com/ on November 20, 2007.

18. The Associated Press (March 31, 2005), "Doctor Defends Prescriptions for Steroids," published in *The New York Times* (online edition), retrieved from http://www.nytimes.com/ on December 8, 2007.

19. The Associated Press (September 21, 2005), "S.C. Doctor Indicted on Steroid Distribution Charges," published at USAToday.com, retrieved from http://www.usatoday.com/ on December 8, 2007.

20. The Associated Press (September 30, 2005), "Report: NFL Players Linked to Doctor Will Be Tested," published at USAToday.com, retrieved from http://www.usatoday.com/ on December 8, 2007.

21. Ibid.

22. The Associated Press (December 2, 2005), "Doctor Advised Panthers on How to Beat Drug Tests," published at USAToday.com, retrieved from http://www.usatoday.com/ on December 8, 2007.

23. Jim Kouri (July 19, 2006), "Doctor Who Gave NFL Players Steroids Headed for Prison," *American Chronicle* (online edition), retrieved from http://www.americanchronicle.com/ on December 8, 2007.

24. Mark Fainaru-Wada (December 13, 2007), "Mitchell Report Sheds Light on What Giants Knew About Bonds," ESPN.com, retrieved from http://sports.espn.go.com/ on December 25, 2007.

25. Duff Wilson and Michael S. Schmidt (November 18, 2007), "A Harvest of Trash and Turmoil for an Agent Fighting Steroids," *The New York Times*, p. 1 (also available online at http://www.nytimes.com/). Korchemy information from Liz Robbins with reporting by Carol Pogash (May 8, 2004), "Examination of Balco Files to Be a Sprint," *The New York Times* (online edition), retrieved from http://www.nytimes.com/ on November 23, 2007.

26. The Associated Press (August 5, 2006), "Balco Chemist Gets Prison Term," *The New York Times* (online edition, retrieved from http://www.nytimes.com/ on November 23, 2007. Also, Mark Fainaru-Wada (August 23, 2004), "Graham Admits Balco Role," *San Francisco Chronicle* on SFGate.com, retrieved from http://www.sfgate.com/ on November 24, 2007.

27. Mark Fainaru-Wada and Lance Williams (February 13, 2004), "US: Drug Ring Aided Top Jocks; BONDS TIES: 2 of 4 Indicted Have Close Links to Giants Superstar," *San Francisco Chronicle* on SFGate.com, retrieved from http://www. sfgate.com/ on November 24, 2007.

28. Elizabeth Fernandez and Chuck Squatriglia (July 15, 2005), "Conte, 2 Others Admit Distributing Steroids," *San Francisco Chronicle* on SFGate.com, retrieved from http://www.sfgate.com/ on November 24, 2007.

29. David Kravets (October 18, 2005), "Balco Boss to Serve 8 Months in Prison," The Associated Press, published at USAToday.com, retrieved from http:// www.usatoday.com/ on November 24, 2007. Korchemny information: Press Release, U.S. Department of Justice (February 24, 2006), "Final Defendant Sentenced in Steroid Distribution Conspiracy," retrieved from http://www.justice.gov/ on November 24, 2007.

30. Sentencing: KTVU.com, with reporting from The Associated Press (August 4, 2006), "Father of 'The Clear' Sentenced in Balco Case," retrieved from http:// www.ktvu.com/ on November 24, 2007. Additional designer steroid information: Henry K. Lee (August 5, 2006), "Balco Steroid Developer Sentenced to Prison Term," *San Francisco Chronicle* on SFgate.com, retrieved from http://www.sfgate.com/ on November 24, 2007.

31. The Associated Press (July 12, 2007), "Balco Leaker Ellerman Gets 2 $\frac{1}{2}$ Years in Prison," published at ESPN.com, retrieved from http://sports.espn.go.com/ on November 25, 2007.

32. Testosterone/epitestosterone balance information from Mark Fainaru-Wada and Lance Williams (February 13, 2004), "US: Drug Ring Aided Top Jocks; BONDS TIES: 2 of 4 Indicted Have Close Links to Giants Superstar," *San Francisco Chronicle* on SFGate.com, retrieved from http://www.sfgate.com/ on November 24, 2007.

33. Mark Fainaru-Wada and Lance Williams (December 21, 2003), "How the Doping Scandal Unfolded, Fallout from the BALCO Scandal Could Taint Olympics, Pro Sports," *San Francisco Chronicle* on SFGate.com, retrieved from http://www. sfgate.com/ on November 24, 2007.

34. American Track and Field (May 19, 2005), "Collins Accepts Four-Year Suspension," retrieved from http://www.american-trackandfield.com/ on November 30, 2007.

35. Jon Sarche (May 19, 2005), "Sprinter Collins Accepts Four-Year Doping Ban," The Associated Press, published at USAToday.com, retrieved from http:// www.usatoday.com/ on November 30, 2007.

36. Eddie Pells (May 21, 2007), "Doping Days Behind Her, Collin on Right Track," The Associated Press, retrieved from http://findarticles.com/ on November 27, 2007.

37. Jere Longmann (December 11, 2004), "Sprinter in Scandal Is Suspended," *The New York Times* (online edition), retrieved from http://www.nytimes.com/ on November 29, 2007.

38. Mark Fainaru-Wada and Lance Williams (June 24, 2004), "Sprinter Admitted Use of Balco 'Magic Potion,' November Testimony to Federal Grand Jury Contradicts Record-Holder's Public Denials," *San Francisco Chronicle* (online edition), retrieved from http://www.sfgate.com on June 24, 2007.

39. Ibid.

40. BBCnews.com (November 16, 2004), "Sprint Pair Discovers Appeal Dates," retrieved from http://news.bbc.co.uk/ on December 1, 2007.

41. Mark Fainaru-Wada and Lance Williams (December 14, 2005), "Montgomery Banned for Two Years for Doping, World Record Expunged; Gaines Also Banned," *San Francisco Chronicle* on SFGate.com, retrieved from http://www.sfgate.com/ on December 1, 2007.

42. Dick Patrick (December 13, 2005), "White's Words Key in Montgomery, Gaines Cases," USAToday.com, retrieved from http://www.usatoday.com/ on December 1, 2007.

43. Mark Fainaru-Wada (December 15, 2005), quoting Reuters news agency, "Sports and Drugs, Montgomery Says He's Done," *San Francisco Chronicle* on SFGate.com, retrieved from http://www.sfgate.com/ on December 1, 2007.

44. Mark Fainaru-Wada and Lance Williams (July 23, 2004), "Olympian Accused of Doping in Sydney; Jones' Husband Told Investigators He Injected Sprinter," *San Francisco Chronicle* on SFGate.com, retrieved from http://www.sfgate.com/ on November 28, 2007.

45. 20/20, ABC News (December 3, 2004), "Balco Chief on Sports Doping Scandal," retrieved from http://abcnews.go.com/2020/ on November 29, 2007.

46. Lance Williams and Mark Fainaru-Wada (December 16, 2004), "Marion Jones Sues Balco's Conte for Defamation," *San Francisco Chronicle* on SFGate.com, retrieved from http://www.sfgate.com/ on November 29, 2007.

47. Mark Fainaru-Wada (February 6, 2006), "Balco Defamation Suit Settled," *San Francisco Chronicle* on SFGate.com, retrieved from http://www.sfgate.com/ on November 29, 2007.

48. ESPN.com, attributed to ESPN.com wire services (August 19, 2006), "Sources: Sprinter Jones Tested Positive for EPO," retrieved from http://sports.espn.go.com/ on December 6, 2007.

49. ESPN.com, attributed to ESPN.com wire services (September 7, 2006) "Marion Jones' 'B' Sample Negative; Sprinter Cleared," retrieved from http://sports.espn.go.com/ on December 6, 2007.

50. Ibid.

51. Skip Rozin (November 28, 2007), "The Inside Dope, How Sports Drug Testing Works," OpinionJournal.com (part of the Wall Street Journal online edition), retrieved from http://www.opinionjournal.com/ on November 28, 2007.

52. The Associated Press (January 14, 2008), "Jones (Six Months), Former Coach (63 Months) Sentenced to Prison," published at ESPN.com, retrieved from http://sports.espn.go.com/ on January 15, 2008.

53. Lance Williams and Mark Fainaru-Wada (December 3, 2004), "What Bonds Told the Grand Jury," *San Francisco Chronicle* on SFGate.com, retrieved from http://www.sfgate.com/ on December 2, 2007.

54. Lance Williams and Mark Fainaru-Wada (April 26, 2006), "Bonds Trainer Greg Anderson Subpoenaed in Perjury Probe; Investigation Widens into Whether Giants Slugger Lied About Using Banned Drugs," *San Francisco Chronicle* on SFGate.com, retrieved from http://www.sfgate.com/ on December 3, 2007.

55. Lance Williams and Mark Fainaru-Wada (July 5, 2006), "Bonds' Trainer Going to Prison," *San Francisco Chronicle* on SFGate.com, retrieved from http://www.sfgate.com/ on December 3, 2007.

56. Lance Williams (November 16, 2007), "Barry Bonds Indicted on 4 Perjury Counts, Obstruction of Justice," *San Francisco Chronicle* on SFGate.com, retrieved from http://www.sfgate.com/ on December 3, 2007.

57. Jaxon Van Derbeken and Henry K. Lee (November 16, 2007), "Greg Anderson Released from Federal Prison," *San Francisco Chronicle* on SFGate.com, retrieved from http://www.sfgate.com/ on December 3, 2007.

58. Mark Fainaru-Wada (December 13, 2007), "Mitchell Report Sheds Light on What Giants Knew About Bonds," ESPN.com, http://sports.espn.go.com/ accessed December 25, 2007.

59. Mike Collett (December 5, 2003), "Blatter Admits Soccer Has a Doping Problem," rediff.com, retrieved from http://in.rediff.com/ on November 21, 2007.

60. ABCsport (August 10, 2004), "No Going Back on Anti-doping Deal, Says Blatter," Australian Broadcasting Company (online), retrieved from http://www.abc.net.au/sport/ on November 11, 2007.

61. FIFA press release (April 24, 2006), "Court of Arbitration for Sport Confirms FIFA's Individual Case Management in Doping Matters," retrieved from http://www.fifa.com/ on November 21, 2007.

62. The Associated Press (April 24, 2006), "FIFA Doping Rules Don't Comply with WADA Code," published at ESPN.com, retrieved from http://soccernet.espn.go.com/ on November 21, 2007.

63. Ibid.

64. The Associated Press (June 5, 2006), "World Cup Roundup: The Dutch Limp into Germany," *The New York Times* (online edition), retrieved from http://www.nytimes.com/ on November 21, 2007.

65. Gary Kamiya (August 27, 2004), "The Serious Buzz in Athens," Salon.com, retrieved from http://www.salon.com/ on November 22, 2007.

66. Peter Berlin (August 19, 2004), "Greece's Sprint Stars, Still Untested, Throw in the Towel," *International Herald Tribune* (online edition), retrieved from http://www.iht.com/ on November 22, 2007.

67. Ibid.

68. The Associated Press (December 2, 2004), "Greek Sprinters Cited for Doping Violations," published at USAToday.com, retrieved from http://www.usatoday.com/ on November 22, 2007.

69. Sapa-Agence France Presse (April 2, 2005), "IAAF to Appeal Kenteris, Thanou Acquittal," IOL Web site, retrieved from http://www.int.iol.co.za/ on November 22, 2007.

70. The Associated Press (June 26, 2006), "Greek Sprinters Kenteris, Thanou Accept Ruling," published at USAToday.com, retrieved from http://www.usatoday.com/ on November 22, 2007.

71. Agence France Presse (October 31, 2007), "Kenteris-Thanou Cleared of BALCO Link," published in *The Australian* (online edition), retrieved from http://www.theaustralian.news.com.au/ on November 22, 2007.

72. Eric Schwartz (October 26, 2004), "Rutger Beke's Positive EPO Test," duathlon.com, retrieved from http://www.duathlon.com/ on November 23, 2007. Beke's placing information from Eric Schwartz (August 10, 2005), "Rutger Beke Cleared; Revised Ironman Hawaii 2004 Results," duathlon.com, retrieved from http://www.duathlon.com/ on November 23, 2007.

73. Statement from Chris McCrary, Katalyst Multisport Management (August 10, 2005), published on duathlon.com, retrieved from http://www.duathlon.com on November 23, 2007.

74. John Stevenson (August 10, 2005), "Triathlete Cleared for EPO False Positive," Cyclingnew.com, retrieved from http://www.cyclingnews.com/ on November 23, 2007.

75. Katalyst Multisport Management press release (August 9, 2005), "Rutger Beke Cleared of Doping Charge," retrieved from http://www.katalystmultisport.com/news.php?p=20 on November 23, 2007.

76. Kevin Mackinnon (April 19, 2007), "Rutger Beke Claims His First Ironman," IRONMAN.com, retrieved from http://www.ironmanlive.com/ on November 23, 2007.

77. Rob Hughes (November 27, 2004), "Soccer: Juventus Conviction Casts Aura of Doubt on Sport," *International Herald Tribune* (online edition), retrieved from http://www.iht.com/ on November 21, 2007.

78. The Associated Press (December 14, 2005), "Juve Doctor Is Cleared," *International Herald Tribune* (online edition), retrieved from http://www.iht.com/ on November 21, 2007.

79. Robin Parisotto, *Blood Sports: The Inside Dope on Drugs in Sport* (Pahran, Victoria, Australia: Hardie Grant Books, 2006), p. 143.

80. Charles Pelkey (April 18, 2005), "Hamilton Draws Two-Year Suspension," VeloNews.com, retrieved from http://www.velonews.com/ on December 9, 2007.

81. CyclingNews.com (July 3, 2004), "Anti-doping Measures Get Tougher," retrieved from http://www.cyclingnews.com/ on December 9, 2007.

82. Charles Pelkey (April 18, 2005), "Hamilton Draws Two-Year Suspension," VeloNews.com, retrieved from http://www.velonews.com/ on December 9, 2007.

83. Jeff Jones (September 21, 2004), "Hamilton Fails Blood Tests," Cyclingnews.com, retrieved from http://www.cyclingnews.com/ on December 9, 2007.

84. Charles Pelkey (April 18, 2005), "Hamilton Draws Two-Year Suspension," VeloNews.com, retrieved from http://www.velonews.com/ on December 9, 2007.

85. Gina Kolata (May 10, 2005), "Cheating, or an Early Mingling of the Blood?" *The New York Times* (online edition), retrieved from http://www.nytimes.com/ on December 10, 2007.

86. VeloNews.com (May 9, 2007), "Tinkoff Suspends Hamilton, Jaksche and Hondo," retrieved from http://www.velonews.com/ on December 10, 2007.

87. Neal Rogers (December 21, 2007), "Rock Racing Owner Confirms Hamilton Deal," VeloNews.com, retrieved from http://www.velonews.com/ on December 25, 2007.

88. L'Equipe (August 23, 2005), "Armstrong dans la tourmente," retrieved from http://www.lequipe.fr/ on December 12, 2007.

89. VeloNews.com, with wire services (August 23, 2005), "L'Equipe Alleges Armstrong Samples Show EPO Use in 99 Tour," retrieved from http://www.velonews.com/ on December 12, 2007. Full text: "A Statement by Lance Armstrong Regarding L'Equipe's Article," ThePaceline.com, retrieved from http://www.thepaceline.com/ on December 12, 2007.

90. L'Equipe (August 23, 2005), "Jean-Marie Leblanc troublé et déçu," retrieved from http://www.lequipe.fr/ on December 12, 2007.

91. L'Equipe and Agence France Presse (August 24, 2005), "Les Reactions," retrieved from http://www.lequipe.fr/ on December 12, 2007.

92. L'Equipe (August 23, 2005), "Pound: Un affaire 'Grave,'" retrieved from http://www.lequipe.fr/ on December 12, 2007.

93. L'Equipe (August 23, 2005), "Trois questions à Jacques de Ceaurriz," retrieved from http://www.lequipe.fr/ on December 12, 2007.

94. The Associated Press (August 27, 2005), "USA Cycling Strongly Backs Armstrong," published at MSNBC.com, retrieved from http://www.msnbc.msn.com/ on December 12, 2007.

95. Emile N. Vrijman, Adriaan van der Veen, and Paul Scholten, *Report: Independent Investigation, Analysis Samples from the 1999 Tour de France*, (Amsterdam: Scholten c.s. Advocaten, May 2006), p. 14, paragraphs 1.09 and 1.10.

96. Ibid., p. 18, paragraph 1.17.

97. The Associated Press (May 31, 2006), "UCI Report Clears Armstrong," published at VeloNews.com, retrieved from http://www.velonews.com/ on December 12, 2007.

98. Agence France Presse (June 2, 2006), "WADA Calls Vrijman Report Farcical," published at VeloNews.com, retrieved from http://www.velonews.com/ on December 13, 2007.

99. VeloNews.com (May 31, 2006), "UCI, Armstrong and WADA React to Vrijman Report," retrieved from http://www.velonews.com/ on December 12, 2007.

100. The Associated Press (May 31, 2006), "UCI Report Clears Armstrong," published at VeloNews.com, retrieved from http://www.velonews.com/ on December 12, 2007.

101. Richard H. McLaren, Arturo Marti, and Peter van Beek (August 7, 2005), *The ATP Anti-doping Tribunal Appeal of Guillermo Cañas*, p. 33, International Tennis Federation Web site, retrieved from http://www.itftennis.com/ on November 19, 2007.

102. Maidie Oliveau, Christopher Campbell, and Yves Fortier, *Arbitral Award Delivered by the Court of Arbitration for Sport, Guillermo Cañas v. ATP Tour*, p. 16, paragraph 8.14.4, International Tennis Federation Web site, retrieved from http://www.itftennis.com/ on November 19, 2007.

103. Bonnie DeSimone (March 28, 2007) "Cañas Confirms Return by Beating Federer Again," ESPN.com, retrieved from http://sports.espn.go.com/ on November 19, 2007.

104. Bonnie DeSimone (June 3, 2007), "Cañas Will Run All Day On (and Off) the Court," ESPN.com, retrieved from http://sports.espn.go.com/ on November 19, 2007.

105. The Associated Press (December 5, 2006), "Pakistani Bowlers Cleared of Doping," *International Herald Tribune* (online edition), retrieved from http://www.iht.com/ on December 4, 2007.

106. Reuters (July 2, 2007), "Court Unable to Rule on Akhtar, Asif Doping Cases," Australian Broadcasting Company News, retrieved from http://www.abc.net.au/news/ on December 5, 2007.

107. Jeff Jones (May 23, 2006), "Saiz Arrested on Doping Charges," Cyclingnews.com, retrieved from http://www.cyclingnews.com/ on December 14, 2007.

108. Antonio J. Salmerón (September 24, 2006), "Manzano: Well-Known Footballers Also Clients of Fuentes," CyclingNews.com, retrieved from http://www.cyclingnews.com/ on December 14, 2007.

109. Nathaniel Vinton (June 28, 2006), "Amid Doping Scandal, Ullrich Is Cleared to Ride in Tour de France," *The New York Times* (online edition), retrieved from http://www.nytimes.com/ on December 14, 2007.

110. Jeff Jones (June 30, 2006), "Ullrich, Sevilla and Pevenage Suspended, the List Gets Longer," Cyclingnews.com, retrieved from http://www.cyclingnews.com/ on December 15, 2007.

111. Ibid.

112. Hood, Andrew (July 26, 2006), "Astana 5 cleared by Spanish courts," VeloNews.com, retrieved from http://www.velonews.com/ on December 15, 2007.

113. Laura Weislo and Susan Westemeyer (October 8, 2006), "Puerto Court Orders Spanish Federation Not to Act," Cyclingnews.com, retrieved from http://www.cyclingnews.com/ on December 15, 2007.

114. Laura Weislo (October 28, 2006), "Spanish Federation Drops Puerto Cases," CyclingNews.com, retrieved from http://www.cyclingnews.com/ on December 15, 2007.

115. The Associated Press (November 24, 2006), "EPO Found in Bags of Blood Seized in Doping Investigation," *International Herald Tribune* (online edition), retrieved from http://www.iht.com/ on December 15, 2007.

116. Sal Ruibal, "Italian Cyclist Basso Signs with Discovery Channel," *USA Today* (online edition), retrieved from http://www.usatoday.com/sports/cycling/2006-11-08-basso-discovery_x.htm on December 15, 2007.

117. Susan Westemeyer (February 2, 2007), "Ullrich Gives DNA Sample," CyclingNews.com, retrieved from http://www.cyclingnews.com/ on December 15, 2007.

118. The Associated Press (June 30, 2007), "German Rider Joerg Jaksche Admits Blood Doping from Spanish Doctor," *International Herald Tribune* (online edition), retrieved from http://www.iht.com/ on December 15, 2007.

119. Marca.com (July 27, 2006), "No hay atletas implicados en la 'Operación Puerto,'" retrieved from http://www.marca.com/ on December 15, 2007.

120. Hedwig Kröner and Shane Stokes (December 8, 2006), "Spanish Soccer Clubs Linked to Fuentes?" Cyclingnews.com, retrieved from http://www.cyclingnews.com/ on December 15, 2007.

121. Ben Abrahams and Greg Johnson, with assistance from Susan Westemeyer (May 15, 2007), "FIFA Wants Puerto Documents," Cyclingnews.com, retrieved from http://www.cyclingnews.com/ on December 15, 2007.

122. Susan Westemeyer (December 1, 2007), "German Court Orders Fuentes Testimony," cyclingnews.com, retrieved from http://www.cyclingnews.com/ on December 15, 2007.

123. Laura Weislo, with assistance from Susan Westemeyer (September 23, 2007), "Ullrich's 'Suspicious Cash Withdrawals,'" Cyclingnews.com, retrieved from http://www.cyclingnews.com/ on December 15, 2007.

124. Neal Rogers (October 29, 2007), "What in the Worlds? Angry Bettini Ends Bizarre Week with Second Consecutive Rainbow Jersey," *VeloNews*, vol. 36, no. 20, pp. 43–46.

125. Jeff Adams (June 14, 2007), "Spinning Out of Control," Adamsmania.com, retrieved from http://www.adamsmania.com/ on December 9, 2007.

126. Randy Starkman (June 13, 2007), "Wheelchair Champ Suspended, Athlete to Fight Cocaine Suspension," *Toronto Star* (online edition), retrieved from http://www.thestar.com/ on December 9, 2007.

127. CBC Sports (June 12, 2007), "Olympian Jeff Adams Suspended Over Cocaine Test," retrieved from http://www.cbc.ca/ on December 9, 2007.

128. Ibid.

129. Randy Starkman (June 13, 2007), "Wheelchair Champ Suspended, Athlete to Fight Cocaine Suspension," *Toronto Star* (online edition), retrieved from http://www.thestar.com/ on December 9, 2007.

130. Jeff Adams (August 16, 2007), "The Latest Developments," Adamsmania.com, retrieved from http://www.adamsmania.com/ on December 9, 2007.

131. Floyd Landis, with Loren Mooney, *Positively False* (New York: Simon Spotlight Entertainment, 2007), pp. 152, 153.

132. BBC Sport (August 8, 2006), "Landis Blames Testing Procedure," retrieved from http://news.bbc.co.uk/sport2/low/other_sports/cycling/5254402.stm on December 28, 2007.

133. Floyd Landis, quoted at Trust But Verify (November 28, 2006), "Tuesday Roundup," retrieved from http://trustbut.blogspot.com/ on December 16, 2007.

134. Transcript of Proceedings, May 14, 2007, U.S. Anti-Doping Agency vs. Floyd Landis, pp. 1218–1220.

135. Christopher Campbell (September 20, 2007), *United States Anti-doping Agency v. Floyd Landis*, American Arbitration Association No. 30 190 00847 06, North American Court of Arbitration for Sport Panel Award.

136. The Associated Press (October 16, 2007), "Giro Champion Di Luca Banned Three Months for Doping Charges," Yahoo! Sports, retrieved from http://sports.yahoo.com/ on December 16, 2007. Also, VeloNews.com (December 17, 2007), "Italian Doctor Given Life-time Suspension," retrieved from http://www.velonews.com/ on December 17, 2007.

137. Childs Walker (January 25, 2007), "NFL, Players Agree to Get Tougher on Steroid Use," retrieved from http://www.baltimoresun.com on June 23, 2007.

138. Brendan J. Lyons (February 27, 2007), "Albany DA Raids Florida Steroids Center, Yearlong Investigation of Internet Drug Sales May Expose Use by Pro Athletes," *Albany Times-Union* (online edition), retrieved from http://timesunion.com/ on December 18, 2007.

149. The Associated Press (February 28, 2007), "Prosecutors Allege That Sports Players Got Steroids from Online Ring," published at USAToday.com, retrieved from http://www.usatoday.com/ on December 18, 2007.

140. Michael S. Schmidt (September 24, 2007), "US Arrests 124 in Raids on Global Steroid Ring," *The New York Times* (online edition), retrieved from http://www.nytimes.com on December 18, 2007.

141. George J. Mitchell (December 13, 2007), "Report to the Commissioner of Baseball of an Independent Investigation into the Illegal Use of Steroids and Other Performance Enhancing Substances in Major League Baseball." New York: Office of the Commissioner of Baseball, 2007.

142. Interview with Dr. Paul Strauss on October 16, 2007.

CHAPTER 7

1. *MedicineNet.com*, "Definition of Human Gene Therapy," retrieved from http://www.medterms.com/ on January 1, 2008.

2. Kristen Philipkoski (Februay 21, 2003), "Perils of Gene Experimentation," *Wired.com*, retrieved from http://www.wired.com/ on January 2, 2008.

3. The Associated Press (July 26, 2007), "Gene Therapy Patient Dies, Trial Shut Down," published on *CNN.com*, retrieved from http://www.cnn.com on July 27, 2007.

4. H. Lee Sweeney (July 2004), "Gene Doping," *Scientific American*, pp. 62–69.

5. Christen Brownlee (October 30, 2004), "Gene Doping: Will Athletes Go for the Ultimate High?" *Science News Online*, retrieved from http://www.sciencenews.org/ on November 20, 2007.

6. Ibid.

7. Gretchen Reynolds (June 3, 2007), "Outlaw DNA," *Play Magazine*, published by *The New York Times*, retrieved from http://www.nytimes.com/ on January 4, 2008.

8. Ibid.

9. Owen Slot (February 2, 2006), "Apocalypse Now: Fears of Gene Doping Are Realised," *The Times Online*, retrieved from http://www.timesonline.co.uk/ on January 4, 2008.

10. Gretchen Reynolds (June 3, 2007), "Outlaw DNA," *Play Magazine*, published by *The New York Times*, retrieved from http://www.nytimes.com/ on January 4, 2008.

11. Rupert Guinness (February 10, 2006), "Designer drug 'undetectable,'" *The Daily Telegraph* on FoxSports.com.au, retrieved from http://www.foxsports.com.au/ on January 4, 2008.

12. *Ibid*.

13. Wade Roush (April 7, 1995), "An 'Off Switch' for Red Blood Cells," *Science*, Volume 268, pp. 27–28.

14. Sal Ruibal (December 5, 2006), "New tool to catch sports cheats: Gene-doping test," *USAToday.com*, retrieved from http://www.usatoday.com/ on 1/3/08.

Index

About the Author

DANIEL M. ROSEN is a graduate of the School of Journalism at the University of Missouri, Columbia. Since 1982, he has worked as a photojournalist, technical writer, multimedia developer, and instructional designer. In his spare time, Rosen publishes "Rant Your Head Off" (http://rant-your-head-off.com), a blog which covers a number of issues, including various sports doping scandals. He is an avid cyclist.